International Management and Language

Globalization processes have resulted in the emergence of business and management networks in which the sharing of knowledge is of crucial importance. Combining two contemporary and important subject areas – namely that of international management and also language and communication in multi-language contexts – the author of this book presents a wealth of ideas, examples and applications taken from international and global contexts, which show that 'language matters' in the pursuit of international business affairs.

The book establishes the theoretical core of its main ideas by introducing two orientations (social construction and linguistic relativity) and demonstrates how they can be drawn on to frame and understand the activities of managers. In particular the role of the English language in international communications is explored through a detailed investigation of its emergence as a lingua franca, the debates surrounding it and the impact it has on knowledge transfer. The book then provides several in-depth case studies of issues, themes and organizations pertinent to the subject matter of international management and languages. In its concluding part, it provides novel approaches to understand international management from a comparative perspective and to approach its dynamic character as processes of translation.

Highly innovative and topical, Susanne Tietze's book will appeal to students of international management and international human resource management as well as those studying intercultural communication. It is also useful for managers and practitioners who work internationally.

Susanne Tietze is Professor of Human Resource Management and Organisational Analysis at Nottingham Trent University.

Routledge Studies in International Business and the World Economy

International Management and Language

Susanne Tietze

Routledge
Taylor & Francis Group

LONDON AND NEW YORK

First published 2008
by Routledge
2 Park Square, Milton Park, Abingdon, Oxon OX14 4RN

Simultaneously published in the USA and Canada
by Routledge
270 Madison Ave, New York, NY 10016

Routledge is an imprint of the Taylor & Francis Group, an informa business

© 2008 Susanne Tietze

Typeset in Times New Roman by
Taylor & Francis Books
Printed and bound in Great Britain by
Antony Rowe Ltd, Chippenham, Wiltshire

All rights reserved. No part of this book may be reprinted or reproduced
or utilised in any form or by any electronic, mechanical, or other means,
now known or hereafter invented, including photocopying and recording,
or in any information storage or retrieval system, without permission in
writing from the publishers.

British Library Cataloguing in Publication Data
A catalogue record for this book is available from the British Library

Library of Congress Cataloging in Publication Data
International management and language / Susanne Tietze.
p. cm.
Includes bibliographical references and index.
ISBN 978-0-415-40393-1 (hardcover) – ISBN 978-0-203-92935-3 (e-book)
1. International business enterprises–Management–Cross-cultural studies.
2. Language and culture. 3. Communication in management–
Cross-cultural studies. 4. Intercultural communication. 5. Corporate
culture–Cross-cultural studies. I. Title.
HD62.4.T54 2008
658'.049–dc22
2007037782

ISBN13: 978-0-415-40393-1 (hbk)
ISBN13: 978-0-203-92935-3 (ebk)

Contents

Illustrations

Contributors

Gerhard Fink, PhD, is Jean Monnet Professor for applied micro-economics in European integration and director of the doctoral programme at Wirtschaftsuniversität Wien (Vienna University of Economics and Business Administration). He was director of the Institute for European Affairs (Jean Monnet Centre of Excellence) during 1997–2003. Professor Fink is author of about 200 publications in learned journals and author or (co-)editor of about 15 books; in 2005 he was guest editor of the Academy of Management Executive, one of the leading management journals in the USA. See also http://fgr.wu-wien.ac.at/institut/ef/cvfinkde.html.

Nigel Holden, PhD, is Professor of Cross-Cultural Management and Director of the Institute of International Business at Lancashire Business School at the University of Central Lancashire. He has previously held professorial appointments in the UK, Germany and Denmark. He is author of *Cross-Cultural Management: A Knowledge Management Perspective* (2002), which has been published in Chinese and Russian versions, and is Associate Editor of the *European Journal of International Management*. He has given over 100 invited lectures and keynote addresses to academic and professional audiences in several European countries, as well as Japan, Taiwan, USA and Russia.

Luchien Karsten, PhD, is Professor of the History of Management at the University of Groningen, Faculty of Business and Management, where he is also head of Department of International Business and Management. He studied economics and philosophy in Groningen as well as history at the École des Hautes Études in Paris and earned his PhD from Groningen University in the Netherlands. He has coordinated a project of cooperation (1988–2004) with the faculty of Economics at the University of Ouagadougou (Burkina Faso) and has been director of a consortium for international business together with the University of Stirling (Scotland) and the Business School Ceram in Nice (France). His research interests focus on time and management, the transfer and translation of management concepts and history of multinationals. He is a member of the editorial board of the *East Asian Journal of Management*.

Olga Kuznetsova, PhD, is a Senior Lecturer at the Manchester Metropolitan University Business School, UK, where she teaches Business Environment and International Business. She writes on multi-dimensional interactions between business and society and institutional aspects of business environment with emphasis on Russia. West–East managerial knowledge transfer is among the latest additions to her research portfolio. She has translated Russian literature into English.

Rebecca Piekkari, PhD, is Professor of International Business at the Helsinki School of Economics, Finland. Her area of expertise is international management, with a specific focus on language issues in multinational corporations. She has also written about the use of qualitative research methods in international business. Her articles have appeared in the *Journal of Management Studies, European Management Journal, International Journal of Cross-cultural Management, International Business Review, Management International Review, Corporate Communications* and *Business Communication Quarterly.* Her most recent book is the *Handbook of Qualitative Research Methods for International Business* (with Catherine Welch), published in 2004.

Gina Poncini, PhD, is Associate Professor in the Department of Economics, Business and Statistics at the University of Milan, Italy, where she teaches *English Business Communication* in the European Economics degree programme. Her research and publications focus on business meetings, intercultural business communication, financial communication, videoconferencing, and communication in the tourism and agro-food industries. She is the author of the book *Discursive Strategies in Multicultural Business Meetings* (2004), winner of the Association for Business Communication 2005 Award for Distinguished Publication on Business Communication. She is Vice President Europe of the Association for Business Communication (ABC) and has managerial experience in the international banking sector.

Hiromasa Tanaka, PhD, is Professor at Meisei University, Tokyo. He received his doctoral degree from Temple University. His research interests include English and intercultural communication curriculum development in business corporations. Since 1999 he has completed education need analysis projects for several companies including the most recent project in Japan Gasoline Corporation.

Carole Tansley, PhD, is Professor of Human Resource Innovation in the HRM division of Nottingham Business School, Nottingham Trent University, UK, and has widely published her ethnographic research on the developing HR Global information systems in enterprise resource planning (ERP) initiatives in multi-national organizations. She has led a number of funded research projects, most recently research on talent management for the UK Chartered Institute of Personnel and Development. She has published in leading scholarly journals such as *Journal of Management Studies, Management Learning* and the *Journal of Managerial Psychology.* Her current interests are in the philology of organizational terms such as 'management' and 'talent'.

Susanne Tietze, PhD, is Professor of Human Resource Management and Organisational Analysis at Nottingham Business School, Nottingham Trent University, UK. Her research focuses on language and discourse as used in work contexts and she has also conducted studies on emergent forms of work organizations. She has worked for several UK and European universities and consulted on topics such as organizational communication, management development and home-based telework. She has published in leading scholarly journals such as *Organization Studies, Journal of Management Studies* and *Journal of Business Ethics* as well as in practitioner journals such as *Organization and People, Teleworker* and *HRM Digest International.*

Elisa Turra is a lecturer at Bocconi University, where she teaches Italian for business and academic purposes to international economics students. She is currently completing a PhD in Applied Linguistics at the University of Lancaster, UK, with her doctoral research focusing on consensus and conflict at business meetings conducted in English and Italian. Her research and publications focus on corporate communication in the agro-food industry, corporate websites, e-commerce and intercultural communication in institutional settings.

Luc-Jan Wolpert, PhD, studied Economics at the Faculty of Economics at the University of Groningen and subsequently became a junior consultant at Rijnconsult where he was invited to research on AKZO's organizational change activities. This research led to the successful completion of a doctoral thesis and the award of a PhD by the University of Groningen. Currently he is Director of Vending@work.

Acknowledgements

Susanne Tietze wishes to thank Patricia Steele for her patience and help in adding the final editorial touches to the manuscript. Terry Clague of Routledge has supported this project from the very beginning and has promptly and competently addressed all of my queries and questions throughout the process. I appreciate the permission given by the journal *Language and Intercultural Communication* to reprint the article 'Spreading the Management Gospel – in English'.

Nigel Holden and Carole Tansley warmly thank Dr Edgar Hoffman of the Institute of Slavic Languages of the Vienna University of Economics and Business Administration and Professor Anrei Kuznetsov of the University of Central Lancashire for valuable assistance in the preparation of Chapter 8.

Rebecca Piekkari expresses her appreciation for the input by Professor Denice Welch, of Melbourne Business School, Melbourne University, Australia, for her contributions to Chapter 9.

Luchien Karsten and Luc-Jan Wolpert acknowledge the support and input of Chairman of the Board A. A. Louden – both for the research project in general and for this chapter (Chapter 10) in particular. They also express their gratitude to Susanne Tietze for her help in the editorial stages of writing the chapter.

1 Setting the scene

This is a book about language as it is used by a particular professional group, namely managers, including those who manage across national and cultural boundaries. The activities of managers – as well as other organizational and professional groups – are intrinsically linked to the use of language and acts of communicating meaning. However, managers – more than other professional or organizational groups – need to possess superb communicative skills as they are perpetually talking and communicating with different professional, hierarchical or functional groups in order to achieve their organization's goals and objectives and also to realize their own personal interests and projects. Apart from such communicative and skill-based functions, the use of language has a deeper meaning for managers: it is their most used and least understood tool for creating professional identity, status and credibility to the extent that managers could be seen as created through their own language use. Large parts of this book will be dedicated to explore this claim.

Their main tool for communicating is in most instances, of course, their own *native language* or mother tongue. Additionally, concomitant with the increase in the professionalization of management, managers draw on the *discourses of management* – by which I simply mean the specialist vocabulary and techniques acquired through management education and practice. In brief, managers use both their native language and the discourse/s of management to pursue organizational (and personal) projects. Examples of such discourses are the vocabulary and techniques/practices of Human Resource Management, Marketing Management, Strategic Management and so on. International managers are then those people who manage across national and cultural boundaries and, in doing so, they too perpetually use language and discourse. Much of their communication involves the use of their mother tongues as well as, or even exclusively, the use of the English language as the lingua franca of international business (Bargiela-Chiappini 2006). Therefore, international managers use both their native language as well as English and the discourse/s of management to pursue organizational (and personal) projects.

Linguistic turns

The reason to write this book is to bring together the knowledge, which the field of management studies has accumulated about a) 'language' and its use (as in 'the German language'; 'the Japanese language'; the Finnish language; the Russian language etc.); b) discourse and its use; and c) the use of English as the lingua franca of international business and management.

The broad field of management and organization studies has indeed already taken on board the importance of language and communication in managerial work and undertaken what has been labelled the 'linguistic turn' – i.e. it increasingly concerns itself with managerial and organizational use of language and discourse (Deetz 2003a; Holman and Thorpe 2003; Tietze *et al.*, 2003). The underlying premise to this linguistic turn is based on social constructionist ideas about reality and knowledge and acknowledges that when managers are communicating they are not merely 'talking' or exchanging information; rather they are actively creating social and organizational worlds of work. Similarly, international managers are doing much more than merely 'communicating in English' across national, cultural and organizational boundaries; rather they are contributing to the creation of increasingly global realities. Thus, the axiomatic premise of this book is that 'language matters'.

Of course, there is already much knowledge about the relationship between language, reality, management activity and practices – as quite an impressive body of literature dedicates itself to its exploration. However, different sub-fields of the overall field of organization and management studies have undergone slightly different 'linguistic turns' and pursued different areas of interest and have therefore focused on different themes and topics. For example, the sub-field one can describe as 'organization studies' has made the study of discourses in and between organizational contexts its major concern. Research projects have provided deep insights into the processual, complex and contested character of managerial activity and drawn attention to the discursive character of organizations. The sub-field of international management has focused on the use (or non-use) of languages including that of English as the shared corporate language and scholars within this tradition have looked, for example, at language proficiency and its consequences for social exclusion/inclusion. The sub-field of international business has adopted an explicit focused on English as the lingua franca in international business contexts and its research focuses on the role of English in internal communications of global firms, as well as the emergence of multiple 'Englishes' and possibilities for resistance and reflection.

To repeat, the commonality between these sub-fields is the overarching interest in language and the realisation that it is at the core of management processes and that these processes can indeed be understood and approached through a linguistic lens.

Ironically, despite this shared interest in all matters related to language, discourse and communication, these different, yet related, fields do not 'talk to each other'. In other words there are no instititutionalized (e.g. shared conferences, journals, courses) ways of communicating across these fields, nor have particular research ties been developed between researchers from these different traditions. Thus, in the field of organization studies, the investigation of 'discourses' rules at the expense of any consideration of the role of native or national languages in general and the role of English as the 'lingua franca' in particular. In the fields of international management and business (which are more closely related to each other), there are hardly any investigations of the use of discourses, managerial or otherwise.

Such 'non-communication' seemed to me to be a shame and this book aims to overcome this separation and to build on the commonalities between different traditions and fields.

A global context

The broad context for this book is that of 'globalization' – in other words it is assumed that currently the world is changing and becoming more global and that these processes can be approached from a linguistic perspective. I want to stay clear of hyperbolic language – claiming that change is 'unprecedented' and globalization is the inevitable fate of humankind – but rather within possible positions vis-à-vis globalization, the book takes a 'transformationalist position', which is explained below.

In terms of discussions and debates about globalization, one can differentiate between three perspectives. The *hyperglobalist thesis* sees globalization as a new epoch of human history which features radically different changes in trade, finance and governance. Economic factors are seen to be driving changes in cultural, social and political structures (Ohmae 1990). Within this school of thinking these developments are either celebrated as a utopia of individual freedom based on free-market principles or seen as oppressive and enslaving from a neo-Marxist position. The *sceptical thesis* argues that claims about the existence of globalization are exaggerated. Hirst and Thompson (1996) suggest that current developments are not new at all and that globalization is little more than a contemporary myth. The *transformationalist thesis* sees globalization as a force which drives social, economical, political and cultural changes. Held *et al.*, (1999: 16) offer a definition, which can be positioned within the *transformationalist* thesis and which also provides a useful backdrop for the position of this book:

> A process (or set of processes) which embodies a transformation in the spatial organization of social relations and transactions – assessed in terms of their extensity, intensity, velocity and impact – generating transcontinental or interregional flows and networks of activity, interaction, and the exercise of power.

It appears that this understanding of globalization acknowledges its existence, but also expresses that transformations are multiple and varied and that there are therefore different types of globalization, which can exist concurrently. Held *et al.* describe these different types of globalization as thick, diffused, expansive and thin – in other words, it is thinkable that some practices have indeed become widespread and expansive, yet that others remain diffuse and do not converge into more universalistic patterns. Also, globalization here is not defined as an exclusively economic phenomenon, but is seen to consist of diverse power networks set in economic, political, environmental, technological and cultural domains. Thus it is a complex socio-historical process that generates dynamic processes of cooperation as much as of animosity and conflict (Faria and Guedes 2005). Thus framed, the existence of globalization does not imply the arrival of a boundaryless world (Ohmae 1994) or a world in which national and cultural borders do not matter any more: national idiosyncrasies are as abundant as ever and even the most transnational of corporations retain a form of national identity, despite their global presence. Rather, it depicts a world which is becoming more complex, perhaps less stable, and more interconnected. It does not deny the existence of boundaries and borders; rather it proposes that some might have become permeable or eroded, but others might have become firmer and more defined. Thus managers can still be viewed as communicators across different organizational as well as national and cultural boundaries. However, the character and relationships between such boundaries has become more complex and frequently complicated.

The terms 'language' or 'discourse' are conspicuously absent in the above definition – a fact Phillipson (2003: 3) points to when he says that 'in the copious literature on European integration and globalization, the language dimension tends to be absent, except in specialist works on the sociology of language and nationalism'. It is my hope that this book does go beyond the specialism of a particular discipline or school of thought in that it pulls together the topics and themes from the field of management studies as well as linguistics and in doing so raises the profile of language and discourse in global processes.

However, it would be premature and unfair to say that language and discourse have been completely sidelined and ignored in scholarly works. There are indeed plenty of contributions in different fields which are related to global as well as linguistic processes – to reiterate: the purpose of the book being to create some intellectual synergy between them. Three areas, which have received scholarly attention are introduced here as they provide important parameters for the purpose and rationale of the book. They will be revisited in more detail in subsequent chapters.

- English language: There is a huge body of literature which describes and assesses the role of the English language in global contexts. There are different strands of literatures, each of which focuses on different aspects. For example, there is a strand which looks at globalization processes in the light of language teaching and in particular English language teaching (e.g. Block and Cameron 2002) whereas other strands look at (national or European) language policies (Phillipson 2003) or the consequences of language competence for national and individual identities (Pavlenko and Blackledge 2004). The literatures of international business and management focus on the use of English and/or other languages in international or global organizational contexts (Bargiela-Chiappini 2006; Nickerson 2005); whereas a more general-oriented strand of literature discusses the consequences of the spread of English for other languages and cultures, the entailed possibilities and dangers (Crystal 2003).

- Global discourses: Scholars have claimed that there are discourses which are becoming increasingly spread and which transgress national and cultural boundaries. These discourses provide both the words and accompanying practices for describing and understanding the global world. Fairclough (2002) provides the discourse of 'new public management' (i.e. the transferability of the private sector as a role model for the public one) as one example of a discourse which has transcended national boundaries. Gee *et al.* (1996) refer to 'Total Quality Management' and 'teamwork' as similar examples of 'words and practices' which have achieved a globalized meaning, i.e. which are recognized as meaningful and important in multiple and diverse organizational contexts. Also, they argue that such globalized discourses have consequences for the identities of people who use them or are subjected to them.
- Global identities: A theme which criss-crosses several of the strands of literatures addresses issues of changing and emerging identities. Some scholars comment on the emergence of global identities, which quite often they see formulated within the global discourses (Gee *et al.* 1996), associated with the use of English as a global communicative means. Their evaluation of such possibilities of identity construction is varied, though the academic literature tends to be sceptical and reserved vis-à-vis claims that such identity convergence exists and/or that it might be a beneficial development (Elgin Haden 2000; Tietze 2004).

Thus, there is indeed a plethora of contributions – however, they derive from such diverse traditions and approaches, that they have yet to develop common projects and interests. Indeed, up to date there is only a handful of studies which concern themselves with the relationship between both language and (management) discourse – which entails questions about whether it matters that the discourses of management are mainly produced and reproduced in the English language; whether the incorporation of English/American management idioms and terminology into other languages and cultures implies an increasing convergence of their values and identity. Whereas such questions have been addressed by linguists and culture researchers in their own respective domains, they have not been examined from a combined language and (management) discourse perspective.

Rationale, purpose, audience

The overall reason to write this book is to create synergy between these mentioned fields and in doing so to advance knowledge. Although it is a theoretically informed book, it is not necessarily exclusively written for scholars. Rather its target audience also includes teachers and students in the field of organization, management and international business studies. Also, teachers and students of culture and language might find aspects of this book interesting as discussions about the relationship between language and culture feature in this book. Finally, the book is also written with practitioners and managers in mind. I am aware that – in the words of my colleague Professor Nigel Holden – 'the word communication lights up eyes', whereas the word 'language makes them glaze over' – and that a book on communication, in particular an intercultural one, would render the book more interesting for particular audiences. However, there are two good reasons not to write a book on communication: a) a useful body of materials already exists and I have nothing new to add to the books which have been published in the area of (intercultural) communication; b) I believe that understanding how communication works is not possible without an understanding of how language works and the role it plays in social life. Such understanding can be achieved by providing a theoretically grounded understanding of language. Rather than providing prescriptive advice to the imagined readership, the book's philosophies can best be expressed in the words of the linguist Deborah Cameron (2000: 180): 'a competent speaker is one who understands the "grammar of consequences" and can judge which of the available choices will come closest to producing the desired interpretation in a particular set of circumstances'. Practically then, the book provides a repertoire of ideas, theories and examples to inform and guide the making of choices in an increasingly complex and connected world.

Structure of the book

Before I proceed to present a chapter-by-chapter outline of this book, it is necessary to comment on its hybrid character. It is difficult to pigeonhole this book using established categories. It is not a conventional textbook, although it does present overviews over particular bodies of knowledge and also includes features associated with textbooks (such as case studies; text boxes; questions for the reader). It is not a straightforward review of the literature – although it does present and comment upon a large volume of research materials from across the world. It is not a research monograph – although it is a theoretically – and conceptually informed book and includes (in particular in part two) original research findings. On reflection, I wonder whether it is possible to claim that the very hybrid character of this book expresses something not unlike the blurring of clear-cut boundaries that seem to be associated with globalization processes and which are indicative of different ways of framing and thinking about a subject.

Taken as a whole the chapters of the book complete different intellectual tasks, including theoretical positioning; conceptual clarification; discussion of empirical research and assessment of theoretically grounded research; presentation of empirical work and discussion of the presented material.

The book is divided into three parts. Part I sets out the theoretical orientation of the book and introduces its 'working tools', i.e. concepts and ideas. It also outlines the different research approaches and studies conducted by scholars in the field of management. It would be misleading, though, to describe Part I as being of a purely 'theoretical/conceptual' nature as it also includes many examples and applications taken from work contexts. Part II consists of seven case studies, which are contributed by fellow academics. These colleagues are engaged in exploring global, international and inter-relational realities from a language perspective and they present compelling evidence that 'language matters'. Part III is relatively short, consisting of two chapters. Chapter 14 introduces a novel approach to the comparative study of managers and management as 'philology' is introduced as a frame to understand similarities and differences in ideas and practice. Chapter 15 provides a synthesis for the diverse literature, approaches and themes which constitute the field of a 'linguistically' turned management and organization studies. The chapter borrows from the field of translation studies to create a space to open up further debate and to, perhaps, inform future activities in the field of international management.

Part I: 'Theories, ideas and approaches'

Chapter 2: 'Language matters'

In this chapter the theoretical orientation of the book is set out. It provides an overview and discussion of two approaches which provide a framework which makes language and discourse central to the understanding, explanation and enacting of the social world. The two approaches are 'social constructionism' and 'linguistic relativity'. The first approach has been closely associated with the analysis of discourses; the latter is more closely aligned with the role of native languages in the categorization and ordering of human activity. Together they provide a framework to extrapolate four different dimensions of language: a) as a representative symbolic sign system, which allows us to describe and categorise the world; b) as having phatic function, which views talk and communication as ways of forging social cohesion; c) as a performative force, through which the social world is made; d) as an hegemonic function, by which is meant that through use of language and discourse particular worldviews, values and ideas become normalized and can be used for purposes of manipulation and control.

Chapter 3: 'Management and language'

In this chapter the terms 'manager', 'management' and 'managing' will be briefly explained and put in a historical context. Particular attention is paid to the professionalization of management through the provision of increasingly internationalized management education. Management is shown to be a 'discursive activity', which requires the acquisition of particular discourses and which sees the manager as a 'practical author' who (through the use of language and discourse) contributes to constructing social and global realities. This chapter also includes examples of management and global discourses.

Chapter 4: 'International management and language'

This chapter presents an overview over the work conducted in the fields of international management and business. A series of recent research studies will be reviewed and contextualized within the themes and topics of this book. The activities of international managers are described from a language perspective and evidence is provided that linguistic as well as discursive ability are necessary prerequisites to participate successfully in the pursuit of organizational goals. In addition, the chapter challenges current assumptions that the territory of International Management is the management of cultures. It does so by discussing the relationship between language and culture and argues that the two can only be understood in the light of each other.

Chapter 5: 'English as the global lingua franca'

This chapter presents a comprehensive overview over the emergence, spread, scope and role of English as the established lingua franca in a global context. The chapter establishes the notion of Business English Lingua Franca (BELF) as an increasingly important variation and development of the English language. It is shown that English is no longer a monolithic language. The chapter also introduces the debates which surround the advance of English as a global language – in particular it introduces the notion of 'linguistic imperialism' and ends on a consideration of the simultaneous occurrence of English as the (business) lingua franca and increasingly powerful management discourses.

Chapter 6 'Spreading the management gospel – in English'

This chapter addresses the issues of how global discourses, English and (managers') identities are mutually implicated. It discusses whether the combination of a shared global language, the spreading practices of neo-liberal economics and associated management practices lead to a global convergence of identities, economic and cultural systems. This chapter is based on a reproduced article by myself, titled 'Spreading the Management Gospel – in English'. It was first published in 2004 in the *Journal of Language and Intercultural Communication*. However, at its end the content and discussion are commented upon in the light of ideas and concepts, research studies and evidence presented in Part I.

Part II: 'Applications'

Part II provides applications for the issues and ideas introduced in Part I. They are mainly based on original research findings and located in diverse national or cultural contexts. Some are country-based case studies, while some are set in one or even several organizations and focus on micro organizational issues.

Chapter 7: 'German: a language of management designed for Klarheit' (by Holden)

This chapter examines the evolution of management in Germany since the early eighteenth century Prussia, its ascendancy in the nineteentth century as German, its further development in the Nazi period and its manifestation in the current post-unification phase. This diachronic study reveals that German management still retains its Prussian core and reflects a society in which economic artefacts and achievements are considered components of culture, and has evolved a discourse that is strikingly different from management language in other cultures.

Chapter 8: 'Russia's long struggle with Western terms of management and the concepts behind them' (by Holden, Kuznetsova and Fink)

It examines the influx of Western management language since the collapse of the Soviet Union in December 1991. It develops a cross-cultural management perspective, which views the exchange and generation of knowledge as acts of translations. Through the case study of the difficulties in translating one particular book (written in English) into the Russian language, it is shown that translators had to act as catalysts to create common ground between Western experience, knowledge and values with Russian ones. The chapter argues that the world of management practice, education and research is dominated by English, which is indifferent to the impact of language barriers as they influence the intercultural transfer of management knowledge. It shows acts of translations to be a conscientious quest to bring Western knowledge in harmony with Russian experience as it is now.

Chapter 9: 'Language and careers in multinational corporations' (by Piekkari)

This chapter is based on empirical materials taken from a variety of empirical settings, inclusive of the Nordea case study from a Finnish/Swedish context. The chapter takes issues with the notion that language competence in international careers can be reduced to a mere technical skill. Rather, it is suggested that language competence has much deeper implications for career paths and development. The chapter reflects on language competence from a variety of perspectives such as the existence of a 'language glass ceiling', its effects on diverting a person's career, as a requirement for expatriation and as an outcome of the expatriation process, and on its role in shaping personal networks.

Chapter 10: 'The business-unit concept at AKZO and the interpreting role of the CEO' (by Karsten and Wolpert)

This chapter focuses on the Dutch tradition of 'social dialogue' and how it is practised between social partners. It draws on research set in a Dutch company (AKZO), which was faced with urgent needs to change its organizational structure to become more flexible and closer to its markets – business units were introduced as part of the structural change. This idea was incorporated following the visit of the senior manager to the United States and the help of consultancy companies was enlisted to 'translate' the label into practice. However, the 'meaning' of what a business unit actually 'is' and 'what it does' remained unclear to all involved parties. Through a series of dialogues a meaning was finally created and established this new category and structure. The chapter is based on extensive historical accounts of minutes of the board meetings and interviews and shows that even within a context of power and shifting alliances, AKZO succeeded in creating a new structural reality.

Chapter 11: 'Communication strategies and cultural assumptions: an analysis of French–Japanese business meetings' (by Tanaka)

This chapter is based on a case study outlining Nissan (Japan)–Renault (French) interactions. It uses video-recorded data of a marketing meeting between Renault and Nissan employees with English as the working language. The description of the meeting shows that Renault participants dominate the meeting, while Nissan participants are generally quiet with the exception of one active Nissan participant, who had previous international experience. The analysis shows that a Western management discourse underlies the discussion and that particular contextual factors shape the processes as well as the outcome (i.e. the final decision) of the meeting. This case demonstrates how local Japanese management beliefs implicitly affect communicative patterns such as communication styles as well as the utterances made in English by Japanese participants.

Chapter 12: 'An Italian perspective on international meetings, management and language' (by Poncini and Turra)

This chapter explores management and language in Italy by using cases and examples drawn from research and interviews with Italian managers. It first provides historical background on specialized language and conventions used by professional groups to explain why it remains difficult to identify an 'Italian way' of doing management. By contrast, American organization and management literature has had strong influence on the curriculum of Italian business schools and has contributed to unifying linguistic conventions, leading to a use of specialized English terminology in Italian corporate settings. Two themes are presented: first, the use of English as well as other linguistic features in meetings conducted in Italian; second, multicultural business meetings organized by an Italian company and conducted mainly in English are examined.

Chapter 13: 'Humour and management in England'

This chapter introduces the historical and cultural reasons for the particularly widespread use of humour in English society and in its work organizations. It is shown that the use of humour symbolises particular values such as the intolerance of pomposity or undue solemnity, which are exposed and undermined through its use. Humour also services as an important equalising and socializing lubricant which enables the management of potentially difficult and ambiguous situations. It is argued that the particular use of humour and the value put upon it is a typical feature of English society and English management, which continues to differentiate it from other cultures.

Part III: 'Conclusions'

This part consists of two chapters which provide commentary, summary and synthesis of the previously presented materials.

Chapter 14: 'Management in other languages: how a philological approach opens up new cross-cultural vistas' (by Holden and Tansley)

This chapter argues that philology, the branch of linguistic science which focuses on relationship among languages and chronicles the history of words, can provide insights into management in diverse socio-cultural contexts. The chapter briefly summarizes some of the more traditional approaches to comparative management studies. These approaches use 'cultural variables' as their main device to understand and frame management thoughts and actions and they continue to dominate the comparative approaches. The chapter highlights the potential contributions of a comparative approach based on philology. This approach is supported by treating the words 'management', 'managing' and 'manager' from a historical and linguistic-comparative perspective across several countries and languages. The chapter makes the case for the development within management studies of a new field called management linguistics as a counterpoise to the cultural domination in the characterization of management worldwide.

Chapter 15: 'Conclusion: international management and translation'

This chapter draws together the theoretical/conceptual ideas of Part I and the practical applications of Part II. It uses ideas taken from translation studies as a means to synthesize the diverse ideas on language and discourse. It is argued that framing the work and practices of management as acts of translations can be helpful in understanding and enacting a world in which questions of mutual intelligibility are addressed in the context of global network structures and dynamic knowledge transfer.

Part I

Theories, ideas and approaches

Introduction

Chapters 2–6 explain the ideas of the book, introduce the key concepts and terminology and set out the theoretical background for a language-sensitive study of management and business. They provide the intellectual 'toolkit' and 'working utensils' for framing the activities of (international) managers as language-based and exploring them through a linguistic lens.

The purpose of theory is to provide a bedrock within which to conduct systematic analysis of language behaviour in organisational and management settings. In other words theory contributes a way of understanding the myriad activities of the empirical world and in doing so it bestows a sense of order and direction on to what otherwise would remain a chaotic and ungraspable flux of experience. It will be argued that theoretical orientation and practical activity are not as clearly separated as it is sometimes assumed – rather they are in a mutually informative relationship and constitutive of each other.

The two theoretical traditions which will be used are 'social constructionism' (or social construction) and 'linguistic relativity'. Both orientations have been developed from a language-sensitive perspective and make language central to understanding the processes of the social world. Yet, the foci they have taken differ in that the former's thrust of enquiry is directed on discourses and meaning systems, while the latter's is on the grammatical and morphological structures of different languages and consequent social and cultural behaviour. In Chapters 2–6 these theories are introduced, research work grounded in these respective traditions is discussed and it is suggested that in future the study of international management may constructively draw on both traditions to inform 'what we know' and 'how we understand' international management.

2   Language matters

This chapter presents ideas and concepts about 'language' and 'reality'. It establishes certain connections about their relationship – in other words it 'theorizes' about what connects 'language' and 'reality', how words and worlds are implicated in each other. It achieves this by presenting some theories which propose certain links between the two concepts and establish the importance of language in the making of social realities. Theories are, of course, simply a way of understanding the world and its phenomena and offer a systematic framework to make sense of the world.

Nothing as practical as a theory

McAuley *et al.* (2007) argue that theories have a strong practical use as they influence every aspect of our daily lives, how we understand it and act upon it. Theories entail the deployment of an explanation of some apparent aspect of our worlds:

- Theories are linguistic, conceptual devices that try to tell us things about the world by representing them in a causal manner.
- They define, classify or catgorize aspects of the world.
- They propose reasons that explain the variation of particular phenomena in terms of the effects of the action.
- They identify the situations or contexts when these causal relationships will operate.
- They can therefore guide our actions, because they enable predictions.
- They are not divorced from our everyday lives and behaviour.
- They influence what happens to people: they are used to describe, to explain and equally significantly to justify the things that we do and how we do them.

For example, the words 'market', 'supply' and 'demand' are conceptual abstractions, which provide a framework for myriad actions in local, regional, national and global contexts. They are put into a particular relationship (the market is based on the unencumbered interplay of supply and demand mechanisms), which becomes enacted in the world. Theories then are not 'aloof' from life; rather they explain it and as such set a framework for action. Such abstractions ('market', 'supply' and 'demand') are linguistic creations, which have substantial effects on the ordering of the 'real world'. They are also not necessarily 'neutral' or 'objective' representations of 'words become true'. On the contrary, they are imbued with assumptions (e. g. that a 'market' exists and is indeed 'free') and values ('that it is a good thing' to have such market mechanisms to order the economic affairs of states and organizations). Theories then always present world views and are based on assumptions and inscribed with values.

Two theories which are introduced here (social constructionism and linguistic relativity) provide the vocabulary which informs later discussions and therefore they are reproduced in some detail. Both orientations[1] make language central to the perception and making of social realities. At the end of the Chapter 4 dimensions of language are differentiated (descriptive/categorical; phatic; performative; ideological) and discussed in the light of each other.

Social constructionism

Social constructionism can be viewed as a theoretical orientation, which provides underpinning points of reference for many different disciplines. Burr (2003: 11) provides an extended and insightful expose of social constructionism (albeit in the context of psychology), which she sees as associated with postmodernism as a 'rejection of the idea that there can be an ultimate truth and of structuralism, the idea that the world as we see it is the result of hidden structures'. Thus, social constructionism 'denies' that there is an objectiveable, ultimate truth, which can be 'discovered' through scientific means.

As an orientation, social constructionism has been taken up with great enthusiasm by scholars of organization and management, who have found it a useful way of thinking about the role of words and language in the construction of organizations (Tietze *et al.* 2003; Westwood and Linstead 2001). The intellectual roots for the works of many of today's organizational scholars are provided by a book by sociologists Berger and Luckmann (1966), *The Social Construction of Reality*, in which they argue that the seemingly objective social world is in fact constructed by human actions and interactions. Thus 'society' (or the social world) is constructed in continuous, circular processes by human beings, which is perceived as a (seemingly objective) reality which they must obey and respond to. Fundamental to the process of construction is humans' ability to create symbols and categorizations as they can be detached from the 'here and now' and used in many different situations. Ultimately, humans' shared use of symbolic systems constructs huge social structures that seemingly exist and originate outside human activities:

Language now constructs immense edifices of symbolic representations that appear to tower over the reality of everyday life like gigantic presences from another world. Religion, philosophy, art, and science are the historically most important symbol systems of this kind.

(Berger and Luckmann 1966: 55)

Returning to the example about market, supply and demand, which was given at the beginning of this chapter, the process of social construction could look as follows: One might be born into economic structures which are based on the ideas of the free market and supply and demand as its ordering mechanisms. The words and concepts of 'market', 'demand', 'supply' constitute a symbolic system whose meanings can be transported across particular local contexts and be applied elsewhere. Furthermore, growing up in a market economy one takes certain institutions (banks; shops; institutions of education such as business schools) and practices (saving and spending money in exchange for goods and services; acquiring the skills and knowledge to gain a competitive position in the labour market) for granted – i.e. they are accepted as being 'overwhelmingly and irrefutably' true as well as useful. Moreover, free-market capitalist societies are based on the principle of competition – i.e. individuals and organizations compete with each other for jobs, market share or profits. Competition is a fundamental feature of social and economic life, which requires (and produces) 'competitive' people and organizations with certain individual and organizational characteristics. Thus, people think about themselves in terms of a number of dimension of competitiveness (e.g. degree of determination and energy, focus and application) – from a social constructionist point of view this is not because there are any pre-given personality dimensions, which express the essence of competitiveness as part of human nature. Rather competitiveness and its dimensions are seen as (constructed) outcomes of the prevalent economic and social reality at a particular time.

Some features of social constructionism are:

- A critical stance towards any 'taken-for-granted' assumptions. Categories such as 'competitiveness', 'the market', 'the organization' are treated as constructed entities – rather than being seen as inevitable pre-givens. Social constructionism does not 'deny' the existence of social or organizational realities (as it is sometimes accused of). However, it is more likely to ask questions such as: Where do these particular words and practices come from? Who uses them/does not use them and in which contexts? In other words, it questions the 'normality' of words and the social practices they constitute. Consequently, it offers an avenue to better understand the provenance of the 'status quo' as well as to critique and change it. For example, an innovation popularized by fast-food outlets was a re-consideration of what constitutes 'normal' customer behaviour. Rather than assuming that customers need to be served at a table, they became incorporated into the collection of food and the disposal of empty plates and finished dishes. The concept of 'the customer' was, of course, never in doubt, but what constitutes 'normal' behaviour was re-thought.

What's in a name?

In England a number of educational institutions have recently changed their name as they have been given permission to change their title from 'Institute of Higher Education' or 'College of Higher Education' to 'University'. As reported in the *Times Higher Educational Supplement* (August 2006), one of the new vice-chancellors commented: 'Gaining the University title has been really significant for us ... People previously did not really know what an Institute was, but they know immediately what a university is.' In a year when for most universities final recruitment figures are declining, the vast majority of the new universities have announced a 'bumper year' with between 4 to 40 per cent increases.

It is very unlikely that over one summer of recruitment the activities inside these new universities will have changed – the teaching and administration of courses is likely to be very much as it was the year before. While over time some changes might occur such as a stronger focus on research, the immediate 'reality' of these organizations and how students will experience them remained the same. Yet, the change in the name has attracted many more students than before. This might be because universities enjoy a higher status than institutes of education – but it is also a point of knowledge and carrying a 'meaningful label', which is recognizable by potential applicants. Thus a mere change of label has made a tremendous difference for the status, revenue streams and future developments of these organizations:

- An appreciation of the historical and cultural situatedness of knowledge: The categories and concepts which frame our understanding of the world are indeed culturally and historically bound. There are no absolute and universal categories which transcend cultural and temporal boundaries in such ways that they would carry the same meaning in every thinkable context. To give an example, the notion that 'leadership' is important for the successful strategic development of organizations is very much an established 'truth'. It would be difficult to deny this without sounding nonsensical, provocative or seditious. However, it has also been shown that 'leadership' means a great many different things in different contexts, is enacted in multiple ways and its exercise is not necessarily the only way of developing organizational knowledge and expertise. Thus, the word 'leadership', despite its instant appeal and widespread recognition, does not imply the existence of a universal and uncontested 'reality' of leadership.

- An emphasis on everyday social processes: Social interactions as they happen in everyday contexts are of particular interest to social constructionist studies. This is because of its stance that through the investigation of micro contexts, the very process of reality construction can be approached and understood. The mundane looking 'going-ons' between people are viewed as practices through which a shared version of world is sustained and created and common knowledge emerges.

- A recognition of the importance of language: The everyday 'going-ons' would not be possible without the use of language. It provides a means to categorize the world through its function as a symbolic sign system. Thus, we can label a person in different ways – a manager, a career women (but not a 'career man', perhaps?), a chief executive, a labourer, a professional, a secretary, a trainee, a union official. We can also label our actions in different ways indicating normalized ways of behaviour when interacting with particular people – with managers we are likely to 'have discussions', 'sort out problems', 'discuss the business agenda'. We can further describe people and behaviour by adding adjectives and adverbs – 'This rather nice chief executive, I talked to' implies a different meaning from 'This rather pompous chief executive, I talked to'. Being able to 'name' and describe situations, behaviour and people is an important mechanism to categorize our reality and in doing so to create a sense of order and purpose. This implies that language has indeed a descriptive function – in that it provides us with words (and rules how to order these words) to capture our experiences and perceptions. This does not imply that there is a permanent and universal reality behind the meaning we attribute to words and that language 'mirrors' an objectively existing reality. Rather, through using language one draws on and evokes (culturally agreed, but otherwise arbitrary) categories which assist us in describing and acting (in) the world.

- An emphasis on language as a form of social action: Beyond its descriptive and categorizing function, using language also implies 'acting in the world'. In this regard language is more than a bag full of words which we can dip into to describe the world. In using language we perform social actions, which can range from having a chat about the weather with a colleague at the coffee machine, delivering a presentation to a group of fellow sales managers, interviewing for a job or emailing a report to a business partner across the world. All of these actions use language and create social cohesion and belongingness, set the agenda for future action in the sales department, present someone as a professional and competent person and provide timely information to advance a collaborative contact. All of these actions only make sense in a world of business, competition and commerce – at the same time they also confirm and create the very world in which they take place. Thus, language and labelling, action and reality are mutually implicated.

Personality versus identity

People think about their personality as more or less stable and unified. While many people acknowledge a degree of change over time, on the whole one's personality is seen as mainly consistent, as a pre-given sets of traits which define 'who we are'. In particular in some fields of psychology the idea that people have personality characteristics and that these make people behave differently from each other has taken foot. In work contexts these ideas have been applied in particular to recruitment and selection procedures, where personality tests, which measure certain traits of one's personality, are often used to assess the suitability of person to job.

In contrast, from a social constructionist perspective such a view of 'personality' does not exist – within this tradition the word personality is replaced with the word 'identity'. A different choice of word signals that from this perspective the notion that human beings have personalities, which can like objects be measured, does not hold any water. On the contrary, who we are and what we feel is seen to be contingent on who we are with, what we are doing and the reasons why we are doing it. Thus, a social constructionist would not describe someone as having a competitive nature, though in certain contexts the person might very well display competitive behaviour. This is because identities are not seen to reside unchangeably and forever true in the inside of a person, but they derive from the social realm, which is of course constituted in and through the use of language as described in earlier sections of this chapter. This is not to say that identities are either accidental or determined by society – but rather that individuals can draw on those languages (or discourses) available to them at any given time to provide descriptive labels for 'who they are'. Identity is viewed as a 'process in which individuals construct categorical belonging, both for themselves and for others with whom they come in contact' (Joseph 2004: 84).

Critique of social constructionism

There are two main criticism of social constructionism, which express important views on its possible limitations, dangers even. As they do raise fundamental concerns about its (potential) moral void as well as its flawed logic, they are explained here with a view to establish the position of the book:

Social constructionism is morally bland and equivocal. This critique is often associated with a position of relativism which denies the existence of absolute and ultimate standards, which could be used to judge variations of behaviours, practices and values. Different constructions of the world exist and can only be compared with each other rather than to an ultimate truth. Consequently, it seems to be difficult to develop any consistent attempts to develop ethically grounded guidelines for action. How can one group or culture or country claim that its practices and values are universal and therefore superior compared with those of other cultures? How can one group justify its particular cultural, political or commercial preferences if there is no way of asserting that what constitutes a perfectly reasonable choice of (business) behaviour for one group of people constitutes a morally rejectable, oppressive move for others? These are difficult questions to answer from a social constructionist position and will be returned to at the end of this section.

The second criticism posits that entailed in a social constructionist position is the claim that 'language is all there is' as nothing has a 'real existence' beyond the symbolic sign system itself. Thus, the effects of the flow of financial resources, the price of oil, the existence of wars or technological advances are merely happening in language as 'there is nothing outside the text' (Derrida 1978: 158) and therefore they do not have any 'real' material consequences. Returning to the notion of 'globalization' a critic could then argue that from a social constructionist perspective globalization does not really exist, as it is a mere linguistic symbol without any roots in an objectifiable reality. However, this position would be misleading and is, in my opinion, not a social constructionist one. From this perspective one would not ever deny the 'reality' of globalization (note bene: the magnus opus of social constructionism is called 'The Social Construction of *Reality*' – emphasis added) – though one would not treat it as an objectively given entity. Rather, it would be viewed as a process in which different agents come together, using their material and symbolic resources, including power, to forge, negotiate and shape the processes of globalization. As a social constructionist one might be careful when to apply the label of 'globalization' (being aware of its constructed – but not unreal! – character), one might be sceptical about any utopian or exaggerated claims of what this label can achieve (attempting to establish the contexts within which the label is used; to which purpose and by whom), but one would not be blind to the material consequences, both negative and positive, that globalization can bring about for different groups of people.

Thus it appears that the criticisms levelled at social constructionist positions are based on an exclusive 'either–or' logic: Either one has universal (god-given) values and parameters to measure and judge human behaviour or, if not, one glides into moral blandness at best and into nihilistic chaos at worst. Either there is an objective, universal reality or there is only language-based illusion or even falsehood.

Social constructionism recognizes both the material world as well as the role of language. Language use always happens within existing social and cultural contexts, which in turn shape what can be expressed and said. In this regard language mediates reality. I noted earlier that the term 'career women' is a label that can be attached to a woman who pursues a career (rather than focusing on household affairs). It is a meaningful term in the context of labour-market developments which saw the entry of women into the world of paid work. However, talking of a 'career man' is somewhat 'odd' – as men have traditionally been assumed to be grounded in the world of paid work and there was no need to differentiate between differently located men. The context of labour-market developments sets a degree of constraint of 'what can be said' and 'of what makes sense'.

Thus the relationship is a mutual one in which through language use social realities are constructed, challenged and changed, while at the same time the existing social realities provide the (constraining) context in which language and meaning unfold. When it comes to making judgements about values and practices a social constructionist position takes into account the exercise of power and influence in the making of the social world. This is to say that there is no assumption that all human beings have equal opportunity to create life worlds which they would find acceptable; on the contrary some individuals or groups are more influential in shaping social realities in such ways to further their own ambitions or projects (Hardy *et al.* 2000). Thus, when making assessments about the ethical circumstances of a situation or case, from a social constructionist position, one takes into account the exercise of power and control, the means via which it is employed and the consequences it entails. Such assessments are therefore more likely to be context-driven, comparative and specific, rather than drawing on generalized or universal standards.[2]

Applications

In the field of organization studies there are different themes and directions within which social constructionist approaches have been applied. Studies range from an exploration of linguistic resources such as stories and metaphors (Gabriel 2000; Grant and Oswick 1996) to attempts to apply constructs such as scripts, conversations or frames to organizational processes (Fairhurst and Sarr 1996; Ford and Ford 2003; Gioia *et al.* 1989); studies which have researched social practices and symbols and how they are mutually implicated and unfold over time (Boje 1991; Musson and Tietze 2004) and how and why linguistic resources are used by organizational members to confirm, challenge or change existing organizational structures and processes (Boden 1994; Weick 1995). Whatever their specific approach, all studies share a common assumptions about the centrality of language in the making of organizational and social worlds. Organizations are likened to texts (Putnam *et al.* 1996) or indeed sometimes it is assumed that they 'are texts' (Taylor and Van Every 2000), which can be read, understood, edited and (over)written just like the text of a book. Managers are of particular importance in the process of 'writing' the organization as they are in a position to wield more influence compared with other groups. Thus, they have been likened to 'practical authors' (Shotter 1993; Shotter and Cunliffe 2003), who have recognized the formative power of language (Holman and Thorpe 2003) and are particularly active in shaping organizational talks and texts.

Managers as theoreticians

Industrial sociologist Tony J. Watson conducted a participant observation study at a telecommunications manufacturing and development plant in the UK (Watson 1996). The company was going through a period of deep-reaching changes and managers frequently found themselves in difficult and ambiguous circumstances, in which they had to respond to corporate discourses of empowerment, teamwork and development while at the same time they had to implement cost-cutting programmes and often redundancies.

Watson shows that – despite managers' honest claim that they do not much theorize about their actions – they nevertheless developed certain patterns in their thinking which informed their actions. These managers did 'theorize' about the company's circumstances, their actions and consequences in a systematic way. Watson shows that 'The principles which appear to underpin their [managers'] thinking are ones which combine moral categories with pragmatic conceptions of what "will work" – what will work in the sense of helping managers carry out their tasks for which they are responsible.' (Watson 1996: 339)

Linguistic relativity

The second theoretical orientation which expresses an interdependent relationship between world and words derives from the discipline of linguistic anthropology and is referred to as linguistic relativity. Linguistic anthropology looks at language as a set of cultural practices and draws from a variety of approaches within the humanities and the social sciences, but focuses on the nature of speaking and its role in the constitutions of society and the interpretation of culture (Duranti 2005: 21). It is based on ethnographic methods, which means that a researcher explores customs and ways of living from the point of view of the natives. Linguistic anthropology explores languages as its starting point to understand culture. Linguistic anthropologists start their work by learning the language of the tribe or people they are studying, paying particular attention to how grammar and vocabulary structure the reality of the people under study. Thus, linguistic anthropology focuses on the native language of different groups of people.

This is an important difference from the works of researchers in a social constructionist tradition, who sometimes, too, employ ethnographic methods, but who study the language as it is used by particular occupational groups, the stories told by organizational members, the ways women talk differently from men, why and how particular organizational or social group carry more 'voice' and power than others and so on. Apart from very few exemptions, they do *not* study the structure and impact of different native languages on processes of construction, they do not question whether it matters that the vast majority of their contributions is set in English-speaking contexts or at least reported in English and published in journals which are published in the American/English language.

The linguistic relativity hypothesis

The linguistic relativity hypothesis states that members of one linguistic culture think differently from people in other cultures as each language divides the world up differently and therefore speakers of each language perceive the world differently from each other. This means that one's native language shapes in a deep way one's very thoughts and experiences in and of the world: a native speaker of Japanese, for example, sees and experiences the world differently from a native speaker of American English. This 'hypothesis' is attributed to the linguists Benjamin Lee Whorf (1897–1941) and Edward Sapir (1884–1936) (although neither of them ever articulated it and the totality of each of their work is more complex than captured in this 'hypothesis'). The contribution of these researchers is to state that grammar and vocabulary (and its use) cannot be separated from the world and how it is talked about. Two different languages are then no longer just two different ways to talk about the same reality. Alternative languages carry with them different theories of what reality is.

> The real world is to a large extent unconsciously built up on the language habits of the group. No two languages are ever sufficiently similar to be considered as representing the same social reality. The worlds in which different societies live are distinct worlds, not merely the same world with different labels attached.
>
> (Sapir 1949: 161)

There are two different version of this thinking, one called the strong or radical version, one called the weak version. According to the strong version (or linguistic determinism), one's native language determines the way one sees the world, how one thinks about it and the consciousness one can possibly have about it. Agar (1994: 67) explains that it would be like 'a prison with no hope of parole. Translation and bilingualism are impossible'. The strong version has generally been rejected by most researchers – whereas the 'weak version' has been debated and empirically tested. It claims that human perceptions of reality are structured and constrained (not determined or controlled) by human languages in interesting and significant ways. One's native language is like 'a room you're comfortable with, that you know how to move around in. ... But familiarity does not mean you can't ever exist in different rooms' (Agar 1994: 68). Linguistic relativity then means that one's native language influences the way one sees the worlds, behaves towards it and makes sense of it. There is no objective reality which any language can describe through syntax and vocabulary; rather the very description creates 'relative realities', which are contingent on and interlinked with language.

Whorf became famous through his work with the American Hopi Indian's language. He argued that Hopi was a 'timeless' language, radically different from conceptions of time by speakers of American English. Indeed, he argued that with the proper institutional support the Hopi would have articulated the theory of relativity as they do not objectify time, i.e. for them it is not a thing, which can be subdivided into units and segments. Therefore, it cannot be 'counted, saved or wasted'. One of the fundamental metaphors of industrial societies, viz. that 'time is money' (Adam 1995; Tietze and Musson 2005), would therefore make no sense to Hopi Indians (at least those at Whorf's time), not so much because they did not understand systems of exchange, but because the metaphor presupposes that time can be quantified, standardized and counted. In the Hopi language and worldview such a possibility does not exist. Time is part of a flow of events.

Whorf looked at Hopi verbs and grammar and showed that verbs (i.e. words denoting actions) are marked with 'validity' – i.e. Hopi Indians do not put great value on when an event happened, but rather on the evidence that supports what they say. Following Agar's (1994: 63–64) summary and commentary of the use of verbs, it can be stated that: 'He runs' in Hopi is *wari*. But *wari* does not mean he + run + present tense. Rather it means 'running, statement of fact.' *Wari* could mean he is running, ran, has run, he used to run, is going to run, just has started running, etc. as long as the statement is based on what both the speaker and the hearer know to be a fact. *Era wari* on the other hand has a different validity: it means 'running, statement of fact from memory'. So, one would use *wari* if both speaker and hearer had witnessed the running, one would use *era wari* if only the speaker witnessed the event. *Warikni* means 'running, statement of expectation'. *Warikngwe* means 'running, statement of law' (the running person is likely to have been in a race).[3]

Compared with this understanding and marking of verbs, the English language is quite different. When using verbs English speakers have to use a tense marker – they have to acknowledge different times in which action takes place.[4] There is no way round this: when using the English language, the world is in the first instance divided into temporal categories – past, present, future – rather than into categories of validity. Thus Whorf argued that speakers of American English and speakers of Hopi live in different worlds. The first group lives in a world of clocks, calendars and deadlines and the latter live in a world of unfolding events. This observation raises the question again of whether the inhabitants of different linguistic worlds live in the same world at all. In terms of linguistic relativity (and social constructionism) the answer is 'yes, to an extent'. Looking at the concepts of validity (memory, fact, expectations) there is some commonality with temporal concepts (past, present, future) – an argument which can be supported by the fact that Whorf wrote in English about the Hopi language. This is only possible if Hopi concepts and meanings can be translated (albeit not perfectly) into other meaning and language systems. Also, the English language can find ways of expressing concepts of validity, though they do not form part of the basic grammar and taken-for-granted assumptions.

Thus expressions of validity are less easily codable in the English language, i.e. there is no ready made language-tag one can use to express different degrees of validity easily – though they are still translatable, though one might have to use a whole phrase in the target language to communicate the concepts expressed in the original language with only a single word or language-tag.

Time is money – a global metaphor?

Explorations of how 'time' is understood and lived provide rich insights into the fundamental orders of societies and cultures and into the very basic assumptions which underlie the understanding of human activity in time.

According to Lakoff and Johnson (1980) metaphors are much more than mere embellishments, rather they express the basic conceptual devices through which human beings see, interpret and make sense of the world. A particular dominant metaphor is 'time is money', which establishes a relationship between 'time' and 'money' in which time becomes a measurable and limited resource that can be planned, controlled and efficiently administered. We can measure time through dividing it into sub-unites and live by calendars and clocks. Encoded into this metaphor are also certain prescriptions for behaviour: If time is scare (limited) we must not waste it; rather we must 'manage' it in such ways as not to squander it and to apply it effectively in each situation. Effectiveness also implies working to achieve targets in line with deadlines. In order to stick to deadlines we must stay in control of time and conduct ourselves as disciplined employees.

While this metaphor is often related to industrial production as it provided a framework to manage time in line with the production process, the question arises whether it is becoming a concept that gained global presence and global recognition. Propelled by IT technology it is now possible, perhaps, to respond speedily and effectively to all kinds of requests and requirements.

In many regards the features of linguistic relativity are very similar to those of social constructionism:

- A critical stance versus 'taken-for-granted' assumptions. Whorf's work has shown that one of the fundamental principles of understanding human beings' position in the world, i.e. time, is tied into language and that no universal concept of time exists. These observations are confirmed when looking at the work of cultural anthropologists such as Hall (1973) who show that 'time' and 'space' are culturally bound concepts, which are expressed differently in different contexts.
- A recognition of language and an emphasis on everyday language and social processes: Many of the early researchers were trained linguists as well as

anthropologists. Therefore, their focus on language, everyday linguistic and social processes was the point of departure for their work. They often lived with the people they were observing and kept detailed diaries and notes about their observation. Such work included learning of the native language, drawing up its grammar and words and thus inferring about the worldviews. Thus they approached the understanding of culture very much from a language perspective, in which the social and the linguistic are very closely aligned.

- An emphasis of language as a form of social action: The categorization of the world through the use of words and the ordering of the world through the use of grammar is linked to viewing the world in particular ways and acting in the world in particular ways. For example, the Hindi language has a much richer vocabulary to describe and express family relationships compared to the English language. There are different words for 'aunt' and 'uncle', depending whether they are from the paternal or the maternal side as well as on their age. Implied in these categorizations are different ways of relating towards them and different ritualistic ways of behaving towards them. Of course, such differences can also be made in other languages, though one would have to add on more descriptive explanation. However, other languages do not connote these particular ways of thinking about peoples' status, the respect they are owed and how to conduct oneself in their presence – i.e. these words also express particular worldviews (about family relationships and orders) as well as prescribe action in this social context.

Taking care of the Ganges

The river Ganges in India is used for bathing, washing and religious rituals of many kinds as well as for disposal of waste and even corpses. Health workers were getting concerned about the level of pollution in the water and the effects this had on the health of people bathing, washing and praying in the Ganges. Despite the use of the same language (English) in discussions involving all constituents there was no meaningful exchange between the different parties. In the Hindi religion the river is sacred (a belief that does not have its roots in English) and how can something sacred be polluted? Thus, any suggestions that the river might be polluted did not make any sense at all – the mere suggestions that the river might be polluted was also considered to be a terrible insult to this holy being. The source of this quandary is the world 'pollution' and its meanings and connotations. After many prolonged and difficult discussions with people along the river and strenuous efforts to explain the meaning of pollution, a shared understanding began to emerge: 'The river is holy, but she is not pure. We are not taking care of her the way she needs us to.' Thus, the river was considered not so much to be polluted, as neglected.

From then on, health workers began to say – in English – 'the Ganges is suffering' rather than 'the Ganges is polluted', despite the fact that in the order and logic of the English language, a river cannot suffer (as 'a river' is categorized as an inanimate object, but not as a person or being). With this new way of defining the situation it can now be talked about and addressed without giving offence. (See Elgin Haden 2000)

Applications

The insights of linguistic anthropology have been taken up and applied by a different set of scholars, who work in the field of international management and business. Piekkari and Zander (2005: 4), in their editorial article about language and communication in international management, frame the contributions in the tradition of linguistic anthropology as they quote the words of linguistic anthropologist Duranti (2005: 337) as a underpinning precursor 'to have a language not only means to have an instrument to represent events in particular ways, it also means to have the ability to interact with such events, affect them or be affected by them'. Contributions in this field are sometimes similar in tenor and focus to those written by their organization studies colleagues, though their focus is on native languages as well as on the role of English as the global lingua franca of international business. Scholars have researched the frequent linguistic and social inequalities associated with particular language practices (Feely 2003), language proficiency and its consequences for social exclusion/inclusion; the use of English as the shared language in multicultural teams and consequent misunderstandings (Henderson 2005); its role in the internal communication of global firms (Poncini 2004) and reflected on ethical implications of English as 'the passport to a successful life' (Bargiela-Chiappini 2006; Gee et al. 1996). As a recent innovation, scholars have turned their attention to the role of English (and other languages) in the very process of knowledge generation and research (Marschan-Piekkari and Welch 2004). Some of the contributions of this field will be rehearsed in more detail in Chapter 4, where the activities of international management are explained and discussed through a linguistic lens.

Human-resource implications of a common corporate language decision in a cross-border merger

A research team investigated the consequences of adopting a common corporate language following a cross-border merger between two Nordic banks, viz. Finnish Merita Bank and Swedish Nordbanken to merge into Merita Nordbanken (MNB). It was decided that Swedish would be the common corporate language. The introduction of a common corporate language aims at achieving a variety of aims such as enabling formal reporting as well as informal communications;

fostering a sense of belonging. The research team investigated the Finnish viewpoint concerning the language choice through an ethnographic case-study approach. In particular, the decision to use Swedish as the common corporate language had human-resource implications – some of which are listed below:

- Performance: The Finnish-speaking employees experienced difficulties in communicating effectively and conveying their views and expertise in meetings, where their insufficient skills rendered them silent although 'professionalism' would have required active participation. Also, performance appraisals were not always held in Finnish, but sometimes conducted through an interpreter – thus making it difficult to convey expertise and competence in occupations which require a high level of conceptualisation and abstraction.
- Career paths and promotion: In order to advance one's career to the top echelons, fluency in Swedish was a prerequisite. Thus, some reorientation of career paths of Finnish-speaking employees occurred, and some evidence suggests that employees might have left the bank partly due to the existence of the common corporate language.
- Key personnel: Many Swedish-speaking Finns benefited from the new language policy, finding themselves in influential positions within the post-merger organization. They fulfilled important gatekeeper and liaison roles and acted as 'language nodes' between various groups. However, they also found themselves used as 'translation machines' and experienced degrees of overwork.

(Adapted from Piekkari *et al.* 2005)

Given that English is the language of banking and that many of the professional employees of the two banks were accustomed to communicating in English, do you think the adoption of English as the common corporate language at MeritaNordbanken would have helped to avoid some of the disintegrating effects described in the study?

Social constructionism and linguistic relativity

The two theoretical orientations introduced in this chapter have informed and provided the intellectual sustenance for a series of scholarly explorations of language and how it is used in organizational and social contexts. The two orientations share certain characteristics. They make language central to their understanding of what constitutes reality and broadly speaking they understand their relationship as a mutual one. In both traditions language is the topic of research, which means that researchers are studying the use of language in different contexts and collect 'data'. In both traditions it is also a resource – i.e. the means through which data is analysed. The two orientations are also beset by the same moral questions and dilemmas – as they can be accused of moral relativism and ontological evasiveness as once one surrenders the belief in essential and absolute categories, analytical and moral rigour become harder to attain.

Yet there are also differences between the two traditions. The first is that they derive from different disciplines (sociology; linguistic anthropology) and have therefore been taken up by different communities and have been applied to different situations and circumstance. Following on from there their respective subjects of interest and attention are different, too. In the field of management studies, social constructionist ideas have been taken up by organizational scholars to explore discourses, i.e. meaning systems and their use. What these scholars have not included into their studies at all is any consideration of language as a system of vocabulary and grammar, i.e. as a native language. Thus, in this field of study there is no exploration of whether, let's say, discourses of management are the same and have the same effects notwithstanding whether they are used by a group of American managers or by a group of French managers. Nor has this field considered the effects and consequences of what might happen in exchanges between such different groups of language users – wouldn't linguistic relativity at least require us to ask questions about the impact of their native language on their exchanges? If English is the language of exchange, what are the consequences and effects of having a shared communicative instrument for the relationships, the definitions and understanding of contexts and tasks? This kind of question, to a much larger extent, has been addressed by scholars who work in the field of international management and business. However, in their studies one seldom finds any references to the multiplicity of discourses in organizational settings, the contested ways of negotiating meaning, the rhetorical means employed to do so. Janssens *et al.* (2004) make a case for more interdisciplinary work between what they call organizational communication scholars and scholars in the field of international management and business to join their complementary insights to understand the production of international companies. A call to which this book is, perhaps, an initial response.

Dimensions of language

In the title of this chapter it is claimed that 'language matters'. This claim is based on the argument that language and social reality cannot be separated. Two theoretical orientations and examples of applications were enlisted to provide a reasoned case for establishing the relationship between language and social reality.

It is therefore possible to distil different dimensions of language, each explaining how language is part of making particular social realities:

a) Descriptive/categorizing dimension: Language is a symbolic sign system, which combines 'signs' with 'meanings' (for details see Tietze *et al.* 2003: 17–31). While there is always a certain degree of flux and changeability in this relationship, there is nevertheless also the possibility to create descriptors, labels and abstractions. These provide important categories, which act like signposts in the world which tell as 'what things are', how to relate to them and behave towards them. These categories are both constructed and real. Often, this descriptive function of language is played down as it is denied that language can 'represent things as they are'. This is not the position of this book, though, in which language is attributed with a descriptive function.

b) Phatic dimension: In speaking to people it is quite often unimportant what is said. In the words of a former linguistics professor of mine: '90 per cent of what people say is actually redundant' – by which he meant that most of the time people talk without communicating any particular important, interesting or new information. So, why do people talk so much? One reason could be that the very act of speaking is a social act, which allows us to establish and confirm relationships with other people. Phrases of politeness (which, according to social anthropologist Malinowski 1923: 476, are as common among savage tribes as in a European drawing room), enquiries about health, the weather, greetings are all language acts which create social cohesion. The phatic function says that the content of what is being said is not as important as that something is being said as it is a way to create a sense of unity and commonality between people.

c) Performative dimension: This is perhaps, the most frequently cited function of language as it expresses most explicitly the creative power of language. The expressions was coined by the philosopher J. L. Austin (1962), who said that certain verbs do more than just describing (representing) a situation, rather they 'do' something. In saying 'I declare you husband and wife' or 'I name this ship Elizabeth' or in placing a bet ('I bet you'), people are performing certain actions. Language 'does' something: it changes the world in the way that two people have got married; a ship has been named; a bet has been placed. Despite their symbolic character, there are material consequences in all three instances in that two individuals have changed their legal status; a ship may now (legally) enter the nautic waterways and systems where it can be registered and controlled; a bet must be honoured and money (or other means) will be exchanged.

d) Hegemonial dimensions: At several occasions in this chapter it was said that not everyone has got equal means to use language in such a way that would allow them to make a world which would be conducive to their success. It was also said that managers – at least in organizational contexts – are sometimes more powerful than other organizational groups to forge alignments between words and world in line with the projects they pursue. Their words and action express a 'common sense logic' which it is difficult to fault or argue with. In a similar vein Phillipson (1992, 2003) argues that the arguments in support of English as the global lingua franca have taken on an almost intuitive common sense logic, which equates English with progress and prosperity. However, behind this 'common sense' lurk the interests of dominant groups who pursue their own interests under the cover of common sense. In other words their words and actions (i.e. discourse) reflect the dominant ideology of particular groups only, but they have been accepted and internalized as normal by the dominated groups. Hegemony is the word which describes the process by which dominant ideas become taken for granted. The nexus of ties between discourse, language and hegemony will be discussed in more detail in the next chapter.

These different dimensions explain why language matters. Of course, such a clear division of language into four neat dimensions is a 'mere construction', albeit a helpful one as it allows reflection on different elements of and reasons for defining language as a creative force. The different dimensions feed of each other and in particular when working with empirical data or even just when reflecting on one's own experience, it becomes clear that they are connected. Let's return to one example. Getting married necessitates the saying of certain words in certain contexts, thus descriptors such as 'husband' and 'wife', 'priest' or 'registrar' are used; without these abstractions it would not be possible to go through the ritualistic process. In the wider context of the event itself many words will be spoken as people meet before and after the ceremony. Most of these words are 'redundant' as they do not carry any particular novel information, yet these words have a purpose: They tie the attending people together from a loose assembly into a purposeful convention, which shares the emotions of the occasions. This, of course, means that the phatic dimensions of language performs a social function. A further performative function is that the status of 'boyfriend' and 'girlfriend' has been changed to 'husband' and 'wife' expressing the change in the cultural and legal status of a person with long-term and significant consequences. The ideological dimension is linked to issues of power. This can simply mean the use of the power of office as only particular office holders are entitled to marry two people. Second, despite recent cultural changes, it is still considered to be 'normal and good' that people get married. An early strand of feminist literature has argued that marriage is a patriarchal institution which benefits men (the dominating group) more than women (the dominated group), yet that women buy wholeheartedly into the idea that in order to achieve fulfilment and purpose in life they need to be married. In terms of these feminist writers marriage is a form of hegemony as it normalises the unequal relationships between man and woman.

In sum, each of the dimensions of language 'does something' in the world. In this regard they could all be subsumed as having a performative, i. e. a creative function. However, they perform quite different things and work in different ways. In differentiating between them greater conceptual

Table 2.1 Dimensions of language use

	Descriptive	Phatic	Performative	Hegemonial
Function	Categories and abstractions which can be transferred across contexts	Group cohesion; emotional ties	Shapes all social relationships and interactions	Common-sense nature of status quo
How	Provides symbolic sign system, which links signs and meanings	Exchange of pleasantries, greetings, small talk	Use of language in general	Normalization of certain practices and ideas

clarity is achieved. In the next chapter the hegemonial function is discussed in the light of the connection of ties between management and discourse.

Questions

1. Why is it harder to speak of a 'career man' than of a 'career woman'? Discuss this question in the light of the four dimensions of language.
2. Can you think of instances where your arguments 'were not heard' or seemed less convincing compared with others'? Why do you think this was the case? Try to phrase your thoughts in the light of social constructionist terminology.
3. If you are bilingual, can you think about any grammatical differences in the two languages, which might constitute a source of different world-views?

Notes

1 From hereon I will use the word 'theoretical orientation', rather than theory, when referring to social constructionism and linguistic relativity. Both provide an explanatory framework for the relationship between world and words, but also both are extremely difficult to prove right or wrong. As explained in the chapter there have been specific attempts to 'prove' or 'disprove' the claims made by linguistic relativity, but as Elgin puts it (2000: 63): 'the jury is still out' whether the posited connections between world and words can be upheld or not. A similar reasoning holds true for social constructionism, which is difficult to prove 'right' or 'wrong' – although, in this area, too, debates rage about its value and the (lack of) potency of explanatory value. For these reasons I talk about 'theoretical orientations' – this term is looser as it includes the possibility to 're-orient' one-self when working with words and languages.

2 Some sources differentiate between social constructionist approaches and those of 'critical realism' (Sayer 2000). Critical realists subscribe to the position that societal structures and processes are historical and culturally contingent not pre-given or ordained categories. However, they are more likely to use concepts such as power and ideology when analysing the 'making of the world'. Critical realists see and describe the social world in terms of power relations, which underpin the ways they are talked about and enacted. For the purpose of this book, no further

distinction between social constructionist approaches and critical realist approaches will be drawn. As I have mentioned several times in this chapter, a social constructionist perspective does not exclude considerations of power in the processes of making the world. For example, managers have been identified as a particularly powerful group whose worldview is often given priority over those of other groups.
3 This section is adapted from Agar's book (1994) titled *Language Shock. Understanding the Culture of Conversation*. The book provides a 'tour de force' through the history of linguistic and cultural studies by reviewing and commenting upon the works of prominent linguists and anthropologists. This is done in a very personable manner and interspersed with anecdotes and examples.
4 It is sometimes said that the English language is easy to learn. As someone who had to acquire English as a second language, I tend to disagree. It is, perhaps, possible to quickly learn some words and phrases to conduct a basic communication (but then again this would be true of many other languages, too). The more one studies English, the harder it becomes to master its complexities and idiosyncrasies. The multitudes and uses of different tenses is a good example. English possesses temporal markers which are quite sophisticated and which either do not exist or are not used to the same extent in other languages.

3   Management and language

In this chapter we turn to a closer examination of the provenance and definitions of the terms 'management', 'manager' and 'managing' as they are used in work organizations and beyond. To this purpose we shall provide some comments about different approaches to understanding the terms 'management' and 'manager' and also delve into the etymological foundations of these descriptive words. The spread of management as a general practice as well as an occupation, both of which are accompanied by particular ways of thinking and acting in the world, is considered in the next section. It is shown how the occupation of 'management' and 'managing' are linked to the acquisition and mastery of a specialist language of management, which is reproduced through the institutions of management education and informs the enactment of organizational realities. In this context discourse is introduced as the ways and means through which such enactment occurs, with managers being influential agents to shape their work environments. Also, the notion of 'global discourses' is defined as providing a universal set of meanings, which is recognized and can be applied across spatial-temporal boundaries.

Approaches to management

The emergence of management as an identifiable social and organizational group and as a hierarchical function within organizations is to be seen against a tapestry of economic and social change rather than as a 'necessary' and 'pre-given' development. Of course, activities which can be described as 'managing', i.e. the direction of effort and resources to obtain particular goals, have existed before the period of the Industrial Revolution – one might think here of the building of the pyramids or the Great Wall of China, not to mention huge military operations which all preceded the British Industrial Revolution. However, the growth in the scale and complexity of capitalist enterprises in the nineteenths and twentieth centuries required the development of a new group of specialists to co-ordinate and direct the extensive activities. Consequently, managers became an important and identifiable group, which could be distinguished from the workers – i.e. the origins of modern management can be located within the period of the Industrial Revolution (Pollard 1965: 35):

> Like the generals of old, they [managers] had to control numerous men [sic], but without power of compulsion: The absence of ... unfree work was not only one of the marked characteristics of the new capitalism, but one of its most seminal ideas ... Again, unlike the builders of the pyramids, they had not only to show absolute results in terms of certain products and efforts, but relate them to costs, and sell them competitively ...

The differentiation of management as a clear occupational and functional group has been associated with the factory system (i.e. factories are the locality of production), which replaced the home-based cottage industry of pre-industrial times (Pollard 1965). Concomitant with this replacement were particular employment relationships – which 'owed as much to the desire for closer co-ordination, discipline and control of the labour force as to the pressures of technology' (Marglin 1974:180). Thus, through the establishment of the factory system a new division of labour became possible, which in the later stages of the Industrial Revolution saw the emergence of the identifiable hierarchical group of 'management'.

In the USA the evolution of scientific management and its popularization by Taylor (1856–1915) contributed to the development of organizational hierarchies as it legitimated the transfer of control over work processes from skilled workers to management. The separation of 'conception' from 'execution' of tasks (Taylor 1947: 36) together with the identification of 'one best way' through rational scientific analysis propelled managers into a more important organizational function and position. Although he did not always concur with Taylor's methods Fayol (1841–1925) provided the classic definition of management as a series of four key activities that managers must continually perform: planning, organizing, directing and controlling (Fayol 1949), which present 'the universal cycle' of management activity.

During the first half of the twentieth century a second differentiation emerged between those who owned businesses and those who controlled them. Burnham (1941) talked of a 'managerial revolution' which placed corporate control firmly in the hands of professional, salaried managers: The rise of the joint stock company, the diffusion of share ownership and the concentration of capital in more complex units, i.e. the overall increasing complexity of businesses necessitated the employment of non-owning professional managers, who exercised power because of their specialist professional and technical knowledge. Indeed Drucker (1954/1993) in a seminal text, *The Practice of Management*, established management both as a function and a social group, which is viewed as 'an essential, a distinct and a leading institution [is a] pivotal event in social history' as management expresses the basic beliefs of modern Western society. Drucker sees management imbued with the possibility of controlling man's livelihood through the systematic organization of economic resources and that through management economic change can be made the most powerful engine for human betterment and social justice.

Thus, in the twentieth century a remarkable transformation in the social standing of management occurred as management is frequently bestowed with an unquestioned faith in its capacity to act as a progressive and benevolent force in organizations and the institutions of society; its specialized tools and techniques are deemed to resolve the problems of contemporary life (Kranz and Gilmore 1990). In this regard management is akin not just to the exercise of planning, co-ordination and control, but also to the exercise of cultural forms of controlling (work) organizations through providing 'visions' (Champy 1995), transformational leadership (Bass 1999) and generally 're-enchanting' (Kanter 1990) the modern workforce. In many texts written by management consultants in particular there is an implicit notion that the supreme tasks for managers is indeed to manage the values and meanings of their subordinates – achieved through the management of culture by dint of using symbolic management (e.g. Peters and Waterman 1982).

Our modern understanding of management as an occupational group that organizes, coordinates and makes decisions about what work is done, how and by whom relating to production, finance, marketing and human resources and as a group who uses particular techniques and tools – inclusive of culture management and the provision of meaning and vision – is the outcome of particular technological, social and historical developments.

This very brief sketch[1] of the development of management and attributed conceptualizations shows management to be a social construct as it changes its meanings over time and as such it provides us with a 'category' to order the world into different social and occupational groups. Parker (2002) and McAuley *et al.* (2007) stress that these developments are not 'inevitable', but that both historically and contemporaneously, alternatives for organizing economic and social affairs exist.

Thus, the term 'management' as a generic expression for 'managers', who are an occupational group which has gained status and importance throughout the twentieth century and which employs a series of techniques and knowledges to coordinate the affairs of work organizations, is not an innocent, neutral label, but a constructed category which brings with it particular ways of being in the world.

Frames of managers and management

Over the decades different ways of thinking about management have emerged, been criticized and amalgamated into what constitutes our knowledge about management. Below are three such frames, together with some comments about how language has been treated within these different frameworks.

Scientific management

This approach to work organization was pioneered by Frederick W. Taylor (1856–1915) while working as superintendent at the Midvale Steel Company in Pennsylvania, USA. It presents both a set of management practices and a system of ideological assumptions. Taylorism's approach to work organization and employment relations is based on division of tasks into their simplest constitutent elements, with decision-making power lying with managers. Skill requirements should be minimized as this reduces a worker's control over work. Following scientific-rational principles, Taylor posited that it is possible to find a universal, one best way of organizing work and work tasks.

Language does not figure as an issue of importance in this approach to management as the relationship between language and reality is considered to be unproblematic. Vocabulary and grammar represent an objective world, which can be described and explained through the application of scientific means to the organization of work.

Reflective practitioner

This term was introduced by Donald Schön (1993) in his book *The Reflective Practioner*, in which he criticizes that managerial work can be understood as a scientific and technical activity. Rather Schön stressed the importance of attending to the social and political context in which problem setting, definition and solving occurs. 'Reflection-in-action' is used in unique and uncertain situations and focuses, for example, on the need to frame a situation and impose an order – but without taking recourse to pre-given theories, but relying on an array of personal and theoretical knowledge. In doing this a new situation is created, frequently through discussions and exchanges of what a situation or problem 'means'.

Here, language is quite central to practice, though it remains part of the background to professional practice. In the index of Schön's book, one finds fives notes relating to language and, indeed, he does liken the reflective practice in his examples to learning particular languages and repertoires (Schön 1993: 157–159). Thus, this work is written within a tradition that sees language as performative and creative and applies this insight to the context or problem definition and solving.

Practical author

This term has been coined by management and communication scholar John Shotter (1993). He likens managers to practical authors, who use language in organizations as they are aware of its performative role and its centrality to processes of organizing. Indeed, good managers are those who recognize this formative power and who create particular types of conversational activities. Their working tools include the use of metaphors and other poetic devices to create a shared 'imaginary' organizational landscape and these very tools also equip them with the collective creation of such a landscape. What differentiates a manager from a non-manager is that managers make a 'comprehensive set of connections and relations between' (Shotter and Cunliffe 2003: 33) the specific roles and tasks in an organization.

Here, language is recognized as a creative force, the intelligent and appropriate use of which is a (pro)active way to pull the different strings of the organization together as to formulate a shared and collective sense of purpose. Indeed, managers are differentiated from non-managers, because only the former are engaged in 'writing the overall organizational story' without losing the plot in the myriad of actions and words which constitute an organization. In contrast to Schön's work, Shotter 'foregrounds' the importance of language and makes it his point of departure for understanding organizational and managerial activities.

An interesting word

The word 'management' and its derivations is a fascinating word as it has much more than just one meaning and changes its connotations according to social, cultural and historic contexts and the purpose and intentions of the speakers. In the face of such multiple meanings and bewildering possibilities, a dictionary is always a useful place to begin contemplating words and their meanings.

According to the *Oxford English Dictionary* (1970), the verb 'to manage' is likely to derive from the mediaeval Italian word *maneggiare*, which in turn comes from the Latin *manu agere*: to drive animals (in particular, horses) by hand – thus the forebearers of the modern word 'to manage' refer to the handling and training of horses. The first three letters *man* indicate the Latin meaning of 'hand' (*manus*). In this derivation the word manage was a masculine concept to do with taking charge, in particular in the context of war. The French word *menager* in contrasts implies a more household based, gentler and perhaps feminine usage (Wesley 1996: 39), with Isabella Beeton's (1861) book on household management providing an example of the general organizing and people management function in the context of a large Victorian household.

Management is 'everything it is place'

One of the most successful books on management ever written was Mrs Beeton's (1836–1865) *Book of Household Management* (1861), a 1,112 page book which sold 60,000 copies in its first year of publication. The household Isabella Beeton wrote about was the equivalent of a small business, with between five and 30 full-time resident employees, plus part-time workers. According to Wesley (1996), Beeton's three principles of good management have stood the test of time: a) setting an example and giving clear guidance to staff; b) controlling the finances; c) applying order and method in all management activities. Wesley also shows through a closer reading of the book that her principles transcend the realm of 'operations management' and

include reflections on moral conduct as well as the provision of values
and goals:

As with the commander of an army, or the leader of any enterprise,
so it is with the mistress of a house. Her spirit will be seen through the
whole establishment, and just as she performs her duties intelligently
and thoroughly, so will her domestics follow in her path (Beeton,
quoted in Wesley 1996: 45).

The meaning of the word management only acquired an association with
business affairs by about 1600, whilst the word 'manager' meant one skilled
in co-ordinating and controlling these very affairs. This understanding
points to modern connotations of a manager as a skilled handler of business, finances and organizational interactions. In Chapter 14 Holden and
Tansley point to another possible root of the word management as it can be
seen to be based on the Latin term *mancepts*, which refers to a head of a
company commissioned by imperial Rome to supply bricks for roads and
armour for the legions. Here, for a contemporary reader, an understanding
of management, which differentiates between manual and conceptual
workers, is recognizable. However, the first 'real' managers emerged only
much later in history and were little more than agents of owners or those in
charge of public institutions such as workhouses. As we have seen in the
previous section, the increase in the size of work organizations in the nineteenth century was concomitant with the emergence of 'management' as a
body of people acting for the owners (Mant 1977).

Apart from such etymological considerations, which point to a variety of
possible interpretations of management and its activities, there is, of course,
the issue that most of the modern and contemporary definitions are
expressed in the English language and therefore they do not express the
enormous semantic range of meanings for 'management' used in other languages. While the English words 'management' and 'to manage' have
entered most European languages, they continue to be connoted with different meanings. Holden and Tansley provide detailed linguistic insights
into the meanings of management as they cover five European languages
and investigate the cultural and historical idiosyncrasies which both shape
and express the meanings attributed to these descriptors. The list below
provides one such abbreviated example of meanings of management taken
from the French language:

Diriger: being in command
Directeur/directrice: not necessarily associated with membership of the
board.
Dirigeant: member of the board with a distinctive leadership role.
La gestion: abstract term for management relating to processes and proce-
dures.

Cadres: top management, come under the *directeurs*.
Le management/le manager/le leader: refer to running of companies.

The Anglicisms, however, are considered to form a shallow (*pauvre*) language. Holden and Tansley also discuss how these different words are imbued with an all-important sense of hierarchy. While it is not impossible to find similar words in the English language (e.g. *la gestion* could be translated as administration), using these words is more than expressing a technical relationship, as they evoke (for those in the know) a hierarchy of different relationships and orders, which carry their own norms for conduct and behaviour. These differences get 'glossed over' if one were to use the generic terms 'manager' and 'management' indiscriminately to describe the French conceptual framing of managers and their activities: According to Caulkin (2005: 5) the use of English is like 'a one way membrane that all too often filters out the rest of the world'.

The first part of this chapter shows that management carries many different meanings, both historically and linguistically. Historically, we can understand management as an occupation, which only rose to prominence and power in the second half of the twentieth century. The roles, activities and the legitimacy of management has changed throughout the decades and continues to be a contested 'label' – these statements are in line with a social constructionist view of management. Linguistically, we can see that the word 'management' carries different meanings in different languages and that the use of the Anglicism 'management', 'to manage' and 'manager' do not capture the nuances of meanings attributed to them in different languages – these statements are in line with a linguistically relative position. To reiterate the message of Chapter 2, both theoretical orientations offer useful insights into the meanings of management.

The spread and spread of management

Management emerged as an identifiable organizational group and function in the nineteenth and twentieth centuries. Gaining increasingly in status management has been likened to a 'professional discipline' on a par with medicine, law or engineering (Squires 2001). A profession is constituted through having a body of knowledge which is learned and used by a body of people – it has an epistemological as well as a social aspect. Whether it is useful or not to differentiate clearly between 'an occupation' or a 'profession' is still debated (see Reed and Anthony 1992; Squires 2001; Watson 2002). For our purpose it suffices to see management as one of the emerging 'organizational professions' (Reed and Anthony 1992) rather than one of the traditional professions such as medicine or law, which require the acquisition of formal diplomas and qualification before practice. Nevertheless, it can be argued that increasingly management has become 'professionalized' as it has developed institutional structures such as networks of business and management schools, professional bodies which establish and guard the knowledge and membership of its functions as well as a network of conferences, seminars and training courses to share and disseminate knowledge. There are also identifiable bodies of knowledge with are studied, learned and for which qualifications can be obtained. These, in turn, are both passport into the profession as well as 'badge' of being a member of the profession. Professions, of course do claim to have special status and to be experts in their areas of activities – i.e. to be able to describe oneself as a 'professional manager' is more than a pure descriptive statement – one also makes a claim to expertise and superior understanding. Thus, there is an argument that the occupation of management emerged throughout the Industrial Revolution and beyond, but that management strove for and successfully acquired increasingly recognised professional status in the later half of the twentieth century. This is not to say that one has to hold a management qualification in order to practise management – however, increasingly people do embark on formal management education. The number of students who study business and management as part of their degree or indeed as their main degree subjects, continues to increase for both undergraduate and postgraduate education. The Master of Business Administration (MBA) also continues to grow as a qualification which is perceived by many as a prerequisite to a successful management career. Grey (2005) reasons that management education has a socializing function and that its point is less the skills and knowledge it imparts, than its capacity to develop a 'certain kind of person' (Grey 2005: 113) – i.e. 'the right kind of person' who can advance in the profession, speaks its language and embraces its values.

Other than the establishment and spread of management as an occupation, function and a profession, there is a second argument which relates to management as an activity, albeit an activity which is carried out in everyday contexts. Willmott (1984: 350) comments that it is possible to be engaged in management without being a manager as it can be seen as a 'reflexive social action', 'intrinsic to human agency' as in all 'societies, people are involved in the complex and demanding business of organizing their everyday lives'. Each of us engages in a daily struggle to accomplish ordinary tasks and maintain normal routines. This management of routines is something we all contribute to, and are knowledgeable about – it is 'second nature' (Alvsson and Willmott 1996: 9). In this regard we are all managers as we all juggle, co-ordinate and arrange a multitude of activities and strive to achieve a sense of order in our lives. These very efforts of keeping a balance and a sense of order point to the notion that there is a precariousness in 'managing' whether in or outside the work context. Watson (2002) has made explicit this link between management, a fear of ontological chaos and efforts to keep a sense of order and perspective. In this regard acts of managing can be seen as a coping mechanism to keep the abyss of chaos at bay. Using the words and techniques available to particular social and organizational agents could then be seen as a means to keep anxiety at bay.

In the light of such an interpretation, does it matter that most people will 'organize' their lives through drawing on the language of management in one way or other? According to some writers this might depend on the degree to which we incorporate the techniques and vocabulary of management into our everyday lives, including the degree of awareness we have about how and why we manage our very selves in particular ways. In this context Grey (1999: 577) issues some cautious words as he sees a spread of management activity into all areas of human relations as potentially dangerous and reductionist as it furthers the

> ascription of the term 'management' to various kinds of activities [which is] is not a mere convenience but rather something which has certain effects. The use of words is not innocent, and in the case of management its use carries irrevocable implications and resonances which are associated with industrialism and modern form of Western forms of rationality and control.

Thus, for example, applications of 'time management' to our private lives and the advice dispended in many magazines, in self-help books and by life consultants, and so on are not 'innocent activities and words' but make us behave in line with principles of efficiency (make a list of activities; rank them in order of importance), which are also imbued with guidelines for moral behaviour (don't waste time). Hancock and Tyler (2004: 619) posit that the techniques and imperatives associated with the management of work organizations are increasingly 'colonizing the everyday sphere of human communication and sense-making'. In identifying contemporary cultural resources such as self-help manuals and lifestyle magazines they argue that such texts 'constitute a material signifier of what is ongoing managerialist colonization of the everyday life world'. In other words we are all requested (and required) to manage our lives, manage our selves by developing life strategies and having a mission. Hancock and Tyler quote the British life coach Mulligan (1999) whose advice for self-improvement commence with the design and production of a personal appraisal form and questionnaire and continues with a range of formalized tasks (e.g. writing of mission statement). This kind of advice and activity is a far cry from the normal managing of everyday activities or the coping with anxiety, which were mentioned earlier. Rather, it is a quite systematic and strategic approach to managing everyday life with a view to generate 'high quality results' in terms of the final product, be it a person or a relationship. Of course, one could say – so what! What is so bad about adopting some of the terminology and practices of management? Why shouldn't I think of myself as 'a brand'? Why shouldn't I 'manage' my relationship with my husband? In response one might say that such application of the systematic and prescribed ways of management leave little room for any irrational, authentic or even just unmanaged experience of life. In this regard 'framing oneself as a brand' or 'managing one's relationships along quite calculated lines' imposes norms and values based on industrial 'performance principles' – rather than being a self-reflexive enterprise of possibilities and alternatives.

What we have tracked so far is the establishment of management as an identifiable occupation and function, which is 'institutionally empowered' (Willmott 1984) to make decisions and co-ordinate work organizations. In the later decades of the twentieth century management has spread in different ways – as a profession with its own institutions, identifiable and protected bodies of knowledge and qualifications which symbolise and express professional status. It has also spread as an everyday activity, which 'borrows' from the words and techniques developed for the purpose of managing work organizations.

The establishment as a function, occupation, profession and as an everyday activity are based on language – in a way this is quite a commonplace statement as most people (if prompted) will agree that language is important, if only because managers are engaged in 'constant verbal activity to gather information, develop shared understandings of the world and persuade individuals to contribute to collective purposes, such as the adoption and the implementation of new practices' (Green 2004: 654) and as one might indeed argue that all human activity is language-based in one way or another. However, in the above pages I have used a number of particular expressions such as the 'vocabulary and techniques of management', the 'words of management', the 'terminology of management' and so on. We will now take a closer look at the 'language of management' (called management discourse), how it is acquired and whether it can be said that it is spreading to such an extent that some parts of the language and practice of management have become 'global' and universally recognized.

Discourse and management

Much of mainstream writing about management and managers creates the impression that it is a straightforward activity, in which a neutral body of knowledge is drawn upon by trained professionals in order to make efficient and value-free decisions. However, even the previous very brief sketch of the rise and spread of management has shown that different meanings are attached to the word 'management' and its activities; these meanings are based on different assumptions about who is entitled to make which decisions and why.

Management has been established as a recognizable occupation which claims professional status. All professions have established bodies of knowledge and people who use and guard this body of knowledge. In the case of management, professional knowledge is tied closely to language as all of its concepts are language-based – i.e. they are highly symbolic in character and therefore subject to interpretation. Other professions, too, encode their knowledge in language and symbols – one might point to lawyers who must have knowledge about the (text-based) body of laws and their interpretation; or medical professionals, whose training involves the learning and remembering of a vast amount of information taken from biology, chemistry and physics and applied to human bodies. The vocabulary and techniques of both the legal and the medical profession might appear more 'real' as one is concerned with 'concrete and written laws' and the other with the human body and its malfunctions. Yet, the law is a prime example of how meanings and applications of rules are fought over and contested and with regard to medicine, just a brief glance into another cultural spheres shows that Eastern medicine employs a quite different sets of words, vocabularies and meanings to understand and heal the human body. Both professions, then, are language-based and contingent on context and circumstance, rather than being the application of universal rules and meanings.

Management as a professional activity is also bound to words and techniques, which are increasingly acquired through formal management training and education, which can be pursued through attending the classes and exams provided by professional bodies as they offer professional qualifications or through the attendance of a course of studies provided at university level by schools of business and management. It has been argued that what aspiring managers acquire through their course of formal education is a particular 'discourse' (Grey 2005), which they learn to master (Tietze 2004).

Discourse has been defined in myriad ways, ranging from everyday, common-sense understanding to highly specific, academic definitions reflecting particular theoretical positions. Traditionally, the term derives from the discipline of linguistics and has been used to any unit of speech which is more than a sentence (Mey 1993), but it has been adopted and used in both cultural, social and also management studies, where contributions often draw on the opus of French historian Michel Foucault (du Gay 1996; McKinlay and Starkey 1998; Townley 1994). However, its use and application continues to remain quite eclectic. For our purposes, a definition of discourse has been chosen, which is based on Foucauldian thinking, but avoids the deterministic stance which at times characterizes his work (Freundlich 1994). The definition we adopt is:

> A connected set of statements, concepts, terms and expressions which constitutes a way of talking or writing about a particular issue, thus framing the way people understand and respond with respect to this issue . . . [discourses] function as menus of discursive resources which various social actors draw on in different ways at different times to achieve their particular purposes – whether these be specific interest-based purposes or

broader ones like that of making sense of what is happening in the organization or what it is 'to be a manager'.

(Watson 1995: 814)

Thus, when considering the 'problems an organization is facing' we use the language of strategy and markets to define what the problem is ('strategic drift'; 'loss of market share') and we discuss this 'problem' in the concepts and terms which are available to us – i.e. we define and frame the problem in the language of strategy (which is our 'discursive resource'). We could use models to assess the degree of competitive forces in our environment and we could talk sensibly and knowingly about the organization's value chain and how to change it in order to cope with the problem we have defined. Consequently, we would make sense of the organization's situation and our own role and stake in it and we would act in line with our understanding – i.e. trying to change aspects of the value chain in order to realign the strategic direction of the organization which might include decisions about allocating resources and initiating new ventures. The language of strategy has developed immensely in the last two decades and comes with a set of techniques and models to assess, conceptualize and analyse organizations and the environment they are embedded in. Acquiring and mastering the language of strategy, for example, is a prime objective of management education and the notion of 'mastery' implies the virtuoso-like use of words and techniques, which frame how organizations are understood and which actions are taken – in other words management education provides access to and acquisition of discourses, which enable aspiring or practising managers to frame organizational and work 'problems' in particular ways. Grey (2005: 113) argues that the main purpose of management education as provided by business and management schools is to socialize people into the management profession and to develop a certain 'kind of "person". Socialisation equals a process of habituation into managerial language and gaining entry into the language codes of business – be it in terms of the latest jargon and buzzwords or the arcane of computing, accounting and finance' (Grey 2005: 115). Thus being able to use established terms and terminology confidently and competently characterizes the successful managers and differentiates them from other organizational groups.

Certainly, all education entails an element of socialization,[2] which includes the learning of particular discourses by people who then form social and occupational networks on the basis of their shared discourse and worldview. Many management courses offered at universities pride themselves of the international networks they are part of and which students will tap into by dint of taking their degree with them. Even a cursory glance at any given brochure advertising MBA courses in particular shows that buying into a network of existing and future business contacts is a main advertising feature in the attraction of students. In becoming a member of social and professional networks, which share norms and believes and which encompass language (Joseph 2004), the discourse is disseminated and sustained.

It is important to note here that by discourse we do not simply mean 'technical language' or a particular jargon which is used as a way to communicate with fellow experts and also to differentiate oneself from 'non-experts'. While the discourses of management entail a good deal of what can be described as jargon – the term discourse is both wider and deeper than 'jargon'. Discourse in the work context of management evokes a stronger element of identity and reality shaping and also provides a stronger sense of legitimacy for the actions of managers. Jargon can be seen as part of a wider discourse and can be used to achieve the appearance that neural expertise is applied to a set of circumstances rather than exercising power over people.

The use of jargon

Tony Watson (2004) differentiates between weak and strong discursive managerial pseudo-jargon. The weak version is a relatively informal type as heard in meetings and corporate settings and used to make concrete abstract element in organizational life. The stronger version uses more technical, performative language, which assists in mystifying and neutralizing the intrinsically political and value dimension of managerial work. Examples include:

Weak pseudo-jargon	*Strong pseudo-jargon*
From zero to hero	The reward system needs to be aligned with proven performance
Let's push the envelope	Our values need to be generally owned
Everyone needs to sing from the same hymn sheet	Our profit centres will deliver sustainable competitive advantage
Let's do some kite-flying	Changes will be driven through within eighteen months as the contribution of the business units to our core business will be re-evaluated

---

From what has been said so far, one could assume that managers acquire a technical language, a worldview and prescriptions for action, which they then simply take out into the world and 'make it real'. This would be saying that managers are the (willing) slaves to discourses, which dictate actions and interactions. However, this is far from true, we see discourses as elements of a society's culture which are – at least in principle, though not always in practice – available to all social actors. In drawing on such discourses, human beings have a great deal of freedom to utilize discourse in particular ways in order to make sense of their situation in the overall context of their lives or to shape their surrounding realities in particular ways. We see managers here as not simply reacting to a particular discourse, who apply recipes and formulas (i.e. using their discursive resources available to them) to solve problems or increase their organization's performance in a schematic and pre-given way. In using the jargon, models and concepts learned and acquired as part of their education, they are also active agents, who make sense of and 'enact' their environment and circumstances. 'Enactment' is the 'fact that, in organizational life, people often produce part of the environment they face (Weick 1995: 30). Managers' work is characterized by a great deal of tension, paradox and ambiguity and they have to make sense of these circumstances – using the concepts and words provided through their professional knowledge is a way of coping with and imposing a sense of order on otherwise complex and complicated processes. In doing so they 'enact' the environment, not as 'puppets on a string of the discourses they learned', but as active agents who draw on the resources available to them.

Hegemony

To an extent all social and organizational actors are thus engaged in the mutual and simultaneous process of shaping the world while being shaped by it. However, managers are a particularly powerful group which has achieved such a standing and authority that it has become difficult to argue with their logic and reasons. It is difficult to argue with the notion that organizations have to be efficient as it is in our minds so clearly linked to notions of profitability – and who can argue with such a given 'fact of life' that 'organizations have to be efficient to be profitable'. Of course one could argue that efficiency means different things to different people and that there are different ways to achieve efficiency and that it can indeed be measured in different ways – all of which would have quite far-reaching consequences for the decisions and actions an organization might pursue. Indeed, in organizational contexts such debates take place – as ethnographic studies have shown time and time again (Dalton 1959; Watson 1994/2001) – and people do query the costs and sacrifices entailed in decisions relating to outsourcing, cost cutting and efficiency gains. Yet, the dictate and necessity of 'being efficient' has been established as 'self-evident' and 'obvious' and the decisions taken in the light of increasing organizational efficiency tend to be accepted as normal and inevitable – though not necessarily desirable.

The concept of 'hegemony' explains why some ideas or actions appear to be so unassailable and 'true': hegemony refers to dominant ideas we take for granted – they are transferred by a 'hegemonic process' (a body of practices and ideas), by which the majority of people come to accept the ideas, skills and knowledge, the values and worldviews of the dominant group as 'naturally' superior and ontologically 'true' to the extend that they aspire to them, too. Phillipson (1992: 74), in his discussion of the English language and hegemonic processes (to which we will return in Chapter 5), argues that there are always competing and complementary sets of values and practices – in this regard hegemony is never absolute or complete – but that those in power are better able to legitimate themselves and to convert their ideas into material power.

Hegemony has become an important social-science construct, which is based mainly on the works of Italian scholar Antonio Gramsci (1971). It is important to note that hegemony does not imply a conspiracy or malicious manipulation of people, rather it is the capability of the dominant class or group of people to provide intellectual and moral leadership and to pursue interests which can be plausibly presented to be in the interests of all people (Fox and Fox 2004). The brief potted history of management at the beginning of this chapter described to an extent some hegemonic processes through which one group of actors emerged as more important than others and how, consequently, their knowledge, practices and worldviews become accepted as 'normal' and 'superior'.

The beginning of the chapter has shown that management as an organizational group, a function and more recently as a profession has achieved such hegemonial status – which is perpetuated through the discourses which, so the argument went, are acquired increasingly through formal education, which in itself has become a global business and is indeed part and parcel of the globalization processes described in the introductory chapter.

Global discourses

Following our definition of discourse, a global discourse would be a set of meanings and practices which are accepted and recognized across a multitude and variety of cultural, institutional and national contexts. They are available to organizational agents independently of their local, cultural and particular circumstances. They have crossed established boundaries and have achieved a level of familiarity, which establishes their global reach. Indeed, the discourse or discourses of management have been described in such a way which claims that they have become the ubiquitous 'master discourse of modernity' (Brighton 2002: 2), which 'signify a radical redistribution of social and economic power as it is the natural language of business, government and increasingly everything else as well' (Thrift 2002: 19 and 24). A case in point is Ritzer's 'McDonaldization' thesis (1996: 1), which is the 'process by which the principles of the fast-food restaurant are coming to dominate more and more sectors of American society as well as of the rest of the world'. Ritzer suggests that social collectives, including their business affairs, education and social life, are increasingly organized along the dimensions of efficiency, calculability, predictability and control.[3] Thus, he describes a process of convergence which entails the adoption of these principles to all areas and walks of life in a multitude of settings. Ritzer includes comments on (higher) education in his analysis, which he, too, sees subject to such processes. While he does not use the word 'discourse' the thesis he puts forward is an example of a spreading discourse, whose words carry a descriptive as well as a strong prescriptive function.

Many writings and comments on the globalization of (management) discourses are quite critical of its inherent dangers and warn of the loss of 'difference', 'identity' and 'authenticity', which are seen to be subsumed under the unifying practices which accompany the converging of discourses. However, other writers stress the utopian potential as a unifying discourse can establish a sense of stability, community and shared values which transcend the parochial interests of divided groups and people. Ohmae (1990, 2000) and Kanter (1995) might be two such writers who belong to the utopian school and who envisage cosmopolitans as people who are

> ... rich in the three intangible C's that translate into pre-eminence and power in a *global economy* [emphasis added by author]: concepts – the best and latest knowledge and ideas; competence – the ability to operate at the highest standards of any place anywhere; and connections – the best relationships, which provide access to the resources of other people and organizations around the world. Indeed, it is because cosmopolitans bring the best and latest concepts, the highest levels of competence, and excellent connections that they gain influence over locals.
>
> (Kanter 1995: 95)

In the context of this book, these cosmopolitans can be seen as language users – mainly users of the English language according to Ohmae (1991) – and also as users of particular discourses, here described as cosmopolitan, i.e. global economic discourses which provide them with a conceptual toolkit, the ability to practice it in the light of the prevalent (neoliberal) economic ideas and to form 'appropriate' relationships to operate successfully in a global world. Similarly, Ohmae (2000: 18; emphasis added in original) envisages the corporation as an 'invisible continent' which was 'discovered by Americans, but no nation holds a monopoly on entrance to it. *Any nation, any company, any race, any ethnic group, or any individual may enter.* In this sense, it is far fairer than the old world.' Academic writers (Chiapello and Fairclough 2003; Fairclough and Thomas 2004; Gee *et al.* 1996; Halsall 2007) respond sceptically: For example, through a technique known as critical discourse analysis they demonstrate that the assumptions and claims entailed in these texts are frequently programmatic in promoting a 'discourse-led' spirit of capitalism with its concomitant justificatory regime (Halsall 2007). Many of the texts produced by consultants and advisors, so these writers claim, attribute the status of 'greatness' to the cosmopolitan and the status of 'smallness' to the local (Chiapello and Fairclough 2003: 191).

It remains, of course, doubtful, if any discourse can every be truly global – in the sense of being used and dispersed into every corner of the world – so it is equally unlikely that any form of organizational behaviour or workplace practice will transcend all cultural, social and economic differences. Many of the writings of business and management experts are placed in 'an idealized, hygienist organization' in which conflict, resistance and 'talking back' has been banned. Empirical works point time and time again to a more complex reality: the discourses, for example, of Total Quality Management (TQM), teamwork, new public-sector management and so on are global in so far as they are recognized in a multitude of settings and contexts; however, how they are practised and realized is subject to continued and immense variety and complexity. To give but some examples: Holden's (2001a) study set in Matsushita, a major Japanese corporation, shows clearly the tension and discrepancy between the global philosophy discourse and local practice. Watson's ethnography (1994/2001) of ZTC, a multinational IT company, shows that the new discourses of 'empowerment' and 'cost control' did not simply displace existing ones, but rather they clashed, fused, vied for power, intermixed in complex and ever shifting ways – all mediated by managers' interpretation of their meaning and sense-making in the overall context of shifting and slippery organizational dynamics. De Cock's (1998) study of the implementation of TQM and BRP (Business Process Reengineering) discourses in two large British manufacturing organizations demonstrates that these discourses are not as totalizing and unifying as one might expect, but that their hegemonic force is mediated and challenged by local resistance and challenge. Interesting, in both Watson and de Cock's study it is the senior managers themselves who are quite often sceptical about the usefulness, adequateness or logic of such new discourses and, who in their own way, manipulate and mediate how and whether they become enacted reality. In other words they are the active agents, who use and appropriate discourses, but are not determined by them. The relationship between the local setting and the global discourse is a reciprocal one: 'The hegemony of various types of global managerialist discourse is not solid or stale but involves a process of re-negotiations within local contexts (Fairclough and Thomas 2004: 392).

New public-sector management

In a study about new public-sector management – i.e. about the transferability of the private sector as role model for the public sector – Salskov-Iversen *et al.* (2000) show that the discourse of new public-sector management disseminated from transnational organizations such as the OECD, the World Band and the UN, creates certain expectations for change on the local level. The use of NPSM appear like a global imperative, but its assimilation into local practices is hampered as it is re-articulated in line with local conditions, where it is adapted into local languages and only then becomes internalised into social practices.

Conclusion

In this chapter we have had a look at the provenance of management as an occupation and increasingly as a profession. It was shown that the label 'management' and its activities and practices are indeed 'socially constructed' as they emerged in a particular historical period and that they are also relative (not absolute) terms and practices as differences in their meaning continue to exist. The first part of this chapter is an attempt to 'de-naturalize' the concept 'management' by demonstrating that it is a social construct, which carries no universally accepted definition. In the second part it was shown that management is intrinsically tied to language, which was here defined as a particular discourse, which embodies knowledge and which 'empowers' managers to enact the world in line with the concepts and values inscribed in discourse and knowledge.

The discourses of management, so it was argued, are spread (amongst others) through an increasingly international service industry which provides management education. Logically, then this industry shares norms, values and outlooks (all expressed discursively), which are acquired by young generations of aspiring managers. As the numbers of business and management graduates continue to rise, it could be said that an increasing number of people have been equipped with quite similar knowledge and how to apply it in practice – i.e. we might be bearing witness to the emergence of global discourses with hegemonial status which have become so normal and accepted that we do not question their origin, legitimacy or purpose any more. However, evidence was provided that such global discourses might be idealized constructs which simplify the complexities and particularities of contemporary work organizations. In particular, drawing on some of the ethnographic works, it appeared that managers themselves – indeed quite often very senior managers – are very sceptical about universal solutions and the latest management fads and fashions. Therefore, it can be legitimately claimed that managers, while being part of by now established traditions, knowledges and practices (all of which expressed as well as constituted in and through discourses), are not passive subjects to omnipotent discourse, but able of independent thought and action. In this spirit the next chapter will reflect in more detail on the work, words and practices of 'international managers' – in this regard it will pay particular attention to the role of English as their (putative) shared language and on the use of the particular discourses, which they may or may not bring to bear on their particular circumstance.

Questions

1. To what extent to you agree with the statement that much of what managers do is a language-based, symbolic, activity?
2. Can all social and organizational exchange be understood as a form of 'mutual manipulation'?

Notes

1 It is not the purpose of this chapter to provide an in-depth analysis of the genesis and provenance of modern management. The interested reader will find plenty of material in the literature. Pollard (1965) and Mant (1977) have provided detailed accounts of this topic. Similarly, Willmott (1984, 1987) has published overview articles which provide a comprehensive analysis of the images and ideals of managerial work and examinations of conceptual and empirical accounts.

A recent and astute account on the role of organization theory and management, which also includes a detailed analysis of the rise of management, is provided by McAuley *et al.* (2007). The authors present a historical overview over the development of management as an occupation and a hierarchical function and its rise to a prominent and privileged profession. Interestingly, they provide historical evidence that in the transition of the 'cottage industries' (home-based production) to a factory system of production, which gave rise to the establishment of management as an identifiable function, alternative ways of organizing the increasing complexities of production could have been found. They show that the establishment of the factory system was not exclusively driven by technological reasons (the increasing use of water and steam power demanded the concentration of workers in specific geographical locations), but at least equally by the enhanced possibility to survey and control workers within the layout and attributes of the factory system. The authors quote Marglin's comment on the factory system: '[it] owed as much to the desire for closer coordination, discipline and control of the labour force as the pressures of technology' (1974: 180). Thus, the emergence of the factory system and the rise of management is not 'inevitable' but an outcome of technological forces in the context of human interest and influence.

2 Mey (1993: 289) purports that the design and delivery of educational systems is beset by a fundamental problematic, viz. that

> the same classes that have established the institutions of higher education have also been instrumental in structuring that education and organizing its curricula; we are faced with a co-opting, self-perpetuating system that favours those who are most similar to those already in it, *pares nobis*, as the expression used to be.

3 Ritzer (1996) bases his reflections on the works of German sociologist Max Weber who wrote extensively about the emergence and advance of bureaucracy. His discussions were grounded in a broader theory of (formal) rationalization processes. Weber viewed bureaucracies as cages in the sense that people are trapped in them, their humanity denied and anticipated a society of people locked in a web of rational structures.

4 International management and language

Based on the arguments and logic presented in the previous chapter, we can take it as given that the word 'management' is a social construct, which emerged and changed over time and which continues to carry different meanings depending on the context-of-use. Also, we have shown management to be intrinsically intertwined with the acquisition of a particular discourse, a specialist language, which enables managers to cope with the demands of their roles, but which also bestows identity and shapes realities.

In this chapter we turn to exploring the activities associated with international management, which is often set in the context of multinational organizations,[1] which are characterized by a large degree of language difference and have to make decisions about how to deal with a linguistic environment that is diverse and complex. Many companies have adopted English as the common corporate language or use English as part of their interactions. Therefore, the chapter also looks at the role of English in facilitating communication. Finally, some reflections on the relationship between 'language and culture' are offered as, frequently, in the literature and the general expectations of practitioner the activities of international managers are defined and discussed as being primarily related to the management of cultural difference. In suggesting that international management can be understood as a linguistically and discursively based activity, a different viewpoint is offered in this chapter.

Common corporate language – transit language

A common corporate language is 'an administrative managerial tool', which is derived from the needs of senior and top managers in an MNC to run the global corporation (Sørensen 2005 in Frederiksson *et al.* 2006) and provides common ground for communication between organizational units which are often embedded in different language environments. It is introduced to increase efficiency by overcoming misunderstandings, reducing costs, avoiding time-consuming translation and creating a sense of belonging with the firm (Marschan-Piekkari *et al.*1999a).

Sørensen's analysis of 70 Danish corporations, which used English as a common corporate language found that almost all written documents were generated in English as well as in the local language. With the exception of board and executive meetings attended by non-Danish speakers, these companies did not use English as an overruling language, but as a 'transit language' between various parallel local languages. Consequently, cost of translation had been doubled, dissemination of communication had become laborious and been delayed. Moreover, an element of misinterpretation had been added as there is a risk of altering the sense of a text each time it is translated (Sørensen 2005: 59).

International management and languages in the multinational organization

Martinez and Toyne (2000) show that the meaning of 'international' is diverse when it prefaces the noun 'management'. Indeed, international management has been defined in various ways and there is by no means a universally accepted definition. One could ask whether the meaning of 'international' is restricted to business contexts, which cross national borders or whether it should be defined more broadly, entailing also contexts which imply the crossing of cultural boundaries (which are not necessarily overlapping with national ones). For example, Boddewyn (1997) defines 'international' as relating to the fact that business which is conducted in different national states is necessarily embedded in different economic, sociocultural and political contexts. However, most definitions of international management do not treat language as a factor worth considering.

In the previous chapter management was defined as a discursive activity, based on the acquisition of particular discourses, which are spread through increasingly institutionalized and professionalized educational network structures. Building on this discursive definition, 'international management', too, is seen to be constituted and expressed by particular discourses, but in addition international managers are likely to express these discourses in different languages as they are part of multinational organizations, which consist of geographically dispersed subunits embedded in different language environments. The case of language being central to conducting international business and at being at the heart of international management processes has been articulated more frequently and with more urgency in recent years.[2] Piekkari and Zander (2005: 4) place language quite firmly 'at the core of international management processes', creating and reflecting organizational realities'; Barner-Rasmussen and Björkman (2005: 99) see MNCs as being 'multilingual almost by definition', as international negotiations, knowledge transfer and management, headquarters–subsidiary, subsidiary–subsidiary relations and processes pertaining to control, coordination, integration and management of multinational enterprises can neither be conceptualized nor conducted without reference to and use of language as 'the multicultural and multilingual workforce is a reality for many companies' (Harris and Bargiela-Chiappini 2003: 156; see also Holden 2002; Holden and von Korztfleisch 2004; Welch *et al.* 2005).

More specifically and most recently researchers have taken such comments on board and began to seek avenues which integrate the 'languages issue' with the strategic development of multinational enterprises. Luo and Shenkar (2006) make a strong case to integrate language into the articulation and implementation of a global strategy as 'language choice and usage affect information circulation, presentation, and interpretation, which in turn allows corporate headquarters to control global planning and inter-unit coordination'. Barner-Rasmussen and Björkman (2005) have explored how MNCs can gain competitive advantage from inter-unit knowledge sharing and communication – they show that managers' fluency in the languages of interchange (here Finnish and Chinese) is an important factor in stimulating inter-unit knowledge exchange.

These authors argue that international activity involves a multitude of activities such as the management of linguistically and nationally diverse teams, the initiation of inter-unit knowledge transfer, the design and implementation of integrated human-resource management or quality-control systems or the co-ordination of a global-resourcing system and many more. All of these tasks cannot be conducted without taking recourse to language and discourse. Clearly, task complexity varies and requires different language skills. For example, a receptionist needs speaking and listening skills to provide information and exchange (fairly standardized) courtesies; a logistics officer requires reading and writing skills to satisfy the technical requirements of co-ordinating the flow of parts, goods or services; a designer working (even if only virtually) in a multilingual team needs good overall communication skills as well as reading, writing and listening skills in order to interact constructively in a team. Chew's (2005) study on the English-language skills of new entrants in banks in Hong Kong confirms Feely and Harzing's (2003) assumption that language skills and requirements vary across tasks and roles. For example, Chew's respondents were engaged in such diverse tasks as taking notes, processing information into spreadsheets, develop and write procedural guidelines, reading manuals, dealing with customer complaints, translating for non-English-speaking colleagues, writing internal newsletters, reporting to senior managers – all of these tasks were conducted in English and required different levels of proficiency and sometimes posed different training requirements.

Feely and Harzing (2003) put international managers at the pinnacle of the linguistic skills scale as they 'will need excellent language proficiency embracing the full range of rhetorical skills such as negotiations, persuasions, motivation and humour. At this level the capability level might well exceed that of a typical Masters graduate in modern languages.' This is an interesting quote as it assumes that an intrinsic characteristic of being an international manager is being able to express oneself in a (potentially) foreign language in a sophisticated and refined way – combined, of course, with an astute sense of achieving objectives and relevant technical expertise. Holden (2002) adds an important element to an emergent understanding of inter-national management (or to what he refers to as the cross-cultural manager) as he stresses that the managerial function requires ensuring that in all conversations the 'business focus' is maintained and provides direction for actions. Thus, the international manager is different from other professional groups, which might have equal or better language competence, but lack awareness of business goals and objectives. The approach taken by Feely and Harzing and Holden are congruent with the position of this book, which views international managers as working in sophisticated ways with words and techniques to ensure business focus, which are captured and expressed in a multitude of languages. This is then our working definition of international managers and what they do: They work with discourses, i.e. words, meanings and techniques in mainly (but not exclusively) multi-national organizations and need to be able to address tasks and achieve business goals in different languages. I am aware that this is an unusual definition, which is different from other approaches which base their understanding of the identification of international manager roles (e.g. Sparrow 1999). In employing an approach based on language, which is understood as a conduit for gaining deeper contextualized knowledge, one can explore the dynamics and complexities which accompany the processes of international cooperation and exchange.

Language difference in multinational enterprises

Multinational organizations have been shown to comprise a multitude of tongues (Welch *et al.* 2005) – they are sides of language difference. Welch et al. (2005) show that the effects of language influence the integration of dif-ferent parts following mergers and acquisitions such as inter-unit commu-nication, subsidiary role and autonomy, staff transfers, organizational structure and control and coordination mechanisms; moreover language effects also shape the experience of social inclusion or exclusion as well as the exercise of power. These authors claim that 'language is almost the essence of international business' (Welch *et al.* 2005: 11) and enterprises and corporations neglect it at their own expense. While such difference can be a creative force, it can also be an impediment to effective and successful communication – it becomes a language barrier as in the light of such lin-guistic difference, multinational organizations have to take a position vis-à-vis language difference and how they want to manage it.

According to Welch *et al.* language works at various levels – it can be the spoken or written language of everyday communication, but it can also be a form of company idiom (acronyms, special terms and terminology specific to a company) or it can comprise the technical/professional or industry language – the latter being the nearest to this book's definition of discourse.

The different levels of language co-exist and interact with each other, so that language is never a one-sided, easily controlled 'thing'. In this regard, framing language difference as a mere mechanical problem, which can be addressed through technical translation, is a fallacy as empirical studies (cf. Henderson 2005; Poncini 2003, 2004) show. Ponicini, for example, demonstrates through her analysis of an Italian company's meetings with its international distributors (representing 12–15 countries) that participants construct their business relationship through their linguistic choices (eight languages other than English are used in these meetings) and that these are considerably more complex than just 'using English' as the shared lingua franca. The analysis shows that multicultural and multilingual groups develop their own sense of 'groupness' and build relationships in the context of business interactions. It is important to note that this sense of groupness involved the overcoming of different levels of proficiency in English and different communicative behaviours. This sense of groupness was not linked to national cultures. Cases of conflict, for example between the company spokesman and distributors, were not related to different national cultures and their respective behaviours, but were caused by specific business issues.

The group of business people Poncini observed did successfully overcome language barriers, but they had to work hard for this. Language difference can become and remain a genuine barrier, which prevents successful communications across boundaries. Often, companies anticipate communication difficulties and take recourse to the tools of modern-day communication such as video conferencing, intranets, email networks and so on, all of which make information flow faster, but do not guarantee that successful communication will happen as companies have to manage *language diversity* (the number of languages used in the company), which also includes a consideration of *language penetration* (number of functions which are actively engaged in cross-lingual communication) and *language sophistication* (the refinement and proficiency required to successful communicate).[3] Feely and Harzing (2003) suggest a variety of options for managing language problems:

- Adopt a lingua franca; frequently this is English.
- Adopt 'functional multilingualism' – rely on a mix of languages to communicate.
- Use external language resources such as translators and interpreters.
- Train the workforce.
- Introduce a common corporate language, in particular for core functions.
- Deploy 'language nodes' (linguistically skilled personnel) strategically.
- Follow selective recruitment to address language needs.
- Deploy expatriates to manage subsidiaries.
- Pursue inpatriation strategy – employ inpatriate subsidiary personnel into head office operations.

- Use machine translation.
- Use a controlled language with limited use of vocabulary and syntax.

None of these approaches in themselves provide a perfect solution as each presents its own mix of advantages and disadvantages. Feely and Harzing (2003) comment that the challenge is to understand the language barrier well and to mix and match the solutions into a blend that is right for the company context. However, even understanding the nature of the context and problem can be quite a challenge as this requires the cooperation of people working in a second or third language with people working in their native tongue. Miscommunications are likely to occur on both sides of the communication coin: Native speakers who have a tendency to attribute their ideas and feelings onto other people, and over-estimate their linguistic fluency (Gudykunst 1998). Or they find themselves bemused, disconcerted or even angry when second language users switch the communication code, i.e. they confer with each other in their own language. Second-language users often find themselves faced with a loss of rhetorical skills, which in turn has consequences for their professional identity and can undermine the authority and standing of often quite senior managers, who feel uncomfortable with committing to agreements or objectives or processes, which are expressed in a language they have not fully mastered. A personal acquaintance of mine, who is the Managing Director of an international haulage company based in Germany, feels that his whole career has been dogged by his lack of competence in the English language. Despite attempts to obtain a degree of fluency in this language through private tuition, he continued to feel out of his depths in business meetings, where he felt his years of experience and his insights were 'wasted' as he did not possess the linguistic means to express himself.

Feely and Harzing (2003) track some such consequences upon the relationship of actors in multinational corporations. They identify 'psychic distance' where the effect of language difference is an increase in uncertainty within the relationship manifesting itself as suspicion, caution and mistrust. Also, people tend to 'cluster around' other users of their own language, which can lead to the emergence of parallel information networks, which are detrimental to team cohesion and knowledge sharing. Language is the dominant factor in defining group boundaries and compositions and orders how information is screened and interpreted.[4]

So far, it has been shown that language differences have an impact on the functioning and goal achievement of multinational organizations and therefore these organizations have to contain such difference. Frequently, they adopt a common corporate language to ease and lubricate the processes of communication. This language standardization has many advantages as Marschan-Piekkari *et al.* (1999a: 379) point out: it can support formal reporting relationships between units, improve access to company documents and create a stronger sense of belonging to the corporation. In this regard, the use of a common corporate language is not only tied to efficient communication, but to controlling diversity through integration into a corporate idiom. English functions quite often as such a lingua franca, which is defined as an idiom that non-native speakers use with other non-native speakers (Vandermeeren 1999: 276), although its use as a communicative exchange mechanism can also include native speakers of English. Thus, the use of a lingua franca is an attempt to standardize and make manageable language difference. A standardized approach, however, does not resolve language difference associated with daily operations as the level of proficiency is likely to vary immensely between different employees and many of their interactions are unlikely to be a monolingual events. Thus, multinational enterprises in general terms exist in a field of linguistic tension, and the choice they can make is to adopt 'standardization strategies' or 'adaptation strategies' (multiple languages are used in a flexible way). Vandermeeren (1999: 276) suggests that these strategies are not an 'all or nothing' phenomena because most companies mix their strategies of language choice.

Some empirical contributions

This section introduces recent research studies, which provide in-depth insights into some language choices made by multinational corporations and the consequences and experiences of people living and enacting such choices.

Henderson (2005: 69) researched the building of trust and relationships in teams composed of speakers of different languages. Language diversity refers not only to the fact that team members speak a variety of mother tongues but also that they 'hear in a variety of different ways' as they use different interpretive mechanisms to make sense of information they receive. Henderson focuses in particular on the consequences of 'hearing differently' – an example being the use of the fairly common word such as 'team' and 'control' which carry different meanings in different national contexts (cf. 'control' is a more positively connoted word in the United States, and more negatively connoted in France). In Henderson's study a native French speaker, working in an English-speaking team, reported that 'people think they can speak but in fact they feel they can only discuss technical topics and find "small talk" difficult'. Thus, team building and socialization into the team were handicapped as there was a distinction between 'technical talk' and 'small talk', the latter being a source of socialization and integration which was not open equally to all members of the team. Similarly, using English as a lingua franca led to some false assumptions that everyone was speaking the same language and that therefore there would be a degree of equality in the group. However, this was erroneous as, for example, the role of language in self-image and professional competence was considered to be paramount by French speakers, and that foreign speakers using English rarely have the same command and powers of persuasion as when speaking in their mother tongue. It was felt that US managers sometimes made negative assessments of their French partners and underestimated their intelligence because they spoke slowly and had to search for words. It was only through gradual clarification of issues related to perception, interpretive schemes and different meaning systems, which sometimes implied the use of outside consultants, that such trust-eroding processes could be articulated and addressed.

Team metaphors

Gibson and Zellmer-Bruhn (2001) investigated the different meanings attributed to the concept of 'teamwork' across national and organizational cultures. They differentiated between five metaphors for teamwork (military, sports, community, family and associates) which were used by their respondents when they described and talked about their multinational teams. Metaphors are important concepts (Lakoff and Johnson 1980) as they contain important meanings about scope and roles of relationships, norms and expected behaviour and the mental model team members hold about structure and process of the team. People around the globe hold different definitions of teamwork. For example, if they live in a fairly individualistic national culture they are more likely to think of team in terms of sports or associated metaphors. If they are in a controlled organizational culture, military or family metaphors are more likely to resonate with them. These metaphors carry with them expectations for how teams will be managed and how processes with unfold.

Implications from this research could be that international managers cannot assume that their own conceptualization of teamwork resonates with that of the team members whose work they have to co-ordinate. Should some team members' expectations be framed by the family metaphor and imply the existence of clear roles and the provision of unambiguous guidance, whereas the team leader or manager sees a team as a form of community defined by the free sharing of ideas and members' roles as facilitating dialogue, a degree of conflict and frustration is bound to occur. Similarly, a team member conceptualizing a team as a family unit to provide support and ensure family members' well-being might be perceived as ineffective by other members of the team whose understanding of its own purpose is based on competitive sport metaphors.

Frederiksson *et al.*'s (2006) case study of Siemens shows that there was a continuous and powerful interplay between two languages, German and English, which reflects the language proficiency of the language users and which was out of line with the corporate policy of adopting English as the common corporate language. Overall, English was the language most commonly used, but German was also noted as an important everyday language, in particular in more traditional Siemens business areas whereas the 'newer' ones (e.g. telecommunications) relied on English. Similarly, the age of language users made a difference as younger people excelled in English more than their older counterparts; the geographical location was an influencing factor on language choice as German-speaking countries prefer using German in communication with headquarters, as did Eastern European and Latin American ones as well as China. However, overall there was consensus that English would become more dominant and that the former CEO's (von Pierer) comment on English being the corporate language was interpreted to refer to external communications only, whereas the common internal corporate language choice was seen to be left open. In this regard there was some welcome breathing space for Siemens' employees to choose the language of their daily interactions in line with personal preferences. Also, the use of English in the context of highly complex professional and technical situations can be a source of misunderstandings as an incident between Germans and Scottish delegates showed. Their technical discussions were of course combined with non-technical language use, which led to misunderstandings and loss of meaning as the German negotiators had lost the flow of thoughts and argument, but continued to act as if they had understood everything. It took considerable time and effort for the misunderstanding to be acknowledged – this behaviour can be attributed to keeping face as the understanding of the technical language of one's profession is also perceived as a key aspect of being a competent professional.

This study clearly shows that a common corporate language cannot be introduced by management fiat, that language use occurs in the context of administrative heritage, company history and new developments as well as personal choice. Finally Frederiksson *et al.* (2006) suggest, in contrast to much other literature, that Siemens' managing of language difference could be interpreted as a deliberate non-management in form of leaving it ambiguous when to actually use which language. As language choice is so closely linked to identity and power in multinationals, and imposing a language usually results in strong emotional reactions, it is possible to avoid the provocation of such reactions by retaining an element of ambiguity in the choice of the common corporate language.

A study by Piekkari *et al.* (2005) also draws attention to the problematic nature of imposing a common corporate language. In their work on a merger between the Finnish Merita Bank and the Swedish Nordbanken, they show that the introduction of the use of Swedish as the common corporate language had a disintegrating effect on parts of the merged company. The Swedes regarded the choice of language as self-evident and a relief. From the viewpoint of the Finnish-speaking organization, this decision meant that all internal communication aimed at top management had to be conducted in a new language, which was seen as a sign of Swedish dominance as English was seen as a viable alternative to the use of Swedish. For the Finnish colleagues, the choice of the corporate language carried several disadvantages. Their professional competence was diminished as conveying

UNIVERSITY OF HERTFORDSHIRE LRC

views, expressing complex subject matters and contributing in meetings were severely restricted by the lack of access to Swedish. Indeed, performance appraisals themselves were sometimes conducted with the help of an interpreter. Their career paths were dented and promotion opportunities were not always open to them, so that deprived of meaningful career opportunities, many highly trained and competent professional staff left the organization. Different levels of proficiency in Finnish and Swedish saw some individuals catapulted into positions of influence (as gatekeepers and language nodes), but also saw them overburdened with work and being used as 'translation machines'. Thus, this study illustrates that the introduction of a common corporate language backfired to an extent in that it undermined the integration effect it was meant to stimulate.

Lost in translation: recontextualization and language in the asset transfer

Brannen (2004) published an interesting study on the transfer of organizational assets to host countries. She uses Walt Disney's attempts to establish a theme park in Tokyo, Japan and then later in France (Euro Disney) – both initiatives were based on a 'copy exactly strategy', but only the theme park in Tokyo was successful in this respect.

Brannen argues that in the host country the organizational assets and systems 'take on a new meaning in distinct cultural contexts' (p. 595). She develops a conceptual understanding of such transfer processes based on semiotics, i.e. the study of how language produces meaning in situated contexts and investigates the reason for success and failure of Walt Disney's internationalization strategies based on the concepts of 'semantic fit' and 'recontexualization'. She shows how Walt Disney's strategic firm assets (products, practices, ideologies) change their meaning depending on the context in which they are employed and that therefore 'semantic fit' had not been achieved in the transfer process to France. Thus, to give just one example, the meaning of Disney's products differs between the countries to such an extent that the acceptance of the symbolic value of the products influenced buying behaviour and the overall success of the parks (see Table 4.1).

Similarly, two case studies (a globally operating paper manufacturer and a bank operating in the Scandinavian and Baltic countries) of cross-border mergers (both between Finnish- and Swedish-speaking companies) (Louhiala-Salminen *et al.* 2005) concerned themselves with the use of the English language in the process of integrating two previously separate businesses. In one case study English was introduced from the very beginning as the common corporate language as the assumption was that everyone would then have to speak this foreign language and therefore 'staff were at least theoretically on a level playing field'. However, communication challenges remained as the 'complex web of social, historical, and cultural experiences,

Table 4.1 A semiotic comparison

Signifier/Product	United States	Japan	France
Mickey Mouse	All-American boy	Safe, reliable	Le Journal Mickey
Cowboy	Rugged individualist	Quintessential team player	Carefree individualist
Souvenirs	Fun, part of the experience	Senbetsu, Legitimizing memento	Tacky, waste of money

expectations, and resulting assumptions remained, though now they had to be dealt with in English' (p. 403). For examples, differences in what was perceived to be 'polite requests' continued to exist, with Finnish staff being more direct, whereas Swedish staff preferred more indirect expressions. Also, 'foreign-language use' was regarded as the main source of communication problem as nuances of meanings and expressions of opinions, but also answering of phones and participating in 'small talk' are harder to achieve in a foreign language. In the case where English was adopted as a shared lingua franca, it proved helpful in smoothing the difficult post-merger period and its use 'neutralized' potential tensions between the different companies. However, its adoption did not eliminate communication problems, as its use is neither 'neutral' or 'cultureless' because it acts as a 'conduit of the speaker's communication culture' (p. 417).

Research work conducted in a Finnish multinational, Kone Elevators (common corporate language: English; parent language: Finnish) and its diverse subsidiaries showed that staff use language to build particular relationships – when having confined language skills they tended to build supporting personal relationships with language mediators; when having superior language skills they built broad contact networks within the multinational. Also, individuals often used language as an informal source of expert power (Marschan-Piekkari, Welch and Welch 1999b) in an organizational context which is characterized by high language difference. For example, the proportion of foreign employees out of total employment had risen to 92 per cent in 1996 and where 57 per cent of the interviewees of the study indicated that language was a huge barrier to them as it distorted information, prevented meaningful communication about technical problems, impeded negatively on the development of horizontal relationships with other units or headquarter. Even staff at middle-management level could sometimes not participate in offered training programmes due to a lack of competence in communicating in English. On the other hand some individuals with high language competency in both Finnish and English acted as language mediators and acted as bridge builders between different units and often strengthened the status of Finnish staff in inter-unit communication within the company, while non-Finnish employees felt disconnected from decision-making processes and critical information exchanges. Also, in subsidiaries individuals with relevant language skills often led them to have more power than their formal position would normally indicate as it was through them that all-important information flew, was filtered and interpreted. Overall, in this multinational, the formal organizational structure was shadowed by an informal structure based on language. Rather than being based on geographical location, the shadow structure was based on five language clusters (Finnish, English, 'Scandinaviska', German and Spanish) around which personal and business connections and information flows were established. The 'language distance' experienced by these clusters from the headquarters revealed a hierarchy of languages with Finnish and/or English empowering its competent users to engage actively in information exchange and build powerful networks.

A word on the use of the English language

Partly, the role of English as a lingua franca or common corporate language has already been addressed, as all of the reviewed studies concern themselves at least to an extent with the influence of the English language in multinational settings – even if it is just as a point of reference and how it is 'not used' as a universal medium of communication; even if its putative levelling ability is queried and even if questions are raised about its ability to address differences in meanings, which merely get masked over and can result in further communication problems. Even in the case scenario depicted and analysed by Piekkari *et al.* (2005), the dynamics between Swedish and Finnish as the two contesting languages, were finally interrupted by introducing English as the common corporate language as it provided a more 'neutral' communicative medium.

Thus, 'English has become a fact of life for many business people' (Nickerson 2005) as the dominance of English as a lingua franca in international business contexts appears to be beyond dispute (Bargiela-Chiappini 2006; Harris and Bargiela-Chiappini 2003; Nickerson 2005).[5] Some authors argue that it would be better to refer to English in the plural form, as Englishes, as the reality of the use of this language shows that there are more non-native speakers of English than there are native speakers (Block and Starks 1999); consequently a plurality of different Englishes exits.

Kachru (1985, 1992) developed a typology of English-speaking and non-English speaking countries, which he divided into the 'inner', 'outer' and 'expanding' circles. 'Inner circle' countries include the USA, UK, Canada, New Zealand and Australia, where English is the main language – which does not, of course, imply that a multitude of other languages, dialects and idioms are not used and spoken. The 'outer circle' refers to countries where English is one of many languages and has an official or associate official language status – examples here would be Nigeria and India. English is used for a variety of purposes including educational, social and administrative functions (e.g. Singapore, Malaysia and the Philippines). The 'expanding circle' describes English as an international language – the speakers do not have a colonial past and the English they learn is based on 'inner circle' varieties. Language learners have different levels of competence and proficiency in these countries (Japan, Korea and Taiwan) and the number of English-language speakers is rapidly increasing. Indeed Bloch and Stark (1999: 82) pose that 'Business English' should be added on as the latest emerging circle as it is the 'sort of common English that a Norwegian would use when conversing with an Italian. It is, therefore, a *lingua-franca* of non-native English speakers and represents their only possible means of communication.' There are, of course, differences in the kinds of Englishes used – they stretch from linguistic features (e.g. pronunciation; grammar and syntax; orthography) to language use (e.g. oral: code switching, turn-taking; written: developing of logical structures; form of address) and sociolinguistic differences (e.g. tone; politeness strategies) resulting in different usages which come with subtle differences in nuances and shades of meaning and plenty of opportunity for misconception and miscommunication. Nevertheless, it appears that having access to learning English is quite important in order to participate in international encounters, in particular in the area of business and management: 'English is a high priority for management in most companies' (Bloch and Starks 1999: 86), which

> for an elite of highly educated and 'cosmopolitan' business people [this] may be an expected requirements of their job profile that comes as a package with an American or British MBA course; for workers moving across borders in pursuit of economic betterment or simply a survival job, linguistic skills can become the source of social stigma and exclusion.
> (Bargiela-Chiappini 2006: 9)

These comments by scholars engaged in research on the role and use of English in global contexts point to the controversial nature of English as a lingua franca – as its use in international settings is bound up in flows of power and expressive of differences in equality between different organizational agents. It is also referred to as a medium to which not everyone has access and which serves as a tool to spread particular [management] ideologies:

> Corporate language practices are infused with ideology(ies): for example, management terminology is a tangible manifestation of a pervasive ideological stream that emanated originally from America and Britain but through the medium of English is being transferred across geographic boundaries and economic systems.
> (Bargiela-Chiappini 2006: 4)

This quotation resonates with the fourth dimension of language described in Chapter 2, where language use was seen to be tied into the hegemonial spreading of particular 'preferred' ideas and values through the seemingly 'innocent' use of language (English) and discourse (management terminology).

Gee *et al.* (1996) have conducted a series of ethnographic research projects situated in a company they call Teamco, a computer and software developer in California, USA. Through detailed observations of training interactions of shop-floor staff not particularly articulate in the English language, nor particularly fluent in the required discourses of 'self-directed teams' and 'culture change', they show that the purpose of training was not such much knowledge transfer in itself, but rather to create appropriate individuals who were able to buy into the company's vision and to start 'enacting' this vision in their work contexts. The sharing of English as the corporate language was seen as an important step towards creating a harmonized workforce, which fully embraced Teamco's vision. Indeed, their evidence shows that shop-floor staff who were already able to articulate themselves in English were also quicker to learn and use the discourses of 'teams' and 'change' and were frequently in a position to develop more beneficial career trajectories in a workplace which relied on contingent labour. Thus, the ability to speak English is tied into the appropriation of particular discourses (which Gee *et al.* relate to the emergence of global discourses of fast capitalism), which enables some language and discourse users to create advantageous positions for themselves.

Bargiela-Chiappini (2001) provides another rare empirical example which investigates the use of languages (English and Italian) together with the use of management discourses and their impact on the experience of an Anglo-Italia joint venture (called *Novella*). In particular middle managers in the Italian part of the joint venture found themselves caught up in new areas of responsibilities, which were expressed and constituted by the introduction of new job and role descriptions, expressed in English titles, but which did not capture the duties fulfilled by them prior to the joint venture – thus their titles had changed in line with their British counterparts, but their competencies and power had not, thus creating a gap between Italian performance and British expectations. The Italian *quadric* (middle managers) were left to juggle the continuing autocratic practices of their Italian superiors with the new demands imposed by them. Italian managers were quite competent 'to mouth the discourse of Anglo-Saxon management', but they failed to implement it as it was 'too distant from the expectations built into the language of British management practice' (p. 155). Thus, the use of English role and job descriptions was not contributing to furthering collaborative relations, but experienced by the thus re-labelled Italian middle managers as devoid of meaning and substance. Also, the effect of using English terminology on perceptions of self-identity was not limited to job titles – expressions such as 'appraisal', 'briefing' and 'focus groups' had also become part of the Italian managers' idiolect – but indicated to them that business was now done the British way. Bargiela-Chiappini differentiates between middle and top managers, with senior management being the movers and shakers behind the joint venture and the only group that had contact and exchange with their British counterparts. Thus, struggles and incomprehension over words and practices features strongly in this joint venture, more importantly so, in the medium layers of the joint venture company, where work tasks had to implemented. This study shows that the English language is tied in with the use of what Bargiela-Chiappini calls 'management terminology', but what may be better described as management discourse as it comprises both terminology and actions. The English language and a management discourse exposed Italian speaking *quadric* to 'a force' which re-described their role and activities, which they experienced as incongruent with their own understanding and identity, but they felt unable to resist the new language and discourse.

Language and culture

Bargiela-Chiappini's study (2001) shows that 'language' and 'culture' are intrinsically intertwined as the use of language and terminology was expressive and constitutive of (new) cultural values and behaviours in the joint venture company. Mainly, however, researchers and practitioners alike tend to include 'language' into their consideration only as an after-thought, as it is viewed to be part of the 'culture box' and it is treated as 'a part of cultural differences inherent in international business operations' (Welch *et al.* 2005: 23). Most prominently, perhaps, Hofstede (1994a, 1980/2001)[6] expresses the view that 'the business of international business is culture' and that the managing of international business means handling both national and organizational culture differences at the same time. Yet, such thinking can obscure processes at the core of international business operations as they 'mask the impact that language has on the development of information flows and knowledge transfer' (Welch *et al.* 2005: 23) as the previously reviewed research studies have shown. The purpose of this section is not to substitute established thinking on (cross-cultural) management and national cultural differences; rather it is an invitation to address the contribution that a more language-based approach might make to the understanding of complex multinational organizations. Holden (2002), and Luo and Shenkar (2006) are some such researchers who currently attempt to establish alternative ways of framing and understanding international management and business and they point to the role of language as a tool and medium through which such reframing can occur. Holden (2002) in one of the most elaborate attempts to develop fresh approaches to framing international/cross-cultural management quite rightly points out that international managers in their respective fields and industries have to manage and interfere in concrete interactions – rather than being involved in deliberate and theoretical attempts at 'managing cultural difference'. These interactions occur in contexts that are multilingual, multidiscursive and frequently geographically dispersed and international managers have to address such complexity practically while retaining a business focus. The studies, which were reviewed in the previous section, do provide some insights into such 'concrete inter-actions' and the dilemmas they can cause for people involved in bestowing a sense of order upon such complexity. Despite the increasing interest in lan-guage and its role in international management, there is at present no coherent and united body of work, which could propel the field of interna-tional management studies into a 'post-Hofstedian' state (Holden 2002: 41). However, the studies provide evidence that the realities of international managers are indeed characterized by the management of language differ-ences and that they are exposed on a daily basis to linguistic and discursive complexities, which cannot be addressed through the application of stan-dardized '(national) cultural dimensions', in particular as these complexities are also mediated by the functional and industrial contexts they are set in. Holden (2002) observers that in future the ability to create and sustain net-works, through which knowledge and meaning can flow, will be central to what (cross-cultural) international managers do. He sees language and com-munication as fundamental to this process as

> The main medium for the cross-cultural manager as communicator is the mode of language which was designated as facilitating networking and mobilizing synergies. The kind of skills of communication and motivation that are required to facilitate participative competence require linguistic skills of a high order, whether in English or in other common language.
>
> (Holden 2002: 298)

In addition, Holden also mentions the requirement of such managers to retain a business focus, which links into the notion of international man-agers as users of management discourses through which such retention of focus can be achieved.

It is not the intent of this book to 'replace' the 'cultural approach' to understanding international business and management processes – rather it is to channel the readers' attention towards an alternative, language-based, approach. By re-focusing the conceptual part of analysis from 'culture' to 'language', it is not claimed that language and culture are separate entities. Indeed, it has been argued that they are one and the same (e.g. Agar 1994 and his concept of 'languaculture'). In practice, too, international managers might find it difficult to clearly differentiate when they are dealing with 'cultural problems' and when they are dealing with 'language problems'. However, it has also been argued that in times of global networks as described in the introductory chapter the ability to create and sustain knowledge networks is of paramount importance to multinational organizations. As these knowledge networks are in their essence language and discourse based, an approach har-nessing the insights which can be derived from linguistically and discursively informed (international) management studies may prove a viable way forward to manage networked information channels.

Conclusion

In the Introduction globalization was defined as a process (or set of processes), which generates transcontinental or interregional flows and networks of activity, interaction, and the exercise of power. Multinational organizations exist in this force field of flows and networks and international managers are a core group which is bestowed with the task of facilitating and making possible the flow of knowledge by creating networks of activity. We concur with Holden (2002) who posits that in this kind of globalized world models and mechanism to 'manage cultural differences' are no longer relevant as the dynamics and complexities caused by such information flows need to be conceptualized differently. In this chapter it has been argued that a recourse to language and discourse as a conceptual lens to understand these processes in the context of international management provides a deeper insight into how such processes are experienced and played out in multi-complex settings.

The empirical works which were introduced and reviewed showed that multinational organizations have indeed to deal with 'language difference' in order to create and maintain the all important exchange of meaningful information between people and units of business. The evidence shows that such exchanges occur in concrete contexts which are characterized by functional and organizational structures, the professional background and the language preference and proficiency of the people involved, the administrative heritage, existing and emergent strategic directions, technological advances – all of which are framed by the overall dynamic and direction of business activity. If this is the case, an exclusive concentration on 'cultural differences' as the main 'impediment to successful information transfer' will not be conducive to equipping managers with conceptual tools to address such shifting and multi-layered situations.

English as the lingua franca of international business plays an important role in the process of knowledge transfer; however, it cannot be considered to be a panacea as proficiency levels vary, its use can lead to misunderstandings as differences in meanings are glossed over, and it is also associated with inequality of access and in particular with a political and cultural heritage associated with post-colonialism and the dominance of neo-liberal capitalist ideas. These positions are explained and explored in the next chapter.

Questions

1. Do you ever use English as a lingua franca in your conversations? If 'yes' what is your experience?
2. If you are not a native English speaker: Are there any words, expressions or metaphors which are difficult to translate into English or any other language? Is the vocabulary of management and business in your language expressed in English?

Notes

1 In most publications organizations which are geographically dispersed across different nation states are referred to as MNCs – multinational corporations. I have adopted here the expression multinational organization (MNO) as it appears to me to be a more neutral term and also because it is not only corporations which are based on global network structures.

2 In the field of international business and management studies issues pertinent to language and its use in multinational settings have not become part of mainstream knowledge and discussions. Reeve and Wright (1996) describe this field of study as 'neglected', Marschan-Piekkari et al. (1999a) as 'forgotten' – these concerns are echoed in more recent contribution such as Holden (2002) who refers to language as a 'lost content' of international management and in Welch *et al.* (2005: 10) who confirm their earlier observation that

> language issues have been relatively ignored [in international management processes], but may offer a rewarding research avenue regarding the functioning of the MNC ... Thus, while it can be said that there is interest in a language-based approach to understanding international management processes, it is far from becoming part of the mainstream literature, which is still dominated by approaches focusing on cultural difference and 'the management of cultural difference' [see also note 5].

3 Many multinational organizations have not got a strong grasp on the extent and depth of their own language differences. Tools for measuring, for example, language barriers' dimensions exist and are provided by linguistic auditing (Reeves and Wright 1996).

4 This book does not engage in depth with research emanating from the field of intercultural communication – despite its valuable contribution to understanding communication processes across cultural boundaries. This is a deliberate choice taken to keep the focus strongly on 'language'. However, the interested reader is referred to the works of Guirdham (1999), Gudykunst (1998); Gudykunst and Lee (2002), Jandt (1998) Scollon and Wong Scollon (2001) and to the reader by Samovar and Porter (2000).

5 Graddol (2004) suggests that English may ultimately be replaced by languages such as Chinese, Hindi/Urdu or Arabic as the lingua francae of international business. Such changes are, of course, always possible, but given the continuing increase of English being taught as a second language around the world, this is unlikely to occur in the next half century.

6 It can be argued that the field of international management studies (see Holden 2002 for analysis and critique) has been dominated by an understanding which views culture as the paramount influence on international business affairs. Cultures, in particular national ones, are seen as relatively stable, homogeneous and consistent systems of assumptions, values and norms. In so far as cultures are different from each other, comparative management studies can engage with measuring difference and evaluating its impact upon international business. Noteworthy here are the work of Hofstede (1980/2001), Trompenaars (1993) and Adler (1991) of which Hofstede is the most cited author and his cultural dimensions have become established yardsticks for measuring cultural difference. His contribution did in fact create a new landscape for international management studies and has been adopted widely.

5 English as the global lingua franca

This chapter provides an exploration of English as the contemporary 'lingua franca' of global reach. It provides some background to and reasons for the emergence and ascent of English as a shared communicative tool. The role and rise of English as such a communicative tool has been investigated from different positions, and different explanations for its augmented status have been given – e.g. it is associated with the economic dominance of the United States, increases in mobility and travel of large parts of the population, the emergence of networked information societies as well as with the history of British colonialism and imperialism. As the role and function of English have been discussed to an extent in the previous chapter and will again be discussed in the following chapter, this chapter remains a relatively brief one, as it links the themes of the previous chapter with those of the following chapters in part two, which provides applications of the discussed themes.

English as the contemporary lingua franca

Vandermeeren (1999: 276) defines a lingua franca as 'an idiom that non-native speakers use with other non-native speakers, rending it a foreign language for all parties concerned'.[1] Many languages have been used as such shared communicative tools, for example Arabic, French, Greek, Latin, Persian, Portuguese, Russian to name but a few (for a detailed historical analysis see Ostler 2005). Many lingua francae extend only over a small territory, linking, for example the trading populations of just a few countries. By contrast, Latin was more widely used throughout the Roman Empire, although its use was mainly contained at the level of government and not everyone spoke or used Latin for their daily interactions.

According to Crystal (2003) it was only since the 1950s that the need for a truly global lingua franca was articulated as so many international bodies and institutions came into being. Also, particular communities such as the academic and the business ones required the adoption of a single lingua franca as both are involved in generating and sharing knowledge. A situation where a Germany company director needs to meet with contacts from Hong

Kong and France in a hotel in Singapore to start negotiations about a shared joint venture is more easily conducted when using a shared language, rather than a translation process across multiple languages.

Also, people in general have become more mobile – both physically as well as electronically. In particular the use of the Internet and the World Wide Web has enabled people to express and send their ideas in words and images electronically to a multitude of other people; media communication and advertising are new media which reach across cultural barriers and interact with the mindsets of their target audiences (see Martin 2006 for the effect of English on marketing identities in French advertising). Thus, such communication and networking processes require the existence of a shared language as otherwise meaningful exchange is not possible. The use of a shared language is thus driven by a need for mutual intelligibility and the opportunity to have a voice in a global, networked world. English thus can be seen as a valuable instrument enabling people to achieve their respective goals.

The reasons why English emerged as the global language need to be set in a historical context, which begins with voyages to the Americas, Asia and the Antipodes and this expansion of the British Empire continued with the colonial developments in Africa and the South Pacific in the nineteenth century (for a more detailed overview see Crystal 2003; Ostler 2005). Ostler (2005: 457–458) puts the 'propagation period' of English into the context of business and trading:

> In the propagation period, when English speakers begin to travel and settle abroad, the temper of the English, and so by association of their language too, becomes much more worldly, in both literal and figurative sense; the world is opened up to the English, but above all to their business and trading enterprise, with government and Church concerns very much in the rear.

The English language thus became transported and imposed onto other cultures and was associated strongly with 'trade and business'. In the case of colonies, its use as an official and semi-official language was often continued after independence from the colonial forces had been obtained.[2]

Socio-cultural reasons for the adoption and spread of English as the global lingua franca point to the deep penetration of English into political and business life, safety, entertainment, the media and education to the extent that in many of these domains the use of English goes beyond a 'mere convenience', but rather it serves and shapes global human relations and expresses and contains ideas and knowledge. Here, the dominant influence of the United States in the twentieth century plays a crucial role in spreading English as the language of entertainment and commerce, but also as the language of science and education – i.e. the language in which key ideas are formulated, debated and disseminated. Access to knowledge is a prerequisite for participating in the knowledge economy and as knowledge is 'packaged into' the English language, a certain command of its basic structures and vocabulary is a necessity to participate in the flow of knowledge across boundaries and borders.

English and knowledge

The English-speaking world produces most of the leading global players in the arts and humanities, according to academics in the field. All but two of the top 20 universities in the world are Anglophone institutions in the UK, the US, Australia and Canada. ... but there are signs that some institutions are taking action to make their arts and humanities activities more visible on the world stage. As well as publishing more in English, as their science colleagues are doing, they are teaching in English, too. Korea University even teaches Korean Studies in English, although not Korean literature.

(*Times Higher Educational Supplement*, 27 October 2006: 7)

Universities from other [i.e. non-UK] countries are increasingly offering courses conducted in English. ... At a time of intense global competition, Ruhr-Universität Bochum (Germany) is pulling in students from across Eastern Europe and South-East Asia because it offers its courses in English. ... It is alarming ... that in the Netherlands they have 1,000 masters courses being delivered in English. But they have trumped this recently by announcing that all their postgraduate courses will be conducted in English.

(*Times Higher Educational Supplement*, 27 October 2006: 14)

When I lectured in Leiden I found the students in my audience speak English somewhat better, on the whole, with more care for clarity and more respect for tradition, than those I left in Oxford. Still, I should rather see travellers arraigned for noble madness than endure – often ignorantly unaware – the contempt they currently attract as doltish, oafish, lumpish, boorish, brutish and British.

(Fernández-Armestro, *Times Higher Educational Supplement*, 13 October 2006: 13)

Bradford University offers students a list of professional proof-readers to help them correct poor English and improve their marks. The School contends that this implies the opportunity to equalise a relationship in higher education that is weighted toward the home students ... with good command of written English, while other institutional voices describe it as 'spoon-feeding gone mad'.

(*Times Higher Educational Supplement*, 14 April 2006: 1)

> Language difficulties among Chinese students on courses in the UK are so acute that some are resorting to cheating in a desperate attempt to pass their exams. However, institutions are often creating the problem with 'unscrupulous' recruitment strategies and also by relying on standardized testing systems, which are not reliable indicators of a student's ability to cope in an all-English teaching and learning environment. Additionally, some overseas students have unrealistic expectations about how their language skills should improve.
>
> (*Times Higher Educational Supplement*, 7 July 2006: 18)

Business English Lingua Franca

English has been firmly established as the lingua franca of business and management – this may be partly due to its historical origins and the linkages between colonialism, trade and commerce as well as the dominant economic power of the United States in the twentieth century. Business people involved in international affairs take this as a fact. Despite such acceptance, there is overwhelming evidence that it would be more appropriate to talk about 'Englishes' as this language has spread and developed in such a way that no single nation or group can claim to own it.

Indeed as pointed out in the previous chapter Kachru's (1985, 1994) contribution was to provide a deeper understanding of the meaning of what it is to learn English and in doing so he deconstructed the notion of English as a monolithic language, 'finding a pantheon of Englishes where there had been a single Queen's English. ... [bending his energies] to securing recognition for the many Englishes in their own right' (Hasan 2003: 433). Bloch and Starks (1999: 82) expanded the framework offered by Kachru (1985, 1989), which differentiated between 'inner', 'outer' and 'expanding' countries in which English is used as first language, language with official status or taught language to include another concentric circle titled 'Business English', which they describe as 'the sort of common English that a Norwegian would use when conversing with an Italian. It is, therefore, a lingua-franca for non-native English speakers and represents their only possible means of communication'. Thus, in their argument Business English acts as a lingua franca in its own right as it provides a degree of commonality between Englishes, which is derived from the existence of a shared semantic field, i.e. that of business (though the authors do not discuss the character of this semantic field at all).

Louhiala-Salminen *et al.* (2005: 403–404) use the term of Business English Lingua Franca (BELF) as a 'neutral' and shared communication code:

> BELF is neutral in the sense that none of the speakers can claim it as her/his mother tongue ... it is shared in the sense that it is used for conducting business within the global business discourse community,

whose members are BELF users and communicators in their own right – not 'non-native speakers' or 'learners'.

It appears that these attempts to establish English as a lingua franca in the context of business (and management) merge English as a language with a particular 'content', i.e. the vocabulary, genres and techniques of business and management to such an extent that they cannot be separated. This is an interesting development as it provides a conceptual leverage to merge the debate of the status and role of English as a lingua franca with discussion about the role and relevance of professional languages (i.e. discourses), which provide words and vocabulary as well as frameworks for sense-making and action.

Business English Lingua Franca is also not so much associated with particular national or regional cultures, but with particular professional collectives, viz. those who speak English and who also are able to draw on the words, meanings and techniques of business and management.

Debating English as a global language

Intelligibility is of paramount importance in a world which is becoming connected and interdependent, because mutual understanding is imperative for knowledge creation and dissemination. The fundamental value of a shared language is as a resource, which furthers mutual understanding, cooperation and exchange of knowledge. This exchange of knowledge may well include the narration of stories of oppression and liberation. Thus, having a mutually intelligible 'exchange mechanism' is potentially an enormous source for knowledge creation and exchange as well as for empathy, liberation and action.

The benefits which can flow from the existence of a global language are considerable – however, there are also risks. A global language could, for example, cultivate an elitist monolingual class, which is complacent and dismissive in their attitudes toward other languages and worldviews:

> Perhaps those who have such a language at their disposal – and especially those who have it as a mother-tongue – will be more able to think and work quickly in it, and to manipulate it to their own advantage at the expense of those who do not have it, thus maintaining in a linguistic guise the chasm between rich and poor. ... For others, such a world would be a desirable return to the 'innocence' that must have been present among human beings in the days before the Tower of Babel.
> (Crystal 2003: 15)

In addition, the rise of a global language poses questions about its relationship with other languages, in particular minority languages – which can be seen as 'endangered species' (Dalby 2002) and whose disappearance is accompanied by a similar loss of particular cultures and insights (Anderman and Rogers 2005; Ostler 2005). There are also power implications as those members of the academic community, for example, who write up their ideas in a language other than English might have their findings ignored; senior managers who work for companies whose common corporate language is English, but who are not native speakers, might find themselves disadvantaged compared with mother tongue speakers. These effects have clearly been shown in the empirical studies, which were reviewed in the previous chapter.

Loan words

Loan words are words which are incorporated into one language from another language, because the latter does not possess the lexical resources to express certain semantic fields (deficit hypothesis; Kachru 1994). In this regard the existence of English loan words in other language could point to the dissemination of particular meaning fields into the lexical content of this language. In terms of business and management there is no detailed literature to what extent English loan words for the field of business and management have been introduced into other languages or are even 'pushing out' existing expressions and words.

The literature generated in translation studies is more developed as it concerns itself much more with words, meanings and translation. A recent edited book by Anderman and Rogers (2005) concerns itself explicitly with the role of English and its relationship to other European languages. Contributions such as by Johansson and Graedler (2005) look specifically at loan words and do provide some evidence that the vocabulary of business and management as used in Norwegian contexts is indeed entering the Norwegian lexeme – in particular since the late 1980s, a time that can be aligned with the increased use of information technology and the accelerated pace of globalisation.

Thus the need for intelligibility requires some consideration of its concomitant risks. The risks listed above are all associated with the loss of face, and respect, i.e. with people's identity, which in an increasingly connected world becomes subject to converging influences, which require the use of a particular language (English) and discourses (of business and management) in order to participate in the networked flows of knowledge and action.

The need for identity is a fundamental human need to express a sense of belonging to particular groups by distinguishing oneself from other groups (Joseph 2004). Individual and group identity gives people a sense of who they are, of belonging, and a code for behaviour. Language is the most immediate and universal symbol of identity (Crystal 2003; Joseph 2004; Tietze 2004), so that the existence of different language systems are necessary requirements to maintain different identities and associated worldviews, perspectives and insights. House (2003) acknowledges the use of English as a shared lingua franca, the function of which is to provide a useful and versatile tool to assist the exchange of information and the building of relationships in international contexts. In her view English acts as a 'language for communication', but remains a 'mere tool bereft of collective cultural capital', i.e. without any identity shaping ability, which remains associated with the use of one's native language. This is an interesting point as, if compared with Feely and Harzing's (2003) notion of the international managers as the masters of language, one might ask whether and when expert and competent language use take on identity shaping features. We will return to this point later on in this and the next chapter.

Linguistic imperialism

The role of English in the world has been extensively discussed by sociolinguistics, educators and post-colonial theorists. Some groups regard English not as a value-neutral code, but as a locus of power which leads to imbalance in a great many of human endeavours. Sociolinguistics Robert Phillipson's (1992: 47) formulates the position of 'linguistic imperialism' in his so titled book, which contests the political relation between inner and outer circle countries, i.e. between colonial powers and their colonies. Phillipson sees the global spread of English, particularly through English language teaching, as part of linguistic imperialism:

> A working definition of English linguistic imperialism is that the dominance of English is asserted and maintained by the establishment and continuous reconstitution of structural and cultural inequalities between English and other languages. Here structural refers broadly to material properties (for example, institutions, financial allocations) and cultural to immaterial or ideological properties (for example, attitudes, pedagogic principles).

In this analysis the spread of English is part of Western capitalism's global expansion where English must be maintained as the primary language of intercultural communication to help sustain its growth.[3] Thus, a link between global English and global capitalism lies at the heart of the linguistic imperialism theory as notably, Phillipson (1992), but also Pennycook (1994), make explicit connections between colonialism, the spread of corporate capitalism and the globalization of English. From this perspective, corporate language practices would be seen to be embedded in these dynamics and thus as infused with ideology. Management terminology could therefore be described as a tangible manifestation of a pervasive ideological stream that emanated originally from America and Britain and that is transferred across geographic boundaries and economic systems through the medium of the English language.

Halliday (2003) concurs that from a socio-historical perspectives English is now acquiring a new identity as the global language of the late capitalist world. He develops his argument by tracing the emergence of Standard English as it evolved in the context of new demands especially in the areas of commerce, administration and learning. Through a mixture of borrowing of words from other languages (Latin, Greek for example) and the establishment of taxonomic orders of meanings, new forms of knowledge were created, which took on the forms of discourses with 'their own ways of reasoning and arguing, of presenting and marshalling lines of information and control' (Halliday 2003: 408). In discussing the role of Latin and Greek in the emergence of Standard English, he comments:

> Thus Latinate (or graecolatinate) discourse in English carries its own loading of prestige, and when this is combined with the authority of Standard English as the discourse of centralized administration what results, not surprisingly, is a language of power: not just in the sense that it possessed enormous power, through its expanded meaning potential, but in another (related sense) that it gives power to those who control it, and hence serves as a means whereby power structures are put into and maintained in place. ... We are so surrounded today by these dominant forms of discourse that we scarcely notice the any more; it seems quite natural to be told that this certificate remains the property of the corporation and must be presented on request. ...
>
> (Halliday 2003: 411)

Halliday continues his argument by posing the question, whether a language (i.e. English) that becomes internationalized follows the same kind of process and logic and whether this is just an institutional change or whether it creates a whole new function for this language, with new meanings at the potential control of empowered agents. He sees the new context of English as a global one in which the voices of international capitalism build on the heritage of colonial days, but he also differentiates between 'global English' (the English of the inner circles), which is based on new information technology, mass-media advertising, news reporting and all other forms of political and commercial propaganda and 'international Englishes' (the Englishes of the outer circles), by which he understands the plurality of world Englishes, whose very existence he sees as a possibility to resist the 'baleful impact of global English' by transforming it, reshaping its meanings and its meaning potential.

Holland (2002) summarizes the debate about Global English (GE) on a continuum ranging from Global English (GE)-phobe to GE-phile, with a neutralist stance in the middle.[4] In terms of the more extreme positions on the GE-phobe side the main function of English is seen as a hegemonic one, which frames the use of English as a means to normalize the values associated with (corporate) capitalism and neoliberal economics, which privilege the existence of free-market forces as the supreme ordering mechanism of all economic affairs and also increasingly are expanded to define and order all affairs of human and social life. The GE-phile side views English as a benign medium associated with progress and prosperity.

- GE-sceptic: GE is factor in the globalization of a malignant, Western-capitalist discourse. It contributes to the spread of a neo-Orwellian 'globospeak': a set of discursive practices through which, on a global scale, the economically unorthodox is transformed into the politically unthinkable.
- GE-neutralist: GE is socio-politically neutral: for societies using English, it is a means to achieving their own ends. The spread of English is part of a natural and inevitable process of change. It may have socio-political causes/effects, but historically it is nothing very new – except in terms of the truly global scale of modern English language use.
- GE-phile: GE is a factor in the globalization of a benign, Western-democratic discourse. This facilitates the 'export' of free, democratic, and pluralist modes of economic and political organization, encouraging the development of individual freedom and respect for human rights.

(Holland 2002: 6)

In the previous chapter some research studies were discussed – these studies engaged empirically with exploring the role of English and its relationship to other languages, its context of use, the implications for business transactions. The authors of these studies did not blind themselves from the 'fact' that English was in most cases an important, if not the most dominant, of the languages-in-use. As the studies showed, information and knowledge flows, access to networks, personal careers and esteem factors were all tied into the ability to use English proficiently. However, the studies also drew a more complex picture as historical, administrative, cultural and structural factors informed the choice of language use as did personal preferences and proficiency. The authors seem to write from a 'pragmatic position' which reflects an acceptance that there has to be a shared language in order to communicate and that this language, for a variety of reasons, happens to be English. However, in the context of use, it becomes clear that the use of English is far from providing a panacea for language diversity, nor does English replace universally other languages, rather it co-exists frequently – in a more dominant position – with them, is appropriated and used in line with the achievement of individual and organizational objectives. Evidence taken from bottom-up approaches suggests that there is more to language use than meets the conceptual eye and that with the spread of English comes also resistance to its use; new and refreshed opportunities to articulate the complexities of local circumstances and a willingness to challenge and change.

The use of English can offend

In March 2006 Jacques Chirac, the French President, stormed out of an European Summit Meeting in Brussels, because a French delegate elected to speak in English to him.

Many countries have policies on language planning and learning. Sometimes such language policies include the existence of regulations and bodies which protect the native language. In the case of French, which in diplomatic and political circles, for example, is used sometimes as a lingua franca after English, there is a long tradition of cherishing its language. This tradition is embodied in the existence of the Académie Française, founded in 1653, to codify the French language, to protect its purity and eloquence. In 1975 the first consumer-protection language law was passed, officially rendering the non-use of French in certain public domains in France illegal. In 1980 a quota of 40 per cent for French-language programmes and cinematic production on television and radio was introduced. In 1994 the Toubon Law stipulated that French is required in all print, radio and television advertising distributed in France and that if English is used anywhere in the copy, it must appear with an equally legible, audible and intelligible French translation – though this is often not practised (Martin 2006).

Interestingly, studies into the French public's perception of English showed that the public in total was quite open towards the use of English as it felt secure in its own tradition and confident that the French language would retain its integrity and purity (see Martin 2006: 217–219)

English and management discourses

The relationship between English and management discourse is quite simple – they occur together and are intrinsically linked to each other. Risner (2006: 140) describes the concurrence of language and discourse and texts (i.e. meanings) as always the result of a meeting between a linguistic flow and a discursive flow, which 'flow across each other'. One could say that the language/discourse relationship is like those between structure and content; medium and message – in practice they cannot be separated. Conceptually, however, it is sometimes useful to keep them apart to understand their overall importance and impact:

> One could say that discourses flow around in the world, but never without being linked to the expression side of some language or other. Conversely, languages flow around in the world, but never without being linked to a discursive content – perspectival knowledge – of some kind or other – in a more or less fragmentary form.
>
> (Risner 2006: 141)

Given the theoretical frameworks introduced in Chapter 2, the concurrence of language and discourse has certain consequences as – in the terms of linguistic relativity – the use of a particular language shapes the way we perceive and enact the world and as – in terms of social constructionism – the use of discourse is a powerful medium to make and affirm existing structures, which are perceived as given and normal. In Chapters 3 and 4 a case was made that management discourses and the English language have become established as particularly influential forces as they emerged in a historical context which bestowed upon them the privilege of defining what counts as 'normal' and 'useful' behaviour, process and structure – i.e. both exert strong hegemonial influence over the framing and ordering of social and organizational worlds and their concurrence acts as a reinforcing mechanism.

International managers have been shown, both conceptually but also empirically, as users of both English and the discourses of management and business. They can therefore be seen as powerful agents who are at the centre of knowledge and meaning flows. In international contexts they are likely to use English more than any other language, thus perhaps evoking traditions of a language imbued with meanings of superiority, intellectual authority and connoted with the (pre-supposed) inevitability of globalization – a language clearly associated with progress. In using the meanings of business and management similar associations are evoked as historical developments have propelled this meaning system into a position of privilege – i.e. its logic and assumptions about how to best order the economic (as well as social and cultural) affairs of the world are seen as 'normal' and 'logical' as compared with competing approaches and views. Hasan (2003) comments on the relationship between English and business/management discourse (he calls the combination of the two 'glib-speak'). He comments in particular of combing the adjective 'liberal' with the noun 'trade'. He asserts that the meaning of 'trade' is markedly different from 'liberal' or 'liberalize' as trading activities such as buying, selling, lending and borrowing are reciprocal processes in which each party must guard its own interest. 'Therefore "trade" is precisely the converse of 'liberal 'so far as its cryptotypic semantic feature other-oriented is concerned' (Hasan 2003: 441). Through the combination of 'liberal' and 'trade' 'liberal trade' appears more desirable. Hasan (2003: 441) states that 'The ordinary use of the English language does not prepare the listener to interpret this as trade for the benefit of the speaker. But the inventors of this expression are corporate commercial bodies.' The use of the expression 'liberal trade' is an example of the simultaneous use of English and discourse. It implies that there is a hidden meaning in this combination of adjective and noun, which obscures the interest which informs the construction and use of such a label. The recipient of such discourse is not in a strong position to discover its hidden meanings and the flow of powers which inform the use of such expressions. Returning to the theoretical foundations of Chapter 2, the expression 'liberal trade' is a good example of the different dimensions of language as it is (seemingly) a mere descriptive statement – trade is liberal – yet, it also orders the world in a particular way as it labels and groups people, resources, relationships. It could potentially be used in a phatic way to build bridges between people and create a cohesive, if not necessarily equal, network of relationships. It performs the ordering of the world along the normative assumption of neoliberal economics and it is hegemonial in so far as such assumptions carry particular meanings and ideologies which privilege certain groups over others.

Despite criticism of English and discourses it is difficult to imagine a world without this language and these particular meanings systems. A fight against the use of English as a convenient lingua franca would be a rather quixotic venture.[5] Halliday (2003: 416–417) differentiates between international Englishes which have developed and include the meanings of other cultures; whereas global English has expanded as the co-genitor of the new technological age, and is used by those who are able to exploit it whether to sell goods and services or to sell ideas. He sees both language and meaning as continually changed and reshaped through ongoing interactions in the 'semiotic contexts of daily life; and these have now become global contexts, even if those who participate in them are still only a fraction of the total population of the globe'. The empirical studies of Chapters 3 and 4 have shown that international managers are the very participants in the 'semiotic contexts of daily life', which are far from being clear and unambiguous. Managers have to make sense in such circumstances and are guided by objectives and goals of their organizations. Managers have been shown to comply and confirm to converging discourses but they have also been shown to be a source of resistance and meaning change.

Conclusion

The purpose of this chapter has been to link the theoretical position developed in Chapter 2 with the empirical studies of Chapters 3 and 4 against a general discussion of the English language as concurrent with the use of business and management discourses. The next chapter is a reproduction of an article, which was published in 2004 and which investigates in more detail the relationship between English and management discourses and contextualises its ideas with regard to management education and pedagogy. They are seen as generators of management discourses which are spread into the world through the medium of the English language

Questions

1. Do you know whether in your country there are particular language laws or policies to protect your national language?
2. Do you agree with Phillipson's thesis of 'linguistic imperialism'?

Notes

1 In all definitions of English as the lingua franca it is made clear that it is used between two or more non-native speakers of English. However, in practical terms one would assume that frequently interactions occur between native and non-native speakers of English, which still refer to English as a convenient tool. Most studies and definitions tend to ignore this possibility and potential consequences.
2 Commentators such as Halliday (2003) and Crystal (2003) and many others stress that there is no such thing as a standard English language, which 'belongs' to only a particular group of people. Rather it is more appropriate to talk about Englishes, i.e. to understand it as a plurality, which people appropriate in such ways to express their own cultures and meanings.
3 Much of the debate of the influence of English on social relationships and as a global force is articulated within the field of pedagogy and teaching English as a foreign language. Interested readers may refer to Anderson's (2003) review article titled 'Phillipson's children' or to Block and Cameron's (2002) collection of essays *Globalization and Language Teaching* or Hall and Eggington's (2000) edited book *The Sociopolitics of English Language Teaching* for an up-to-date overview of the debates in this field.
4 The debate about the role and nature of English as a global language can be tracked to an extent by following the dispute between two scholars, Robert Phillipson and David Crystal (Phillipson 1999; Crystal 2000); both are eminent authorities in their respective fields and have a keen interest in English and its role in the world. In terms of Holland's (2002) typology they can be positioned on opposites sides of the continuum of Global English sceptic and enthusiast and both provide succinct and informed analysis of the past, current and future role of English
5 Halliday (2003) quips that it is quite difficult to resist the medium of English, even if expressing one's resistance to it. The writer Ngugi wa Thiong'o (1981) has written an important text called *Decolonising the Mind: The Politics of Language in African Literature* – yet, the text is in English and needed to be so in order to be heard. I do not necessarily think that writing in English undermines the case Ngugui is making. Yet, it points to what to me are the beneficial sides of using a mutual lingua franca, which are to share such narratives – even if to reject the medium through which they are communicated at some stage.

6 Spreading the management gospel – in English

Introduction

In this paper I argue that in and through the 'English language' and the 'discourse of management' two powerful forces of (discursive) action combine and reinforce each other in the shaping of an increasingly 'global reality', which is based on the assumptions inherent in these two communicative sources. The English language itself is seen as the conduit through which individual agents acquire the knowledge and language, viz. the discourse, of management and through which they are enabled to construct themselves as 'appropriate individuals'. However, neither 'English' nor the 'management discourse' are seen as neutral and empty structural systems – rather they are expressive as well as constitutive of particular ideologies and situated in specific socio-historical contexts which privilege particular collectives and agents over others and create a unifying system of knowledge and action. Together they express, symbolize and encourage the spread of a particular form of global capitalism. It has been acknowledged that the global spread of English is bound up with many other cultural, economic and political forces and the emergence of a particular 'world order' (Pennycook 1994 and 2000; Phillipson 1992). The contribution of this paper is that it investigates English as a 'global' language and its ties to an increasingly powerful discourse – that of 'management' and 'managing'. Together these two communicative systems form a field of cultural, social and economic forces, which favours the construction of a global world in line with their particular assumptions and ideologies.

The argument of the paper is developed as follows. First, a background of English as the 'lingua franca' of international business is provided. This includes some considerations of the reasons and consequences of this 'rise' and focuses in particular on the different positions which scholars have taken in order to understand and critique the spread of English as an instrument of globalization. The ideological assumptions of English as the global language are highlighted and discussed; particular attention is paid to the role of power and privilege in the construction of the social world. Second, the practice and occupation of 'management' is described and explained as an increasingly global discourse, spread (in English) through institutions of management education. It is shown how it fosters the creation of particular identities through the learning and adoption of particular discursive practices. Following on from here, a third section investigates the consequences of the dynamics created by the combination of English language and the management discourse. This combination creates a force field of power, in which self-perpetuating truths, ideologies and particular identities emerge and are established as 'natural' and 'legitimate'. The final part is a brief reflection on developing a critical management pedagogy, the aim of which is to enable students to 'break open' the tacit assumptions of language and discourse. This, it is argued, can be achieved by introducing a linguistically inspired management pedagogy.

English as the lingua franca of international business

English is indisputably the global lingua franca and serves as the communication tool of many intercultural encounters. This dominant position is also firmly established in the contexts of international trade and business (Rea and Chapman 1995; Scollon and Wong Scollon 2001; Schneider and Barsoux 2001) – in other words a good command of the English language is indispensable when conducting international business and commercial affairs. The linguist Andrew Dalby (2002) tracks this development back historically to the colonization of territories and the establishment of the British Empire as well as to the emergence of long-distance trade relationships. In the twentieth and twenty-first centuries, advances in technology (such as the Internet or ICTechnologies), which originate in the US, further the use of English as a linguistic bridge between speakers from different linguistic backgrounds. Pyles and Alego (1993: 25) propose that it is therefore through a mixture of 'historical chance' that 'it [English] has become the most useful language for others to learn'.

It has been argued that this global spread of English is unproblematic, because English (as any language) is a neutral vehicle of communication which does not carry any cultural, political or ideological baggage. Thus it provides a value-free 'tool' which renders the conduct of commercial affairs easier to pursue. English then acts as the conduit through which 'transfer of technology, the flow of information, and the expansion of manpower' occurs. (Bowers 1986: 398, quoted in Anderson 2003: 82). This position has been challenged, most notably by Phillipson (1992), who, taking a neo-Marxist position, refers to such a conception of English as 'linguistic imperialism', which he sees as being both constituent and expressive of the global spread of Western-style capitalism. The role of English in this approach is seen as the primary language of intercultural communication, which helps to sustain the spread of global capitalism: The advance of English and the spread of global capitalism go hand in hand.

Scholars have since then built on Phillipson's fairly deterministic work (see Anderson, 2003, for an incisive summary and critique of such works). Calls for a socio-cultural sensitive practice of teaching English have been made by scholars such as Holliday (1997), Pennycook (1994) and Canagarajah (1999). Holliday argues from a liberal-reformist position, which sees the use and teaching of English as only partly problematic, because individuals are also able to use English as a resource in line with their own aspirations and wishes. Pennycook and Canagarajah are sensitive to the indoctrinating and ethnocentric perspectives enacted through classroom practices in and through language teaching. They see them in a Foucauldian way as generating 'universal truths' – in line with Phillipson's view of the nexus of ties between the spread of the English language and the spread of global Westernized capitalism these would have to be particular 'Western truths' – which nevertheless claim universal status.

A similar point is made by Cameron (2002) who, in the context of the discourse of communication skills and the norms, genres and speech styles it generates, shows that it originates in the USA, i.e. it is socio-culturally located, but it is nevertheless exported globally as if carrying universal value. Similarly, Block (2002) points to the emergence of 'McCommunication' and associates it with second-language acquisition. This kind of communication is framed as efficient, calculable, predictable and controlled and produces 'streamlined' identities. This understanding of communication, he argues, conceptualizes communication as a process of neutral information exchange and is increasingly 'taken-for-granted'. Gray (2002) points to the bland content of the 'global English textbook', which excludes or glosses over controversial topics such as politics, religion, racism or sex by focusing its content on materialistic and consumerist representations.

Despite their different approaches to understanding the role and function of English as a global medium of communication, these authors share a sceptical attitude towards its alleged neutrality and lay open the hidden assumptions it is based on. It seems then that since Phillipson's contribution scholars have taken up his 'cause' and have developed particular positions. These positions allow – in varying degrees – for less deterministic stances, in that they view individuals as active agents, able to appropriate discourses and meaning systems, and in doing so to resist the normalizing power inherent in such globalized discourse. Gee's et al. (1996) ethnographic evidence is a case in point to this discussion. Gee et al. show clearly how English is deliberately used to promote particular emotio-cognitive disposition as well as specific discursive practices (associated with what they title 'fast capitalism') within groups of multi-ethnic workers at an assembly plant. They show that some of these workers appropriate the discourse in question (a team discourse) successfully to carve out favourable economic positions for themselves. However, it is only a small minority which is able to appropriate the discourse in such a way. Thus their ethnographic evidence bears out Holliday's position only to an extent in that it shows that discourses can indeed be appropriated by the recipients of such teaching/practices and that they are able to develop new meanings and responses to them. The majority of workers in their case study remains quite passively bound by such 'imposed' discourses – affirming Pennycook's and Canagarajah's more sceptical positions regarding the degree of actionable agency.

While the above mentioned contributions and studies differ in their assumptions about the role of individuals in the shaping of discursively constructed environments, they nevertheless share a particular epistemological position, viz. they acknowledge the performative power of language (though I do of course not argue that all these authors would proclaim themselves to be social constructionists). They articulate their positions on the basis of a non representationalist epistemology in which language use is viewed as being actively engaged in constructing social and organizational realities (Berger and Luckmann 1966). In talking, having conversations, negotiating, bantering, and so on, human agents create, confirm, reproduce, as well as challenge and change the ever-emergent social world (Chia 1996). While the authors cited above might arrive at different assessments regarding the role of agency in such processes, they do share the view that language is 'not simply the medium for the transport of meaning' (Alvesson and Kärremann 2000: 138), but it is 'doing things' as a fundamentally social phenomenon through which the social world is constituted, challenged and changed (Tietze et al. 2003). Within this epistemology 'language' is considered as central to the process of constructing social reality, i.e. it is not viewed as a system of representation, but as productive, formative, creative – it makes things happen and gives form to reality (e.g. Austin 1962).

Tollefson (2000: 16–18), in commenting on the hegemony of the English language in the context of language policy, expresses a similar position in that he sees the spread of English as imbued with particular ideological assumptions – language is socially and historically situated and contested, and language ideologies are used to advance different constructions of the world which privilege some groups over others. In this context he raises critical questions (e.g. for which group does the dominance of English provide the greatest opportunity; for which groups does this create barriers?) in order to better understand the reasons and consequences of English as an international language.

Summarizing the critique of 'universal' models of communication as expressed by these writers, a more appropriate understanding of communication can then be described as a creative process of exchanging and transforming meaning between (groups of) agents, who are situated in historical, political and social context and who draw on their available power resources to shape the world in such ways as to lubricate the achievement of their own interests and goals. In other words, power and privilege form part of the making of the social/organizational world. Jackson and Carter (2000: 66–68), reflecting on the constitutive power of language/discourse, express these processes as follows: A discourse defines who is allowed to speak authoritatively on a particular subject; what it is possible to say (and do) and what is not possible to say (and do); where knowledge is located and how it is disseminated and why one speaks about a particular topic. Positioning Jackson and Carter's definition into the context of the above discussion, the ability to express oneself in English enables the individual to speak and act (authoritatively) on topics articulated mainly in English, viz. those of (global) consumerism, business and commerce; to become a location of knowledge, whose legitimacy lies in the mastery of 'English as a language'. This position is unproblematic only in as far as individuals are seen to be free to enter such a language and discourse, to use it at their will and to find a favourable position within it.

However, such a stance assumes that all voices are heard equally in each discourse, that everyone can attain equal access to discourses and can draw on them in an equal manner. This is of course not so (e.g. Hardy *et al.* 2000; Wolfe Morrison and Milliken 2003): Discourses and language systems are imbued with power relationships and inequalities. Roberts *et al.* (1992: 35), for example, provide commanding ethnographic evidence that workers with limited English have no or little power to negotiate a right to be heard and that they are therefore 'reduced as people'. Therefore, having access or being denied access to a language (and the means of expressing oneself in it) is central to positioning oneself in ways which will further one's life projects. Scollon and Wong Scollon (2003: ix) express this with regard of having access to 'English':

> We are writing and publishing in English. This is an observation that is almost entirely invisible until we call your attention to it. Our writing in English and your reading it in English indexes us as members of a particular social group with particular forms of power in the world ...
> A person who does not read English is indexed by the very choice of language in this book as an outsider to this discussion even as we index ourselves as insiders.

Today, the ability to index (or position) oneself as an insider in particular social and occupational worlds is linked to learning English. Schneider and Barsoux (2001: 232) posit that the mastery of the English language provides a power base to the thus educated, because the choice of language in business contexts can create 'winners and losers'. They write:

> The very fact that English has become the lingua franca of business reinforces these power issues: thus anglophones, those most likely to preach empowerment or to favour brainstorming, tend to dominate group discussions ignoring that the differences in ability to speak English create an unequal playing field.

Indeed, 'English' is an established subject in many schools in many countries of the world (see Dalby 2002: 183), which of course contributes to its expansion. In learning English access to the privileged and prosperous worlds of science, art, politics, the professions, including management, may be gained. However, such access 'costs' – while in many rich industrialized countries, a level of education is publicly funded, this is not always the case in other countries and access needs to be (at least partly) privately funded. This 'cost factor' is in particular relevant for management education, an industry which is thriving, and where the acquisition/mastery of English is intrinsically tied into the acquisition of the 'language of management', viz. a specialist vocabulary and idiom.

Management as a global discourse

Managers can be seen as the stewards and agents of (global) capitalism, because it is through them that its institutions and organizations are administered and controlled. It has been argued (e.g. Ritzer's 1996 McDonaldization thesis) that the techniques and knowledge associated with such administration are spreading around the world and that these have become so powerful that they provide their users with important sources of identity construction and legitimacy of action. Indeed, the 'management discourse' is perceived to be so pervasive that its techniques and imperatives are seen to be infiltrating – 'colonizing' – even the everyday sphere of human communication and sense making in increasing measures (Hancock and Tyler 2004).

The spread and ideology of management education

The training and education of managers has burgeoned in the past twenty years. The idea of a professional management education originated in a 'Western context', i.e. the USA where the first MBA programmes were designed and implemented at Harvard and Stanford University. The UK made similar moves towards management education in the 1960s following the Robbins Report (Committee on Higher Education 1963). Today, provision of management education is still located mainly in the USA and UK (see Currie and Knights 2003), with some of the established European business schools gaining only slowly in standing and profile. The following figures give a brief impression of the continuing spread of management education. They are taken from the Association of Business Schools (2001) in the UK, where there are currently 213 management programmes/courses offered by 100 business schools, from which approximately 10,000 students graduated with an MBA in 2000. Note that this figure excludes graduates studying for a specialized management degree as well as the cohort of undergraduates who leave universities every year. According to figures of the Higher Education Statistics Agency the total number of students enrolled on Business and Management courses was 246,780 in 2001/2002. These figures are still likely to expand. These courses, despite their high fees and associated costs, are becoming increasingly attractive to students from overseas, i.e. students who aspire to entry to the world of prosperity and standing and whose first language is unlikely to be English. In acquiring such an education, students become 'experts' who disseminate their expertise and reinforce its importance. The process of education, knowledge creation and dissemination thus becomes self-perpetuating.

Mey (1993: 289) provides a critical commentary on the self-perpetuating nature of such institutions of learning and their ideological base:

> The same classes that have established the institutions of higher education have also been instrumental in structuring that education and organizing its curricula; we are faced with a co-opting, self-perpetuating system that favors those who are most similar to those already in it, *pares nobis* as the expression used to be.

In other words education is never 'neutral' but expresses and reproduces the worldviews and ideologies of an established group of people, who write the curricula and regulate access to educational institutions.

Management education is no exception to the processes described by Mey. It originated in an Anglo-Saxon (US and UK) context and its orthodoxy favours neo-liberal models of market economics in which free and equal agents seek access to resources, which through unfettered supply and demand mechanism constitute a (fair) way to generate and distribute wealth in and across societies. This model and its hidden assumptions continue to dominate management education. It sees management education as concerned with providing the technical knowledge which enables individual agents to play an active part in using and distributing resources in a market context. Management is viewed as rationally directing work organizations by dint of employing special techniques, practices, technologies and terminologies. The role of management education is to 'produce' such technical experts, who are able to construct and control work and business organizations.

The ideological underpinnings of this model of management education are several. First, it originated in a particular historical, social and cultural context – yet it has gained such prominence that its 'truths' and practices are taken to be universally applicable (Ritzer's 1996 McDonaldization thesis) and are transported through the isomorphic processes of management education into other socio-cultural contexts, where they contribute to shaping the social world on the terms of their allegedly universal (and superior) principles. Second, the tools, techniques and imperatives of management are seen as 'neutral' and 'rational' – the inequalities created by them, the 'boundedness' of their rationality (Simon 1960), remain unacknowledged. For example, the application of Human Resource practices such as 'appraisal' or 'performance management' are framed as applying neutral expertise to the 'problems' of controlling individuals and groups in

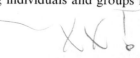

organizations. However, in equal measure they are creating the very roles and problems they mean to address. In doing so they give rise to particular relationships of power and inequality. Indeed, such is the power of discourse that its assumptions become established as 'normal' and 'common-sensical' and its ideologies become harder and harder to discern – let alone criticize or challenge (see Townley 1994 for extended discussion of HRM and discourse).

Management discourse and the creation of identities

As explained in the previous section: A great deal of management education concerns the transmission of 'technical knowledge', which is taken to be a 'neutral' and 'universal' tool for addressing the challenges faced by managers. However, it also fulfils a second, similarly important, though less visible, function, which is the socialisation of the selected aspirants into professional managers. This transformation process occurs in and through the appropriation and mastery of a particular discourse (which in the case of management education is spread and practised mainly in and through the English language). Indeed, the occupation of management is bound to and by discursive practices, which are expressed and spread through the appropriation of language. The salient role of language in 'making managers' has long been recognized. Managers have been described as engaging in 'language games' (Pondy 1978) or able to forge particular images (Conger and Kanungo 1998); they are important word merchants (Bate 1994: 257) whose efforts and tasks are intrinsically intertwined with their ability to use, manipulate and change language. Indeed, they can be considered as a particularly influential group, which shapes the organizational direction in and through their language use (Watson 1994/2001; 2004). In other words, the ability to use language and to use a particular discourse (as disseminated in and through institutions of management education) is core to management and managing in work and organizational contexts.[1]

Thus, having completed the course, MBA graduates, for example, will have acquired a (relative) mastery of the English language itself as well as a particular specialist vocabulary (expressed in English) associated with the profession of management. Such acquisition of language and vocabulary is accompanied by the acceptance of standards for conduct and behaviour and the internalization of particular cognitive and emotive dispositions as part of the students' professional socialization (Watson and Harris 1999).

Indeed, the learning of a particular language – viz. the central, distinctive and discursive activities that typify a particular line of work (Watson 2002) – is closely related to acquiring a particular occupational identity (Whitehead and Dent 2002). In gaining access to and becoming part of the (powerful and advancing) management discourse individuals are acquiring such an identity, which is likely to provide them with the discursive wherewithal to create favourable conditions for themselves. Alvesson and Willmott (2002: 620) see the relationships between identity formulation, discourse and (internalized) control as mutually implicated: 'the self-positioning of employees within managerially inspired discourses about work and organization with which they may become more or less identified and committed'. Managerial identities are then constructed – and controlled – within the parameters and assumptions of the prevailing (Anglo-Saxon) management discourse. They are the key agents and harbingers of this discourse and their 'indoctrination' obliges them to ensure that the discourse becomes enacted reality in the social and cultural spaces under their influence. They are created as 'appropriate individuals' through the transformative processes of management education. These create them as experts, who can speak with authority, and who in turn ensure that they produce 'appropriate individuals' in their respective work organizations. To give just one example: most – if not all – management students are likely to be introduced to a 'team discourse', which defines roles, establishes and enforces particular behaviour and values. These are not superficial exercises in 'mere' language use, but are a 'deeper kind' of exercise (Czerniawska 1998) which uses language to 'instill a common outlook and ideology'. Donnelon's (1996) work on teams, for example, shows clearly that teams do indeed accomplish their work through 'talk', which frames their thoughts and feelings (and actions) in particular ways, enhances (or inhibits) particular relationships. The manager's role in the team is that of a 'coach', a choice of terminology, so one could argue, which 'hides' the control and power aspects of the managerial function by foregrounding the benevolent guidance function of a (sporting) coach. Thus an 'appropriate individual' is a 'team player', who is loyal to the collective, aware of the competitive nature of the game and adheres to the coach's instructions.

Linking 'English' and 'discourse'

The spread of English as the global lingua franca and the spread of a management discourse share a variety of features and characteristics. Both are claiming to present universal standards or truths, which are applicable to all contexts and situations. Both claim to provide trajectories for collective progress and individual empowerment. Their considerable influence on the shaping of social and organizational worlds lies in their having been 'normalized' and the assumptions they are based on as having been established as 'taken-for-granteds'.

Those assumptions, in the case of the English language, go back to the time of colonialism, when English was the language of the dominant classes and exported and imposed upon other cultures and language systems. It was seen as an unproblematic, useful conduit for interactions between cultures, through which knowledge creation and transfer (and imposition) could be initiated. However, both empirical and theoretical investigations have shown that the spread of English is not neutral or 'innocent', but that it carries 'ideological baggage'. Given that language is the first and foremost expression of cultural identities, the dominance of English has potential consequences for the diversity of cultural identities and traditions, which can be seen to 'converge' towards a model of communication and sense-making in line with the 'McCommunication' or the McDonalidization thesis. On the other hand, such access to language can propel individuals into positions of economic and social advantage – but access to this 'medium of identity formation' is not easy and certainly not equally available to everyone.

The discourse of management is making similar claims for universal validity and application. It is based on an economic model which has its roots in the assumptions of neo-liberal economics. The 'truth' of the market is seen as ultimate and therefore as superior to local or situational realities. The stewards of this discourse are managers who through the process of socialization and education acquire technical competence as well as construct themselves (and, in turn, others) as 'appropriate individuals'. However, this discourse is neither neutral nor innocent – rather it is based on a particular Anglo-Saxon model, which carries 'particular truths' and favours the construction of 'particular identities'. As with the English language, access to this discourse is not equally distributed and continues to form significant barriers for those individuals who may wish to 'better themselves'.

What, then, are the ties between the English language and the management discourse? Simply speaking, they occur together: management education happens mainly in English. English is 'merely' the frame and 'management knowledge' is the 'innocent' content of this discourse. However, we now can challenge such an 'innocent' position, because it has been demonstrated that 'English' and the 'management discourse' also share a number of hidden commonalties (identity construction; universal truth claims; hidden ideology of Anglo Saxon model; restricted access) and that there are consequences of participating in 'language' and 'discourse' (construction of particular identities; undermining or even suppression of local identities and traditions; construction of the global world on the terms of a particular economic model). The effects of English as a global language and the management discourse as an increasingly dominant source of meaning and action mutually reinforce each other. This reinforcement creates a vortex of forces, which are very difficult to challenge or resist. In this regard the combination of English as a language system with a management discourse continues and deepens the influence of trends toward cultural imposition and economic dominance.

Discrimination and exclusion, tutelage and patronage are part of these dynamics, but they have become 'invisible' and 'glossed over'. This is because the reasons and consequences of language in its broadest sense (i.e. both as system of language as well as a discourse) as a means of expressing and creating particular relationships of power and hegemony are difficult to see and measure – thus they become difficult to address and change. Furthermore, they are reproductive of dominant social, cultural and economic structures – which become 'doubly' enforced and normalized through the hegemony of English and a management discourse. Thus the mastery of English combined with a conquest of the interpretive frames of the management discourse is a potent source of power which reproduces the world in line with the assumptions of their mutually reinforcing ideologies. What's to be done? Toward a critical pedagogy.

Discourses are not pre-given – they are made by human agents. Therefore they are not inevitable or pure 'closed systems', rather they can be 'opened up', challenged and eventually changed – even if only slowly, due to the normalizing power of discourses. Nevertheless, the cautious optimism of Pennycock's notion (1994) of 'writing back'. and Holliday's postulate (1997: 415–416) that people have the possibility to actively master and use (English) language in line with their own devices are resonant with the notion of language/discourse as an open systems, which can both constrain and empower individuals. It is these very tensions and contradictions in discursive systems, which bestows upon them possibilities for appropriation, emancipation and change.

As in the field of English language teaching, there have been similar developments in the area of management and organization studies to 'break open' the assumptions and techniques upon which 'management' is based (e.g. Grey and Mitev 1995; Reynolds 1999; Willmott 1994). Critical management studies attempt to systematically interrogate such assumptions and challenge their taken-for-granted basis and institutional prerogatives upon which management's hegemony is founded (Alvesson and Willmott 1996). Critical management academics should 'analyse management in terms of its social, moral and political significance' (Grey and Mitev 1995: 76), which implies concurrent changes in the curriculum content and some reconsideration of educational roles (see Dehler et al. 2001; Currie and Knights 2003).

Within the research community of critical management scholars, the role of language in exercising social control, as part and parcel of identity formation and as creating a hegemonial base has been taken up with enthusiasm and has been addressed in depth – this 'movement' has even been given a name, viz. the 'linguistic turn' of organization studies (Deetz 2003a; Holman and Thorpe 2003).

But these insights garnered from a critical engagement with language in organizational arenas and management contexts have not been transported into the class room and have not been made relevant for management education.[2] Whereas in other disciplinary areas the interrelations between education, social control and language are subject to analysis and debate (e.g. Block and Cameron 2002; Cameron 2000; Fairclough 1989; Hall and Eggington 2000) the notion of 'language' as being at the core of the processes of management and managing continues to be ignored or sidelined in the pedagogic contexts of management education (see Musson *et al.* 2007) – even in the debates of critical management scholars – indeed Holden (2002: 225) calls language 'management's lost continent'.

As part of the 'solution' to the 'problem' outlined in the body of the text, the agenda of critical management scholars needs to be broadened by including 'language' into the management curriculum. This implies to transport the 'linguistic turn' into the management classroom in order to 'break open' and reveal the complexities and dynamics implied in language and discursive process.

In terms of the management curriculum, management pedagogues could learn from their linguist colleagues and include critical discourse studies into their teaching so that the topics of the 'hidden' ideology of knowledge and truth claims can be laid open and made subject to discussion and comment. In going beyond descriptive and prescriptive curricula, and in moving towards interpretation and explanation of why and how discourses are produced, students are required to engage with the 'taken-for-granted' assumptions built into management education. Secondly, the inclusion of self-reflective elements about the role of learning, knowledge and the formation of (professional) identities would raise awareness that management education is not the neutral acquisition of a host of techniques, but also informs the 'managing of the inside' (Alvesson and Willmott 2002: 621) and produces 'appropriate individuals'. In the contexts of such discussions, moral and ethical implications can inform the debate in the classroom. The latter is no longer perceived as a neutral vacuum, but as a socio-political space, in which particular roles are enacted, dispositions formed and trajectories for future action laid down. Increasing students' awareness and knowledge that all of this happens because of and through the most 'innocent' of tools, i.e. language, may go a long way in developing their critical abilities.

These 'solutions' are clearly framed within the liberal-reformist position, which acknowledges that people need to identify with particular social groups for both emotional and economic well-being. Furthermore, I do not believe it is possible to 'undo' the development which saw English rise to a global language and which have given potency and authority to a management discourse. Both the use and spread of the English language and the management discourse are as empowering as they are constraining. In the context of this paper, developing a critical management pedagogy is defined as enabling students to 'break open' common-sensical assumptions about the role of language, discourse and management by providing them with theories, concepts and ideas taken from the fields of communication studies and linguistics.

My role as (linguistically inclined management) pedagogue is to promote and further those aspects which I consider emancipatory by raising awareness and increasing knowledge about the role and function of language and discourse. I also believe this to be 'good' management education, because it instils into management students a sense of agency, initiative and possibility as well as sense of structure, context and constraint, together with an awareness that the use of the manager's first and foremost tool (to wit: language) involves a great deal of responsibility.

Conclusion

I assume that the readers of this journal are students, teachers, researchers, consultants or indeed managers – engaged in the creation and dissemination of ideas about culture, communication and discourse. These are inseparably tied in with language, be it as a particular language system or as a discourse. Together, they express a body of particular ideas, identities and relationships, all enacted in a context of power and discipline. Fallows (1995, quoted in Holden 2003: 235) states that: 'The Anglo-American theories have won the battle of ideas – wherever that battle has been carried out in English'. As researchers there is ample opportunity to investigate such claims by focusing our endeavour on exploring the nexus of ties between language systems and discourses. In particular, ethnographically based works focusing on the complex linkages between 'discourse' and 'language system' could provide some insights into the dynamics of emergent orders.

As (perhaps mainly privileged) pedagogues involved in symbolic-analytic work our task is to equip our (perhaps mainly privileged) students with the intellectual and emotive 'arms' to participate in this 'construction of the global world' as autonomously as possible. As critical pedagogues our task is to instil in them a moral disposition, which acknowledges the processes described and analysed in this paper. Pointing to and raising awareness of the very language and discourse processes all parties are using to position themselves in the thus ordered world might go a long way to achieve this. Returning to Grey and Mitev's assertion that critical management academics should analyse management in terms of its social, moral and political significance, I suggest that this can be achieved by making the manager's first and foremost tool (language) subject to enquiry and comment.

Commentary written in 2007

When I wrote this article in 2002/2003 I was starting to explore the connection of ties between 'English' and 'management discourse'. My thinking at the time was based much on a convergence model of globalization and I viewed managerial identities as forged in a particular – and inevitable – force field of forces, that of the English language and the professional language of management, which is taught as a unifying and unfragmented discourse at institutions of business and management education.

As the years have gone by my understanding has shifted as globalization is now viewed as ongoing and diverse processes, which include the possibility of unforeseen outcomes and which can be expressed and created in different ways. Consequently, and also borne out by the empirical studies which were reviewed in previous chapters, the professional-occupational group called international managers can no longer be seen as being formed in any 'inevitable' or forgone kind of manner. Rather, the emergent understanding of the book is that international managers are language and discourse experts, who operate in a multitude of varied, contradictory and contested environments and who make sense of this environment in the light of the linguistic and discursive resources available to them.

A notion arising from this chapter as well as from the previous chapters is the idea that a form of 'Business English Lingua Franca' is now emerging and that this particular lingua franca is not tied to regional/national, cultural or social groups, but to a particular occupational-professional group, viz. business people and managers. This is an interesting thought as it must be the first time that a lingua franca is carried forward through the network of commercial and business ties more than through a network of political and social ties (although of course the two are related). Writers such as Ohmae and Kanter argue that therefore these 'new' networks are open to everyone and democratic in character as they are not built on inherited privilege and that everyone 'who shares in the vision' is able to become a member of this 'new continent'. Critical writers on the other hand stress the notion that 'the new continent' is still based on privileged access and firmly rooted in an economic-social model which is aligned with Western (American) cultural values and ways of living.

The question begs whether international managers in particular are emerging as a distinct group (Gregersen *et al.* 2004; Selmer 2004), which is selected less for its technical expertise as for the ability to 'manage cultural diversity' and to spread 'global awareness'. Micklethwait and Woolridge (2000) and Sklair (2001) describe international cultural elites as people who mix and marry internationally, attend elite universities and then go on to careers with big MNOs. These cadres of people are the likely inhabitants of the 'new continent' envisioned by Ohmae and Kanter in which English is the lingua franca and in which the discourses of business and management are given unheeded priority. Their identity might be that of a 'professionalized elite', which communicates in English and draws on discourses of business and management to make sense of who they are and how to relate to the situations which they encounter in their varied and dynamics careers and lives.

Forester (2000) argues that the emergence of such an international elite remains a myth as managers can never be 'rootless' and even the frequent move from one country/culture to another does not imply that any sense of a home culture and identity is being abandoned – one might suggest that having such a secure base becomes an even greater necessity in the light of frequent changes and adjustments. In the light of the empirical and conceptual evidence provided in this book so far, it appears that the process of internationalization and globalization encourages both linguistic and discursive convergence as well divergence.

The second part of the book is built on practical applications of the ideas of the book provides some empirical evidence for the positions and questions raised in the first part of the book.

Questions

1. As you read this book it is quite possible that you study/practise management, are mobile and interested in processes of globalization. Would you consider yourself as part of an emerging global elite of well-educated, English-speaking and business-minded professionals?
2. The title of this chapter suggests that the management discourse as expressed and spread through the medium of the English language acts like a 'gospel' – an ultimate and irrefutable truth. What is the evidence for this claim?

Notes

1 Of course, scholars in the field of management and organization studies have long made the connection between 'management and discourse' (Grant *et al.* 1998; Watson 1994/2001). They have also engaged critically with the assumptions and ideologies on the management discourse (Hancock and Tyler 2004; Parker 2002). My point here is that such insights have not been transformed into pedagogic insights which *routinely* inform classroom interactions and curriculum development. I shall return to this point later on in the chapter.

2 I acknowledge the contributions of scholars such as Hatch (1997), Jackson and Carter (2000), Tietze *et al.* (2003), Watson (2002) and some others, who have tried to transport the insights of their research on language/discourse into the management classroom. However, these are exceptions rather than the rule.

Part II

Applications

Introduction

This part provides a series of extended examples, case studies and applications to the themes discussed in Part I. They are provided by scholars and practitioners who are engaged with the exploration of language and communication in a variety of international settings. The applications reflect the diversity of the field and the richness of the topic of study as they are different in character and approach, which range from a classic case-study approach to the exploration of particular themes to the integration of personal experience with academic insight. The purpose of providing these application is fairly self-evident as they demonstrate that 'language matters' not just from a scholarly perspective, but that it is the very fabric out of which the worlds of business and management are spun. Below, I provide a brief outline of each chapter, which can be read individually or in conjunction with previous chapters. In order to facilitate a joined-up reading, it is indicated which chapters, ideas or concepts introduced in Part I the application relates to in particular.

Chapter 7 is a declaration of love to the German language and it tracks the evolution of German management over time and also elaborates on German as a language of management (in conceptual terms the arguments of the chapter echo the ideas introduced in Chapters 2 and 3 in particular). It is shown that '*Klarheit*' (clarity) is an ideal to be achieved through displays of expounded knowledge and that in German business culture a manager must be a 'good explainer' (rather than an 'effective communicator'). The chapter also shows how these features are encoded in the language itself which resists any tendency for informality and is extremely adept in creating concrete terms for the hard functions of management. German managers use their language to promote their authority and to show themselves as experts with exceptional and detailed knowledge.

Chapter 8 focuses on the introduction of (Western) discourses of business and management into post-1989 Russia through the medium of the English language (see Chapters 5 and 6 as thematically the use of the English language and the transfer of knowledge are discussed). The vehicle for the investigation is the translation of one particular textbook on knowledge management into the Russian language. The authors show that translating from one language (English) into another language (Russian) is not a mere technical process and not a panacea for addressing problems of communication. Rather acts of translation occur in specific contexts and the meaning associated with (English) business and management vocabulary does not easily translate easily into different cultural and political circumstances. Translators are seen as engaged in knowledge management processes in which words and concepts may become something different in the target language as they enable change so that the new knowledge can be made compatible with the experience of the target culture.

Chapter 9 is thematic in character and investigates the notion of 'careers' in global contexts from a language perspective (aspects of which are discussed in Chapters 4 and 5). Having foreign-language proficiency is increasingly becoming important for managers on foreign assignments, but also for a wider group of people who are employed in multinational corporations. Language proficiency is seen to be more than a mere technical skill, but as integral to the forging of international careers and enabling business success. The author tracks some such language effects on careers by drawing on a variety of research studies. It is shown that these effects refer to expatriate selection, job performance and relationships with local subsidiary staff, but also include a glass-ceiling effect, diversion of career paths and the development of career capital.

Chapter 10 is a case study of a Dutch multinational corporation (AKZO) and traces the introduction and implementation of the Business Unit concept over a number of years (conceptually this chapter is grounded in Chapters 2 and 3 as the case study captures the emergence of a 'new structural reality'). This new concept about the structure and relationship in the organization did not exist either conceptually or empirically before a new CEO, A.A. Loudon, introduced it following a visit to the United States. The authors follow the introduction of this concept through an analysis of the 'monologues', 'dialogues' and 'languaging' processes, which took place in AKZO in order to facilitate the new organizational structure. The case study provides a genuine feel of the longitudinal and sometimes protracted nature of introducing 'a new reality' into an existing setting.

Chapter 11 is also a case setting, but focuses more specifically on business negotiations between Nissan Motors (Japanese) participants and Renault SA (French) participants from an English-language perspective. English is used as the BELF (as explored in Chapters 4 and 5) and it is shown that business interactions remain informed by sometimes conflicting cultural assumptions. It is shown that English does fulfil its role as facilitating mutual intelligibility, but that this is mediated by dynamics and complexities which to an extent undermine the smooth running of the meeting. The author pays particular attention to the role of silence and anxiety in business communication as they are experienced by potential speakers and how they shape communicative behaviour.

Chapter 12, too, focuses on the use of English and its role as BELF and the use of Italian (and other) languages in the context of multicultural and multilingual business meetings set in an Italian context. The authors investigate whether an Italian style of management can be described and they show that to an extent younger Italian managers, who are more likely to have international experience and to have studied at business schools, are more prone to use English business terminology (these ideas are explored in Chapters 4, 5 and 6). However, their discussions also show how the use of English, Italian (and other languages) together with the use of technical vocabulary, meeting behaviour and interactions are drawn upon to facilitate successful communication with a view to build a sense of 'groupness' amongst culturally and linguistically diverse group members.

Chapter 13 is based on personal experience of the use of humour in general and organizational English contexts. The chapter draws on academic literature to demonstrate that the emphasis and value put on the 'use of humour' in England is indeed 'typical' for Englishness and continues to differentiate this nation from others. It is also shown how English managers draw more widely and more consistently than other managers on the use of humour to manage complex and difficult organizational situations. It is argued that through particular historical processes the use of humour has become a widespread and valued means of social interaction, including organizational and management contexts. In this regard understanding the use of humour becomes a prerequisite in international interactions (Chapter 4).

7 German: a language of management designed for *Klarheit*

Nigel Holden

A person who has not studied German can form no idea of what a perplexing language it is.

(Mark Twain, 'The awful German language')

Introduction

If management is a socially definable activity or a bounded reality, then it follows that management both as a practice and as an object of scientific enquiry must be characterized by distinctive language behaviour and a capacity for generating domain-specific lexis. Most people would agree that management in both senses meets those criteria. Accordingly, we need a guiding definition of the language of management which a) reflects a distinctive operational reality in a particular culture and b) recognizes that the terms for management behaviour in the widest sense of the word are not semantically equivalent across languages. For our purposes the following definition of the language of management is offered:

> a set of linguistic symbols, manipulable in a given language (such as English, German, Japanese, Russian, etc.), and incorporating standardised terms and informal elements (such as oblique reference, humour, pretence, etc.), necessary for the conceptualisation, description and execution of management tasks and sharing of management information.
>
> (Holden 2002: 231).

In this contribution there will emerge no more than an approximation of German as a language of management based on the above definition. The approach is tentative but pragmatic, yet also innovative in that the very notion of philologically distinct languages of management has no foothold in the management literature (see Chapter 14). The focus of attention will be on certain social effects of the German language as characteristically used by German managers in the German context and to some extent in their cross-cultural interactions. A key theme of this chapter is that German managers are inclined to use their language as an authority-marking vehicle for impressing on others the depth of their functional knowledge. This tendency would seem to constitute a marked difference in general language use with other business cultures.

Some observations on the German language

It is not customary in the field of management education and research to characterize the general management culture of a nation through the prism of its language. The implicit challenge presents management scholars with the opportunity to make completely new – even unthinkable discoveries – about management behaviour in what one might call home cultural contexts as well as in cross-cultural involvements. An aim of this chapter is to test this claim with reference to the German language. As scholars of German history and culture are fully aware, what constitutes the German language is a tricky conundrum, which is not resolved by merely establishing who counts as German-speakers (Stevenson 1997: 13; see also Clyne 1984 and 1995). For practical purposes the German language will in this chapter be discussed as the national language of the modern Germany following unification in 1989 *and* with some reference to earlier manifestations of the German state including its notable forebear, the kingdom of Prussia.

Having established that as a point of departure, we confront a rather unusual issue. German, it seems, is a language about which non-Germans hold strong opinions. It is indeed a commonplace in the English-speaking world to hear people who have never learnt German to describe it pejoratively – and mistakenly – as 'guttural'.[1] The American writer, Mark Twain (1835–1910), who *did* study the language, famously described it in a witty lampoon as 'awful', protesting that 'there is not another language that is so slipshod and systemless, and so slippery and elusive to the grasp'.

Against that, the award-winning Australian writer Anna Funder (2003: 4) found German, when she started to learn it, 'so beautiful, so strange' and grew to relish the mysteries of its word-building power.[2] Vikram Seth, best known as the author of the novel *A Suitable Boy*, found that learning German was 'an adventure, a love affair under pressure', but when he studied documents of the Nazi period about deportation of the Third Reich's racial enemies for a later book, his pleasure drained. In due course, though, 'my old love [of the German language], now both deeper and more troubled, revived' (Seth 2005: 233–38).

A leading connoisseur of German politics, Timothy Garton Ash (1997: 201), referred to the German language as 'that 'glorious but all-too-powerful instrument'. In a similar impressionistic vein Holden (2002: 232) has observed that the German language 'is elaborate and, like a Mercedes car, is splendidly over-engineered, a precision instrument of great robustness'. The French industrialist and self-declared Germanophile, Daniel Goeudevert (2003: 134), found that German literature led him unexpectedly to 'the discovery of new continents', which was for him the opening up of that much mis-understood entity, the bafflingly tormented German soul (for further discussion on *Angst* see also Ardagh 1987; Kempe 1999; Sereny 2001).

For a more scholarly judgement on the most striking features of the German language in its social effects let us turn to the philologists Priebsch and Collinson (1962: 447) who pronounced:

> The German language brings out in various ways the qualities which the foreigner quickly discerns in the German nation: orderliness and organizing capacity which, if carried too far, lead to dullness and rigidity; a power of abstract thought sometimes too prone to scorn concrete aids; inexorable thoroughness not exempt from the dangers of tediousness; deference within both family and society, at worst tending to obsequiousness: and above all a warmth and depth of feeling which in the finest achievements of its literature strikes a responsive chord in our English hearts.

Priebsch and Collinson wrote that in the 1930s for the first edition of their great work on the German language. It is surely striking that they link German with behaviours such as orderliness, organizing capacity, power of abstract thought and thoroughness. These are after all useful keywords for coming to an understanding of the general nature of German management and the usages of the German language that inform it.

A short review of the evolution of German management

It is possible to trace the beginnings of the distinctive features of German management back to eighteenth-century Prussia, the forebear of modern Germany. That great commentator on German history, Sebastian Haffner (1907–99), has encapsulated the essence of the Prussian state with reference to doing one's duty without feeling sorry for oneself and with decency, but not necessarily compassion, towards one's fellow men. These ideals – Haffner (1998: 47) calls them 'state ethics' – not only stamped the attitudes and behaviour of Germany's industrial magnates in the nineteenth century, but have also left a certain imprint on subsequent German thinking and behaviour.

According to Craig (1991: 104), these 'great industrialists ... were accorded an immoderate degree of admiration and, in some ways, became the culture heroes of their day'. The epitome of them all was Alfred Krupp, who required of his workers 'from on high to the lowest' that they not only demonstrate at work the great virtues of diligence, loyalty and obedience – 'he who defies shall be dismissed' – but lead 'outside the factory' morally impeccable lives (Rother 2003: 187). Krupp, like all the big industrialists of his day, ruled his workforce – and family – like a 'late-feudal baron' (*Schlossherr*) (Rother 2003: 134).

The well-entrenched obedience-seeking style of management became the plaything of the Nazis, who exploited it for their own ends, coercing German managers to align behaviour and performance criteria with the totalitarian needs of the state. According to Tooze (2006: 102), 'German business thrived in this authoritarian atmosphere ... Owners and managers alike bought enthusiastically into the rhetoric of *Führertum*. It meshed all too neatly with the concept of *Unternehmertum* [entrepreneurial leadership] ... as an ideological counterpoint to the interventionist tendencies of trade unions of the Weimar welfare state.' Little wonder then that enterprise management in Nazi Germany has been described by one of its own exponents as 'firm-handed, task-oriented and authoritarian' (Wiederhold 2003: 129). To reinforce their own pre-eminence and flatter their own vanity, Nazi industrial bosses condescendingly termed their employees '*die Gefolgschaft*', a collective noun meaning literally 'followers' but with strongly medieval – and for the Nazis mythic – connotations of fealty and allegiance.

The long-established authoritarian nature of German management, which has its roots in the ideals of eighteenth-century Prussia, is still a prominent feature of German economic life today. Writing some 20 years ago Wöhe, writer of a leading German textbook on management (*Betriebswirtschaftslehre*), declared that the task of management lay in the issuing of instructions (*Weisungen*) (Wöhe 1986: 87), whilst Hermann Simon (1996), a German business professor and consultant, has noted that the management style of German companies tends to be 'authoritarian, centralised and dictatorial wherever the company's principles and fundamental values are concerned'.

These various observations support the notion that 'management activity and orientation is, by its very nature historically "embedded"' (Schmidt and Williams 2002). In the case of Germany, we are dealing with an historical embedding of unusual complexities (see James 2000). In the light of Germany's status as 'a powerhouse at the heart of the continent' (Stürmer 2002) by the late nineteenth century, its involvement in the two world wars of the twentieth century, the Nazi experience in all its horrors, the co-existence of two Germanies from 1945 to 1989, are we in a position to point to some abiding characteristics which can be used as anchors from which to view German managers? A most valuable source for this enquiry is the work of one of Germany's foremost cross-cultural psychologists, Sylvia Schroll-Machl. Based on extensive research on foreign perceptions of Germans, Schroll-Machl (2003) isolated six factors which are discussed by her at great length and regarded *by other nationalities* as key German characteristics:

1. Disposition towards concrete facts (*Sachorientierung*)
2. Appreciation of structures and rules (*Wertschätzung von Strukturen und Regeln*)

3. Rule-oriented, internalized responses (*regelorientierte, internalisierte Kontrolle*)
4. Time planning (*Zeitplanung*)
5. Separation of private and public domains (*Trennung von privaten und ffentlichen Lebensbereichen*)
6. Directness of communication: no ambiguity (*direkte Kommunikation: Keine Doppelbödigkeit*)

Taking these as reasonably well-attested German characteristics, and bearing in mind that, according to Schroll-Machl, different nationalities appear to have a culturally influenced perception of the quality and strength of them, let us now turn to what is probably the most thorough investigation into the relationship between culture and management in Germany ever undertaken, namely the GLOBE (Global Leadership and Organisational Behaviour Effectiveness) study. Engaging 150 social scientists and management scholars from 61 countries, which as the name implies is seeking to understand the impact of cultural variables on leadership and organisations, the GLOBE researchers surveyed 457 managers in 'the top 50 organizations in the telecommunications, food processing, and finance industry' in Germany. 12 per cent of informants were from East Germany (Brodbeck *et al.* 2002).

The GLOBE investigators concluded that the most pronounced German cultural value is performance orientation. The hallmark of German cultural practices is high levels of risk avoidance and assertiveness along with low levels of humane orientation. At work, compassion is low and interpersonal relations are straightforward and stern. They (2002: 16) continue:

> Effective German leaders are characterized by high performance orientation, low compassion, low self-protection, low team orientation, high autonomy and high participation ... A 'tough on the issue, tough on the person' leadership approach appears to explain Germany's economic accomplishments in the second half of the 20th century.

The GLOBE researchers hold the 'stereotypical German business leader' to be perceived as 'a person with a formal interpersonal style and straightforward behaviour, technically skilled, a specialist rather than generalist, neither bureaucrat nor authoritarian, who emphasizes *Technik* as both means and end' (2002: 16). There is nothing then in the GLOBE study which is at variance with Schroll-Machl's six points. In their conclusion the GLOBE researchers cannot resist some finger-wagging: 'Effective leadership is about dealing with people (compassion) as much as it is about dealing with change (future orientation). We think that it is time for German managers to become more effective leaders in that respect.'

It is worth noting how that GLOBE findings and Haffner's characterization of the Prussian state have a good deal in common: the subordination of the individual to a higher need ('duty') and the requirement that those in authority deal with lesser mortals 'honestly and decently', but not necessarily sympathetically. The management scholar Thomas Armbrüster supplies this useful commentary on the matter of relative lack of humane orientation:

> The disapproval, or even ridiculing, of humane orientation in leadership processes is not surprising either, since ... functional authority is based on expertise, and ultimate authority is taken for granted on the basis of positional and personal attitude patterns. Through this lens, humane orientation in leadership processes is considered a nice-to-have in Germany, *but not a feature relevant for effectiveness.*
>
> (Armbrüster 2005: 77; emphasis added)

Such a management system which values expertise is one in which managers at any level derive 'satisfaction from achievements rather than sociability' and in which 'educational depth' is viewed as the 'foundation of performance' (Armbrüster 2005: 151). From this it follows, as Ganter and Walgenbach (2002: 171) have noted, that technical, i.e. job-specific, expertise and not just position in the organization hierarchy legitimizes the authority of German managers. This knowledge-as-authority orientation appears to be a distinctive feature of German management. As an explicit trait it may even be unique in the world's management systems.

German as a language of management

If we accept the characterization of German management as 'management by expert knowledge' (*Führung durch Fachwissen*) (Ganter and Walgenbach 2002: 170), then this suggests that the language of German managers will incline to the formal, jussory (i.e. concerned with commanding) and explicatory. In exploring that proposition we shall consider first some aspects of German language usage in organizational contexts and then consider formal management terminology in German.

Aspects of usage

In this very short contribution it is plainly impossible to describe in a formal linguistic way the grammatical structure of the German language, its morphology and syntax. All in all it might be said that the German language well suits 'the German labyrinthine mind' with its 'liking for holistic and orderly systems' (Hampden-Turner and Trompenaars 1994: 212). We may concede too that the German language fits the temper and thinking habits of a people characterized by the French Germanophile Daniel Goeudevert (2002) as '*gewissenhaft, ehrlich und gradlinig, strebsam und ordnungsliebend*' (conscientious, honest und straight, diligent and order-loving).

We may perhaps suggest that German is a language of management which is striking for its capacity to objectify, to formalize, to analyse (if not over-analyse), and to deliver commands. All this is consistent with a society where 'educated Germans ... have ... idealized rational, analytical knowledge' and where the communication style is 'explicit, fact-oriented and academic' (Nees 2000: 63). This is a language of management with a tendency to remove the human factor – or rather human weakness – from calculations and decisions, whilst expounding a vision whose achievement perforce depends on coercion as a form of motivation.

We can turn to the weighty matter of clarity. Gesteland (2006: 316), a business practitioner who has become a cross-cultural trainer, observed in 'over a hundred meetings with Germans since 1963' that 'clarity of understanding [is] the prime goal of communication' for them. This may appear to be stating the obvious, but what constitutes clarity must be firmly understood in the German context. At the end of discussion in an organization a manager may well ask his colleagues: '*Alles klar?*' (literally 'Everything clear?'). When they respond with an affirmatory '*Alles klar!*', the colleagues are indicating that they have followed the logic of the boss's explanations. It is after all the case that the clearer the boss makes himself (and that may require an exposition of considerable detail), the more are the colleagues satisfied, the more they may respect and admire him (Nees 2000: 55).

In German culture – in German companies – it is as if the ideal is that clarity – *Klarheit* in German – is achieved through displays of expounded knowledge. This clarity–knowledge fusion simply has no place in other business cultures and its function, betraying a deep need for security – a haven from *Angst* – on the part of Germans, seems to be seriously misunderstood by foreigners. If in Anglo-Saxon business cultures it is desirable for managers to be 'effective communicators', in German business culture managers must be 'good explainers'.

If explanations happen to be elaborate, ponderous and pedantic, then that it is a sign of professionalism and competence in German culture. Explanations really must be *wordy*. After all, as Kempe (1999: 46) has knowingly pointed out: 'Germans are often surprised when wisdom can be delivered in but a few words.' Besides, lengthy explanations show that there has been 'painstaking methodological preparation' (Hampden-Turner and Trompenaars 1994: 216) – a German managerial virtue, incidentally that led to clashes between senior German and American managers after the DaimlerChrysler merger. German managers might relish reading '50 page documents before key meetings' (*Economist* 1999: 91); their American counterparts emphatically do not.

All this in turn underscores the point that Germans do not find it easy to engage in small talk, that is to say conversations designed to (temporarily) reduce social distance between people. Indeed the German language does not have an equivalent word for small talk. Germans use 'der Smalltalk', which is, according to the authoritative *Duden* dictionary (1996), 'light, casual conversation'. Small talk in professional interactions, so vital in business cultures as contrasting as the British and Japanese, seems to go against the grain of German assumptions about human interaction for business: that meetings should only take place among professionals when there is something concrete to discuss.

At meetings the Germans can impress their listeners with their knowledge. The American journalist Kempe (1999: 45) goes further. The Germans, he suggests, feel a *need* to impart whatever wisdom they hold 'on whomever will listen'. In German organizational contexts the unspoken rule then appears to be that talk should be restricted to the concrete and the specific (Nees 2000: 54–56). Interlocutors will speak their minds frankly, but managers and others in senior positions will expect due deference from those in lower ranks. So it is that interactions among Germans lack informality, spontaneity and emotional closeness.

An important feature of a language of management is, as we have already been noting, what it reveals about communication within and among organizations. It is well known that there is in the German workplace a preference for formality in work contexts which scrupulously cultivates social distance. Colleagues who have worked together for years will refer to each other using *Herr* and *Frau*, using the formal word for you (*Sie*). Although among young people there is a shift towards the informal forms for you in singular and plural (*Du* and *Ihr*), generally the organization remains 'a *Sie*-zone'.

This encoded resistance to informality in the workplace means that German as a language of management is not designed (as it were) as a nimble interactive communication tool which permits either higher- or lower-ranked colleagues to address themselves on an equal footing. All in all social distance, which is of great importance to Germans in (most) organizational contexts, is reinforced not only through elaborate systems of address but also by authoritative displays of job knowledge. It is a hallmark – if not the very genius – of German as a language of management that it both accommodates and encodes social distance alongside knowledge-as-authority.

In business contexts involving their foreign partners Germans can readily come across as lacking spontaneity and appearing to be too concerned with facts and serpentine explanations. The facts may well have been conveyed, but if the listeners come from cultures that prefer liveliness and easy exchanges with counterparts, German expository performances can induce tedium. The point here is that – especially in professional contexts – the Germans use language to convey their knowledge and to impress others with its depth, comprehensiveness and relevance for a given occasion. Among Germans this is very much the order of things, but it means that foreigners variously note that German business partners, even when using a foreign language, are seen as well-educated specialists, who come quickly to the point, are obsessed with detail (*detailversessen*) avoid questions of a personal kind, and apply rational thinking and objectivity (see Schroll-Machl 2003: 45–66).

So characterized, German as a language of management is surely one that reflects a society and organizational contexts in which the notion of authority-reinforced hierarchy and an accompanying cultivation of social distance are such marked features. In other words it is a language that suits a management culture that is indeed 'tough on the issue, tough on the person', whilst inclined to over-control subordinates. It is furthermore a language which operates in environments where 'good organization' ensures that 'communication is restricted to what serves the main purpose' (Goeudevert 2003: 141[3]). It is a language that rather abhors the extraneous as often unnecessary or potentially distracting. Extraneous matter may include small talk, a joke, or reference to an issue that belongs to another forum of discussion.

Vocabulary

German as a language of management is quite distinct from American with its inventive neologisms and tendency to deploy sporting terminology or from Japanese with its penchant for folksy idioms. It is extremely adept at creating concrete terms for the hard functions of management and many of these terms are incidentally extremely difficult to translate into other languages, sounding awkward and ponderous. Even when seemingly appropriately translated, something can be lost.

An interesting example is the German word for 'personnel management', which predated *das HRM*. The word is *Personalwirtschaft*, which is made up of the two words *Personal* and *Wirtschaft*. In any German–English dictionary the word *Wirtschaft* will be translated as 'economy'. Plainly the expression 'personnel economy' is a nonsense in English. The flavour of the German word is that something is well husbanded, turned to good account: in this case, personnel.[4] Ironically 'human resource management' is a better translation of *Personalwirtschaft* than 'personnel management'!

There is of course plenty of borrowing of management words from (American) English. Practitioners and management writers, academic and non-academic, have no qualms in peppering their discourse with terms such as *das HRM, M & A, das Talent-Management, die Balanced Scorecard* and even *Exzellenz*. If German absorbs nouns (mainly nouns) from English, it is more reluctant to internalize the up-beat metaphors that enliven especially American business discourse. This is explainable by virtue of the fact that a striking feature of German in management contexts appears to be an extreme aversion to the use of metaphors.

Metaphors are affective, convey mood and possibly provoke insights into the otherwise familiar in an imaginative way. This mode of expression in the management context is seemingly not to the German taste, the Germans preferring facts and wanting them in factual verbal formulations. This state of affairs in itself tells us something about perceptions of management in German popular culture. In Germany management is overwhelmingly seen as a practical activity. Unlike Americans German do not ratchet up management to be an almost mystical experience. In German management culture, if something works or does not work, there are good functional reasons to explain it.

From all the foregoing it should not be surprising to learn that the German language has arrays of words for the core English terms 'manager', 'management' and 'manage'. Indeed we find that there are some 50 different words in German to cover everyday senses including activities relating to the running of organizations:

Management: Behandlung, Betriebsleitung, Betriebswirtschaftslehre, Direktion, Führung, Geschäftsführung, Handhabung, Management, die Unternehmungsführung (-leitung),Verwaltung, Vorstand.
Manager: Betriebsleiter, Direktor, Entscheidungsträger, Geschäftsführer, Inhaber, Leiter (Abteilungsleiter, Filialleiter,Verkaufsleiter, etc.), Impresario, Intendant, Manager, Regisseur, Unternehmer, Verwalter, Vorstandsmitglied, Vorsteher, Beschliesser, Haushälter, Hauswirt.
Manage: Mit/ohne etwas auskommen, bändigen, bewältigen, bewirtschaften, gelingen, handhaben, in Ordnung halten hinkommmen, hinkriegen leiten, managen, regeln, schaffen, verkraften,verwalten, mit etwas zurechtkommen.

Readers with a knowledge of German will realize that German makes distinctions that do not exist in English. For example, German has different words for managing large estates, i.e. as owned by aristocrats (*bewirtschatften*), for managing conflict (*handhaben*), not mention pain (*verkraften*), a weapon (*handhaben*) or a celebrity (*managen*). The English word 'manager' is an offered translation for words like impresario as well as 'special' classes of managers such as 'theatre manager' (der *Intendant*), 'estate manager' (*der Gutsverwalter*) and even 'decision maker' (*Entscheidungsträger*) (Duden 1996; Hentze 1995; Langenscheidt 2001).

When it comes to management in and of organizations, the generic terms in German are two words which explicitly connote leading as opposed to managing in a loose Anglo-Saxon sense. The verbs in question are *führen* and *leiten*. When these verbs are used to build various German words for manager and management, the verb *führen* tends to be more significantly associated with the exercise of greater power and authority. The derived nouns for management tell the story. The word *Leitung* often refers to management in non-commercial organizations in contrast to *Führung,* which embraces not only management in the commercial sphere but in other endeavours ranging from politics to sport. The noun *Führung* refers to the process of management as a strategically guiding activity.[5]

Before concluding this section, we should not forget that from 1945 to 1989 two ideologically distinct languages of management developed on

German soil: that of capitalist West Germany (Federal Republic of Germany) and that of the communist East Germany (German Democratic Republic). In the years of division two distinct languages of management were in operation. Since reunification 'almost without exception, West German terms have driven out east German synonyms' (Stevenson 2002: 120) not to mention the entire vocabulary of Marxist-Leninism as a catechism for everyday life.

The old East German language of management, infused as it was in communist terminology, has then virtually disappeared, but this is not to say that the 'West German language of management' has been completely absorbed in Eastern Germany or that all East Germans, especially those who had their formative years under communism, have abandoned every particle of the old mind-set. Evidence from Russia and even from Poland suggests that large-scale exposure to market-economy vocabulary is met with both indifference and even resistance (Hurt and Hurt 2005). We should not forget that in the GDR a) 'everyone suspected everyone else, and the mistrust this bred was the foundation of social existence' (Funder 2003: 28) and b) its citizens created and enacted 'a quasi-diglossic linguistic repertoire, with a clear disjunction between public and private language use' (Stevenson, 2002: 69; see also Fink and Lehmann (2007) on aspects of communication in the socialist workplace). It is hard to drop one's guard even after many years.

Conclusion

Despite the centrality of language to every managerial act and intention, the study of language and management is still in its infancy. In this chapter I have attempted to show how German as a language of management creates a distinctive view of management as an abstract notion and as set of operations. The attempt has embraced aspects of German history, a short commentary on German lexis and a longer commentary of usage. I have to some extent used the language as a kind of meta-language for explaining aspects of German management.

For all the deficiencies of this contribution this approach might be usefully applied to other languages to discover notable culture-specific features which standard methods of cultural and sociological analysis do not always unearth. The implicit challenge to management scholars is significant. First, there is no tradition in management scholarship of incorporating linguistic theories and insights into its models, schemes and assumptions. Second, the dominance of English as the world language of business and management education ensures that what one might call the linguistic exploration of non-English-speaking management cultures is chronically underdeveloped. As has been stated elsewhere in this volume (Chapter 14):

> Very few English-speaking management scholars have any interest in language either as an historical accretion or as a mode of expression of

managers in languages. Such a state of affairs, directly linked to the general monoglottism of the USA and UK management scholarship, leads to the intellectual impoverishment of management studies, whereby the English language, far from acting as a great universal distributor of management knowledge, operates at best as a filter and at worst a distorting mirror of that knowledge.

As Caulkin (2005: 5) has noted: 'English is a one-way membrane that all too often filters out the rest of the world.' Believing as I do that a language, its nature and usages, sheds rewarding light on management in its own linguistic context, let me conclude with these observations of German as a language of management. It appears that German managers use their language to promote their authority and to communicate themselves as persons with exceptional functional knowledge. Behind this may lie a deep need to protect themselves against *Angst*, that particularly German anxiety, which is surely the root of their much-attested risk-avoidance. In their professional contexts managers protect themselves against this troubling state of mind by maintaining cool, correct and uncompassionate interpersonal relationships, demanding from subordinates loyalty and punctilious execution of instructions. The accompanying language behaviour has, if I have it characterized correctly, no obvious correlate in other business cultures.

Notes

1 In linguistics the word 'guttural' refers to sound that are produced in the throat. Strictly speaking, German is not a very guttural language in comparison with, say, Arabic or Danish. It is probable that the word – with its phonetic closeness to the word 'gutter' – became fashionable in Britain during the First or Second World as a pejorative designation about the language of the Germans.

2 Mark Twain in 'The awful German language' whimsically refers to German compound nouns not as words, but as 'alphabetical processions' (2003: 324).

3 What serves the main purpose' is my translation of *Nützlichkeitskern*, meaning literally 'usefulness' (or 'utility core'). This is a good example of a German compound word that is entirely unambiguous, yet extremely problematic to translate

4 The German word for management studies is *Betriebswirtschaftslehre*, which means 'the doctrine of turning an enterprise to good account'.

5 For connoisseurs of leadership studies, German has created a useful compound term *das Führenkönnen*, which combines the verbs 'to lead' and 'to be able'. This German term reminds us that to lead you need the *Führenkönnen*.

8 Russia's long struggle with Western terms of management and the concepts behind them

Nigel Holden, Olga Kuznetsova and Gerhard Fink

Introduction

With the collapse of the Soviet Union in 1991, domestic competence in practically all economic areas and even in many areas of social intercourse vanished virtually overnight. The end of communism marked a new linguistic beginning in that a) the language that described Soviet economic practices and procedures became instantly redundant and b) there followed massive borrowing from the West of business and management terminology. These terms were needed to support the influx into Russia of the new management knowledge and practices through the agency of (mainly) Western providers, who variously descended on Russia as advisors, educators, management consultants and business people. However, despite the efforts of these Western experts and the eagerness on the part of many Russians to embrace this new vocabulary and the skills it represented, the introduction of new terms has not been a smooth process.

By no stretch of the imagination can it be said that Russians at large have already absorbed both new lexis and new way of thinking into their lifeblood. The important thing to realize is that this slow pace was caused by a variety of factors including the vagaries of the economic and social transformation, the complexity of the knowledge transfer process as well as by the condition of the Russian language itself: It simply lacked many of the words necessary to transfer accurately the meaning of the new business ideas that the country urgently needed to introduce the market-economy system. Yet, the importance of the development of the Russian language for management purposes is surely beyond doubt. Indeed the very fate of Russia, whatever path her politicians pursue, and her status in the global economy are directly linked to the establishment of this linguistic apparatus. The complexities of this issue are rarely appreciated in other countries, let alone in Mother Russia herself.

The evolving language of the market economy in the country is not quite Russian. It is the Russian language in a new garb. It may be described as *russgliskii* (Rathmayr 2004), that as yet uneasy amalgam of Russian and English, which, as Pshenichnikova (2003) has noted, will form 'a sub-language that has the potential to develop as a self-sufficient functional variation within the system of literary Russian ... it will fulfil the social, economic and linguistic demands of a new generation of managers in market economy Russia'. The evolving of this quirky hybrid language is in effect an emergency response to the need for a linguistic system that can merge tradition and modernity. It is yet to be seen if *russgliskii* can establish itself in this capacity.

In 1977, when Moscow's prestige and worldwide influence were at their highest, a Soviet philological work declared that one of the most conspicuous features of the Russian language was 'its capacity to express all knowledge accumulated by mankind in every field of endeavour and its semantic universality: from which it follows that its literary language is able to describe human life in its entirety' (Filin 1978; cited in Holden *et al.* 1998: 169). This great language must now be harnessed to the needs of the market economy. The awesome cultural challenge before Russia now is to expand Russian language into unknown territory but not in defiance of, not as counterpoise to, but as a straightforward adjunct of the language of Pushkin and Tolstoy.

On Russian and the language of the market

At the end of the perestroika period, there were, according to the senior Soviet economist Leonid Abalkin (1989), 'fewer than 20 persons with a really sound grasp of finance and marketing' in the entire Soviet Union. Marketing for its part was 'a hazily grasped concept' (Abramishvili 1991) and indeed still remains so in many respects (Jacobs 2001). Yet, since the collapse of the Soviet Union in December 1991 countless thousands of Western management-development documents – everything from training manuals to textbooks – have been converted into Russian. The post-Soviet onslaught of Western management educators and consultants swept in a language that reflected for the citizens of the former Soviet Union completely unknown modes of existence and economic life. The Western experts, eager to communicate their knowledge, and the Russians eager to devour it (or at least some of it), side-stepped the issue of the lack of terminological compatibility between Russian and English (the overwhelming used medium of knowledge transfer).

The outcome of the initial attempts of Western knowledge transfer was that words rather than the concepts they represent have penetrated the emerging Russian business context. Western representatives came with all too highly attractive-sounding words: but the concepts behind the words were all too not clearly understood by an apprehensive and sceptical population.

Not surprisingly, numerous authors have noted the challenge of translating formal Western management terminology into a language which for 70 years shunned that terminology for ideological reasons (Holden et al. 1998; Holden and Fink 2007; Jacobs 2001; Kuznetsov and Yakavenka 2005; Pshenichnikova 2003). As we shall contend, this challenge is not one that has diminished over the years. On the contrary, it has if anything acquired various disconcerting features.

With hindsight we can say that the West never apprehended the significance of the language dimensions of the 'collective culture shock' (Fink and Holden 2002) confronting those 250 million people as of the 1990s. Yet in the very year the Soviet Union disintegrated, the perspicacious American journalist, Hedrick Smith (1991: 660), sized up the situation admirably:

> The language of the market – competition, profits, free prices, and productivity – has come into vogue among urban intellectuals and government circles, but so far these concepts inspire fear, not confidence, among the masses; they cut against the grain of deep-set attitudes. Many little people fear capitalism as a get-rich scheme for a wily minority of unscrupulous speculators.

Getting the knowledge wrong

Western management educators and consultants, when they first came to post-communist Russia, were then largely unaware of the implications of this state of affairs for the efficient transfer of management and market know-how. Their documentation was all too often not adapted but simply translated by Russians without any understanding of Western management concepts and terminology. Interpreters were hired in their thousands to deliver the words of professors and consultants. The entire knowledge transfer process was studded with misleading translations and crass on-the-hoof improvisations by armies of linguists operating outside their competence zones (Holden *et al.* 1998).

From the early 1990s business glossaries and bilingual dictionaries have been available on every street corner in Moscow and other cities. They were, and are, full of errors and misunderstandings, not to mention obscure words and linguistic absurdities. One example is the pairing of the Russian adjective for managerial (*upravlencheskii*) with English loan-word *menedzhment* that gave rise to *upravlencheskii menedzement* meaning literarily 'managerial management'. One glossary of marketing terms in Russian with English and German equivalents produced some quaint, if basically understandable, renditions: 'strategy of marketing', 'strategy of reactive realization', 'product elaboration' (for 'product development'), 'product class cycle' (for product life cycle), 'curve of sale', 'concept of sale', etc. (Dzhincharadze 1991). In another glossary 'advertising' and 'publicity' were translated by the same word (*reklama*), thus perpetuating the Soviet confusion between the two terms (Petrov *et al.* 1991). Another example is the transliteration of the term 'pilot project' into its Russian version *pilotnyi proekt*. When Russians hear the word 'pilot' in Russian it calls to mind aviators, so to many Russians a pilot project might connote a project belonging to an aviator.

Even some prestigious projects financed by international organizations such as the World Bank have been affected by the difficulty of finding adequate explanations to certain terms. For example, in the early 1990s the World Bank sponsored publication of an 'English–Russian Glossary: Banking and Finance'. The latest edition, published in 2006, contains numerous changes and amendments. According to the compilers (Mirkin and Mirkin 2006), these modifications were necessary because the original translations and examples did not correspond to Russian realities at the time of the first publication, because it was not possible to ground the explanations in domestic practice. This suggests that it took more than a decade for the Russian financial sector to accumulate the experience and create new realities that the modified terms and additional entries in the new glossary could reflect.

As Jacobs (2001) has demonstrated, Western textbooks can all too easily be victims of 'errors of translation or editorial tinkering'. For example, a representation of the Boston Consulting Group's growth-share matrix in a translated marketing textbook plainly showed that the principles behind this model had been misunderstood by the translators. As Jacobs (2001), citing the Russian version of Morris's *The Marketing Principle*, records:

> the Boston Consulting Group's growth-share matrix [was] mistakenly discussed as a means to assess business positioning strategy, instead of as a tool to analyse a company's business or product portfolio and also a company's growth opportunities. Moreover, the principles governing construction of the matrix were wrongly labelled: the 'question mark' quadrant is labelled as 'rising star'; the 'cash cow' quadrant inexplicably as 'dead wood'; and the 'dog' quadrant, correctly as 'dog'.
>
> (Morris 1996: 21–23)

Three of the most generic words of the management lexicon, namely the nouns 'manager' and 'management' and the verb 'to manage', have posed enormous problems to translators and interpreters alike. In the Soviet period the Russified forms *menedzher* and *menedzhment* applied strictly to the 'lesser' capitalist species. These words were not used with reference to Soviet *managers*, who might be designated by terms such as *upravlenets*, nominally meaning 'manager', *ekspert, direktor* and, especially in industry, 'chief engineer'. The Soviet 'manager', however he was designated in the Russian language, was a cog in a vast machine. At best he was an organizer for the centralized system; he was never an independent decision-maker.

In the Soviet period the corresponding verb *upravlyat'* denoted decision implementation rather than decision-making. Hence a frequent translation of this word is 'to administer'. Today *upravlyat'* and its related terms (i.e. *upravleniye* and *upravelenets*) do not seem to resonate with the nature of the market economy. So it is that the modern (i.e. post-Soviet) business Russian gives preference to the term *menedzhment* rather than *upravlenie* and *menedzher* instead of *upravlenets*. The latter word has not disappeared, but it has more the flavour of director rather than of manager. Thus the words *menedzher* and *menedzhment* occupy semantic space which is new to the Russian language and its speakers.

Beyond that, the Russian context in turn adds twists to the imported *concept* of management, as managers (*menedzhery*), thanks to the Soviet view of capitalism, tend to be seen as owners of enterprises rather than business people in any generic sense. The Russian-language professional journal *Top-Manager* (note the English title) devoted an entire issue (2006) to a discussion about the emerging role of the manager in Russia. This publication makes clear that that there remains a problem in Russia of understanding the nature of management as professional work, since it does not easily apply to a country where the manager as communicator, mentor and decision-maker all rolled into one was – and largely still is – an unknown quantity.

Here, though, it should be pointed out that even communists – including Lenin and Stalin – had a clear distinction between capitalists and managers, the latter being seen as essential functionaries: Lenin certainly admired Taylorism (Fink and Lehmann 2007), whilst Stalin authorized the translation of books by Henry Ford into Russian. As of the 1990s these words were adopted as porte-manteau words to cover an amalgam of Soviet notions of capitalist management with hints of vaguely understood entrepreneurialism for the transition to the market economy. At the same time the idea that management applied to operational functions as well as profit-driven top management was not readily grasped.

Of special interest too is the word 'buy-out'. During years of extensive privatization Russian business adopted the word 'buy-out', without even translating it, to describe newly privatised enterprises acquired and dominated by insiders. In the West the term 'buy-out' describes the process of an often leveraged sale of the company to specialist financial investors (buy-out specialists) rather than to industry buyers. But in post-Soviet Russia the word 'buy-out' was used to describe largely unregulated and unfettered privatization that took place in socio-economic conditions that were not comparable to those prevailing in established market economies. Thus, when Russians and Western consultants or educators were talking about buy-outs, they were discussing mutually discordant versions of each others' practices and understanding of them. Then, after some years into the transition, Russians become exposed to concepts of transparency, corporate social responsibility (CSR), corporate governance. Here again there is a divergence of realities. It is not unheard of for Russian firms to think that by paying wages or paying taxes on time they are practising CSR (Kuznestov and Kuznetsova 2006).

Defeating the translator: a mini case study

In order to put some of these issues into a more concrete context, we make a reference to aspects of the Russian translation of Holden's book *Cross-cultural Management: A Knowledge Management Perspective* (Holden 2002 and 2005), which was originally published in English in 2002. The Russian edition, which appeared in 2005, not only bears out some of the general points about translation pitfalls, but also gives indicators as to the kind of management terms which present translators with specific challenges. This short review will in turn set the scene for wider reflections on the difficulties of rendering Western management terms in Russian.

The translation of the book in its entirety suggests great difficulties in rendering knowledge management (KM) concepts into Russian, since the very gist of KM has been gravely misrepresented. The translation turned KM into a form of cognitive management (not even 'management of cognition', which would be conceptually closer to the original). It is no exaggeration to say that we are talking about two substantially different books. Co-author of this chapter, Olga Kuznetsova, who is a native Russian speaker, finds that the Russian version offers very little in terms of the academic content, whilst the text is impenetrable in parts and even unintelligible for advanced readers. The Russian publication obviously failed to deliver the intended product to the readership due to incompetent translation.

Even when clearly discussed in the text, some of the English terms (e.g. 'stickiness', 'implicit' and many others) require explanatory footnotes. It was also apparent that there is no agreed translation in Russian for the numerous key terms with 'tacit' and 'explicit' among them. But the translator's difficulties were not confined to KM terminology. A number of management expressions, some of the buzz-word variety, proved taxing. Explanation would either be supplied in footnotes or a 'new' translation would appear in the text. Words in this category include 'stakeholders', 'know-how', 'excellence' 'benchmarking' among many. The latter expression rendered as 'continuous orientation towards the best models.' As for that ultimate buzz-word 'excellence', this term has defied translators in many languages,[1] Russian being no exception.

These observations quickly suggest that Russian remains underdeveloped as a language of management and that it 'suffers from semantic voids pertaining to a wide range of market economy concepts and functions' (Holden *et al.* 1998: 191). Pshenichnikova (2003) also provides an abundance of examples of terminological challenges that face students studying management when their studies require them to work with English (a foreign language) sources. As her analysis suggests, problems related to the transfer of Western terminology present themselves at all levels of the Russian-language system within the managerial-knowledge domain, thus going well beyond conceptual misrepresentations.

There are problems of integrating English language structures and terminology into Russian. These include knowledge absorption, multivariate spellings and non-critical acceptance of Anglicisms even when adequate unambiguous Russian equivalents are available. Inevitably, 'create as you go' has become a widespread and common way of practising, using and developing modern business Russian. Anybody who writes on management or discusses it becomes a creator of terminology. This is demonstrated by the assortment of translations of Hofstede's well-known notion of 'power distance' found in students' reports mentioned in Pshenichnikova's (2003) paper.

From a purely linguistic point of point of view, the mistranslations in all sources that were tested by authors derive from a number of causes, among which:

- Complete misunderstanding of a term in the original (example: mapping/ *kartografiya*; learning history/history of learning; sense-making/understanding; assumptions/axioms; learning by doing/back knowledge; being promoted/becoming more top manager).
- Attempts to demystify English terms by making reference to other English terms that result in profound misjudgement of the original meaning. (Example: Kotler's *Marketing Management* was first translated into Russian in 1980 as *Upravlenie marketingom*. In 1999 it is already translated as *Marketing menedzhement*.) Golubkov (1999), in his endeavour to explain the gist of 'marketing', falls into this trap. His explanations reveal lack of understanding that marketing stands for the process of interaction with market, so marketing management would be a set of actions that allow handling the process in its totality.
- Absence of a close lexical equivalent in Russian (examples concern the verb 'to facililitate' and the nouns 'excellence', 'vision' and, of course, 'marketing').
- Use of circumlocutions and/or free translations that do not convey the meaning of the original (example: analysis of some of the marketing terminology in Russia by Golubkov (1999) and Pshenichnikova (2003)).
- Creation and use of loan-words based on the English originals which in Russified form would be not readily understood (example: *fasilitatsiya, onlinovyi* (on-line in adjectival form), *branding, networking, marketing-mix, controlling, publicity, accounting, benchmarking* etc.).

All in all, the post-communist transformation in Russia can hardly be considered as complete as long as its business language remains in such disarray. Our investigation suggests that Russia still does not have proper access to the modern knowledge base in the field of management and business accumulated in the West at such a critical time for Russia's development. Bad, incorrect or misleading translations of the kind we have been describing simply add to the problems. Other inhibiting factors include the absence of a standardized lexis of management in Russian and a general lack of experience of working in the market environments of other countries.

A caveat

However, what appear to be 'bad' translations should perhaps be seen as attempts to make sense of verbal codified information, which comes from another context (i.e. the West) and does not fit into the prevailing context (i. e. Russia). In the absence of accepted standardized equivalents between English and Russian, the Russian translator will not only resort to transliteration of troublesome words, but will even use his or her skills to create new terms. Sometimes the results are indeed mistranslations, but not necessarily always. Translators can therefore be seen as engaged in a knowledge management process in which words and concepts may become something different in the target language: their 'perceived usefulness and applicability change' (Fink and Holden 2005) so that the new knowledge can be made compatible with the experience of the target culture.

At first glance these mistranslations appear to be symptomatic of occasional professional incompetence. But that may be to miss the bigger point, for it is surely better to regard translators as creative activists in the emergence of a new business culture in Russia, acting as catalysts to create common ground between Western experience, knowledge and values with Russian ones. It has proved to be a task – an experiment, to be more precise – of immense complexity.

Discussion

There is little doubt that the Russian language is generating a new business vocabulary that attempts to reflect generic ideas about the market economy; but yet this lexis remains raw, is not perfectly formed and is therefore not fully operational. Even after fifteen years of transition from communism Russia has still not internalized the language of the market economy. This finding is consistent with the findings of Jacobs concerning marketing terminology (see also: Pshenichnikova 2003). Everyday terms like 'excellence', 'know-how', 'benchmarking', 'performance' and 'vision' sorely test both translators and language users. Some of the terms we mentioned are but the tip of an enormous iceberg comprising between 1,000 and 2,000 of core management terms, this figure not including the specialist vocabularies of functional domains such as marketing, production and information technology.[2]

In other words, Russian is still fissured with lexical and conceptual voids concerning the nature of management for the market economy. It would greatly help if there could be standardization of management terminology in Russian.[3] After all, as Pshenichnikova (2003) has noted: 'There is an urgent need for a normative dictionary of modern business Russian, which would provide proper meanings, possible connotations, orphoepic and grammar characteristics, typical contexts for the key terminology and give recommendations for its proper usage.'

In the absence of such an authoritative work of reference as well as more scrupulously constructed multilingual glossaries Russian is awash with ill-digested management and business terms from English and to a lesser extent from French and German. But the overall terminological uncertainties in the field of business and management are not a consequence of lexical and conceptual voids. They reflect the stresses and strains associated with introducing new values into every level of society. As Kuznetsov and Kuznetsova (2003: 914–15) have noted: 'there is no consistent and comprehensive system of cultural values, but rather an often uneasy coexistence of conflicting values that adds uncertainty to information flows and decision-making'.

Western-management terminology first began to penetrate Russian substantially from around 1985 during the reforms of Mikhail Gorbachev, the last Soviet supreme leader. Reviewing the last twenty years, it is possible to identify classes of Western-management terminology which have proved somewhat difficult to be translated into Russian:

- Figurative terms. Terms like 'benchmarking', 'the bottom line' and 'sticking to the knitting' defy literal translation. They become circumlocutions, which reflect the core idea in neutral language.
- Soft management terms. Modern management uses a vast range of words to cover aspects of communication and motivation (currently fashionable are word like 'team-player', 'coach', 'mentor', 'facilitate', 'empower', 'vision', 'mission', 'deliver', etc.). Many words of this class are virtually untranslatable (except by wordy circumlocutions). Native words which might be used for literal translation are completely inappropriate. For example, the standard Russian word for 'empower' confines its semantic area to high politics.
- Terms in models. Terms in models are often a kind of short-hand for a weighty or complex notion. In Holden (2005) two separate Russian words are shown for 'assumptions' in models. Terms are often figurative, as are 'cash cow' and 'dog' in the Boston Consulting Group's growth-strategy matrix. They too prove exceptionally difficult to render into Russian. Models are widely used in management education and research. A survey of Russian-language versions of Western management would very likely reveal substantial variation in the translations of terms used in models. Iconic terms like 'cash cow' or 'power distance' can be taken to be the tip of the iceberg.
- Terms of organizational life. Two obvious areas are HRM and marketing, for which entirely new areas of vocabulary are being created based on foreign loan-words, especially from (American) English, and reconstituted native word-stock. The absorption of these special functional languages – and

the attitudes that go with them – will take many years, perhaps many decades, to be accomplished.In the Soviet period 'HRM' was the province of the Communist Party, whose representatives were attached to every organization throughout the entire Soviet Union to ensure undeviating commitment to the execution of the great national development plans. It might well be said that Party-inspired HRM existed to nurture *homo sovieticus*, a species superior to *homo capitalisticus* in outlook, social responsibility and indeed moral worth. It might not be an exaggeration to say that Western HRM terminology introduces Russia to a new vocabulary of human behaviour and indeed worth in the form of alien concepts. In this HRM-speak company employees are described as 'resources'. They are subjected to appraisals, for which the nominal translation 'otsenka' ('evaluation') is an inadequate equivalent. They may also have recourse to 'grievance procedures', which also defies neat translation into Russian, as the nominally equivalent words 'pretentsiya', meaning 'a claim' and 'nedovol'stvo', meaning dissatisfaction, are plainly inadequate. It should not be overlooked that traditional Russian society has long taken the view that any kind of law or regulation exists to preserve the privileges of those in authority. The idea that employees can somehow have rights is still a novelty. Marketing by definition had no place in the centrally planned, 'marketless' Soviet economy. It was viewed ideologically as one of the black arts of capitalism, a retrograde system of exploitation devised for and by American big business – if you care to believe the 1970–78 edition of the *Great Soviet Encyclopaedia*. Marketing (see below) was never seen in terms of business planning or customer satisfaction; much less, as some marketers would have put it, as a system promoting the public good. This suspicion of marketing lingered after the collapse of the USSR and may explain why even today so many Russians have grave misgivings about the nature of the market economy with its vulgar commercialization and the creation of super-rich elite. Against that, marketing terminology is something of a translator's death-trap. For a start, the very word marketing which has been absorbed into Russian as a loan-word appears to refer to more to the Russian perceptions of the Western way of doing business than a general principle of business which places the customer at the centre of business activity *in any society*. Except for Russia's wealthy classes, money is not necessarily perceived in the general population in terms of disposal income with which to buy 'the latest thing'. Indeed for countless millions it is a commodity which is all too often conspicuous by its absence for participation in the market economy. It is most immediately needed 'to feed the family' (Rathmayr 2004). One of the most noticeable features of what one might call 'Russian marketing discourse' is the emphasis on marketing as a 'system of management' ever since the term marketing made its first appearance in the 1970–78 edition of the *Great Soviet Encyclopaedia*. In that authoritative tome marketing is described thus:

'One of the management systems of the capitalist enterprise ... The purpose of marketing is to create conditions for the adaptation of products to society's needs, etc.' Compare this with the opening sentence on a chapter on marketing in a book on management published in 2005 and recommended by the Ministry of Education of the Russian Federation. The author (Gerchikova 2005: 189), states that marketing is a system of internal management, which is directed towards the study and evaluation of demand and requirements of the market for a more justified orientation of enterprises' productive activity concerning the output of concrete types of production in pre-established volumes and corresponding to the determined techno-economic characteristics.

Gerchikova (2005), like other Soviet and post-Soviet authors, prefers to treat marketing as a system and not as a process, the latter not the former term being widely used in definitions of marketing in standard textbooks. Marketing then, according to Gerchikova, is still presented to some extent in a Soviet guise, which is surely amazing. And yet it is also not amazing. It is yet another example of the struggle to find the common ground between Russian experience and 'Western' knowledge. Evidently it is easier at this stage of Russia's transition, some 15 years after the collapse of communism, to conceive of marketing as a system of management than the management of processes, many of which are external to the firm. In passing it can be mentioned that the chapter by Gerchikova does not contain a single graphic or model. This persistence of a Soviet practice speaks volumes about a Russian time-lag in the presentation of management knowledge regardless of its content.

Pshenichnikova (2003) notes that expression like 'marketing communications' can erroneously end up in back-translation as 'the marketing of communications' (note the plural form), whilst that problematical concept 'brand' has taken up residence in Russian as 'brend', which to some extent replaces the translation, which literally means 'trade mark.' Russian translators do not always make a clear distinction, crucial to marketers, between 'market research' and 'marketing research'. In the meantime the Russians have taken over the English word 'shop', but this refers to an establishment offering 'up-market goods' (*prestigeträchtige Waren*) (Rathmayr 2002).

Since the collapse of communism in 1991, the Russian language has absorbed a vast number of words and expressions from various languages, but outstandingly from English, in areas of life ranging from business, sport and leisure, media, youth culture, information technology and so forth (Rathmayr 2002). A striking feature of this huge lexical influx is that the vast majority of the imported words are nouns. Rathmayr (2002) lists 177 neologisms, of which all but four are verbs. Of the four verbs, only one is based on native word-stock. Of the remainder two are coinages based on recent imports into Russian. The first verb is *internetit'*, meaning 'to use the

Internet'. The seconds is *vaucherizirovat'*, which can be translated by the non-standard form 'to voucherise'. Another fashionable-sounding verb (not listed by Rathmayr) is *piarit'*, from PA (personal assistant), the verb meaning 'to act as a PA'.

For some reason Russian can Russify foreign nouns more easily than foreign verbs. Russification does not just mean absorbing the foreign word, but will normally entail 'reshaping' it in Cyrillic script and using it with normal case endings. It seems to be more difficult (or unacceptable) to coin verbs out of foreign word-stock. Part of the reason is presumably that Russian has an array of verbal inflections which do not readily graft themselves onto foreign words. There appears to be a reluctance to augment foreign words with the enclitic infinitive form-*irovat*, which is often used for assimilating English verbs ending in-ate (and some German verbs ending in-ieren). Russian has given a home to the English nouns 'manager' and 'management', but there appears to be no Russian verb derived from this root.

This condition of terminological uncertainty ought to be of concern to the management educators for various reasons, the first of which that it extends well beyond Russia. To a greater or lesser extent all former constituent republics of the Soviet Union as well as the former socialist countries of East and Central Europe suffer from the same malaise. From a knowledge-management perspective, the conclusion must be drawn that Western suppliers of management know-how have since the beginning of the 1990s had uneven success in 'creating common cognitive ground' (Nonaka and Takeuchi 1995) for the transfer of this know-how.

The crusade to bring Western management know-how to the former socialist countries has been one of the most expensive exercises in the cross-cultural transfer of management knowledge the world has ever seen. The success has been variable. At the outset it was never grasped that the sine qua non of the success lay in delivering the language as part of the essential knowledge package *and not just as the medium for transferring the knowledge* to transform entire societies along market-economy lines. A contributory factor has surely been a general assumption that Western management terminology is in principle straightforward to translate into Russian and the 50 or so other languages covering the former USSR and former socialist countries of East and Central Europe. All the evidence points in completely the opposite direction, as this chapter should make crystal-clear.

Conclusion

The world of management education and research, dominated as it is by the English language, has traditionally been indifferent to the impact of language barriers as they influence the intercultural transfer of management knowledge. Language barriers by nature are dividers of worldviews as well as creators of twilight zones of interlingual ambiguity and confusion; they slice societies, institutions and even the human heart. Yet, as this chapter has attempted to demonstrate, a language barrier, once penetrated, throws up issues which vary from the singularly fascinating to the downright perturbing.

In the case of Russia it is especially instructive to see this language barrier as a potent factor in the process of transition to the market economy. It has rarely recognized, especially in English-speaking countries, how this barrier imposes such a severe constraint on the smooth transfer of management know-how into the Russian-speaking world. The kind of country which Russia is destined to be is directly linked to how this language barrier is understood by Russians and non-Russians, how its terminological confusions are resolved and how a new and robust lexis of management is cultivated.

It has been well observed that that the 'post-communist transition [in Russia] has proved to be one of those rare historical events in which both the culture and economy experience radical changes simultaneously' (Kuznestov and Kuznetsova 2005). The Russian language may be seen as the key social influence which links culture with the economy, but it too is a state of flux as it shapes and is shaped by the tensions and turmoil which are attending the stupendous process of marketization. The expertise acquired during the Soviet days might be redundant but it will not go away quietly.

Russian universities are still full of academics who were educated before the reforms started. Even if they try to teach differently now, their understanding of the market economy is still influenced by their background. The fact that their first exposure to modern Western knowledge occurred through inferior quality translations, which prevailed during the early years of reforms, does not help. Many modern university courses, even in leading universities, represent a strange symbiosis of borrowings from Western texts and attempts to cross-contaminate them with topics, concepts and approaches traditional for the pre-reforms era. This, however, appears to be not so much an attempt to Russify Western expertise from the linguistic point of view as to salvage some of the self-esteem by the generation of tutors, whose views were formed in the final decades of the Soviet rule.[4]

No one reading this chapter who has professional dealings with Russia can assume from now on that, whatever he or she says, or whatever is committed into Russian about a business arrangement or a knowledge transfer activity, is perceived at the receiving end as if the creation of 'common cognitive ground' were straightforward. More than a decade ago a contributor to the *Financial Times* (1993) characterized business interactions with Russia as 'a cross-cultural minefield'. This is still the case today. This chapter endorses that view, emphasizing that terminological misrepresentations in Russian reflect not so much translators' incompetence as their conscientious quest to bring Western knowledge in harmony with Russian experience as it is now.[5]

Notes

1 The word 'excellence' became hallowed in the Peters and Waterman bestseller *In Search of Excellence* first published in 1982. The key word has defied translation into both German and Danish. The German version of the book uses the word *Spitzenleistung* (lit. 'top performance'), whilst the Danes have opted for a revised title which in back-translation reads as 'What the best firms do best'. It is incidentally of note that Peters and Waterman cannot claim to have introduced the word 'excellence' to the world of management. Excellence was a concept used in Nazi Germany (Wiederhold 2003) and in the Stalin's Gulag in the 1930s.
   In Hitler's Germany, firms which delivered 'outstanding performance' to support the Nazi aims could be designated as 'model enterprises' (*Musterbetriebe*), of which there were 297 in 1940 (Wiederhold 2003: 111, 119). Such honoured firms received from the Nazi authorities an *Auszeichnung*, a certificate of distinction. As those familiar with the German language will know, the associated word *ausgezeichnet* is customarily translated as 'excellent'. In the case of Soviet Russia, inmates of the Gulag who in the grimmest conditions imaginable exceeded production norms were known as *otlichniki* (lit. 'the excellent ones', 'those who stand out); they got no reduction of their cruel sentences, but gained luxuries such as 'single beds with mattresses and blankets, wooden floors and pictures on the wall' (Applebaum 2003: 193).
2 In his compendium of Polish management and business terms Penc (1997) lists 2,300 head-words. *The Concise Blackwell Encyclopaedia of Management* (Cooper and Argyris 1998) lists 900 head-words.
3 Some valuable suggestions can be found in *Guidelines for the Translation of Social Science Texts* (2006) that evolved out of the Social Science Translation project, an initiative sponsored by American Council of Learned Societies but addressed primarily to those who commission/edit translations.
4 We could not obtain relevant information about Russian universities, but some statistics are available for other former Soviet republics. Kuznetsov and Yakavenka (2006) report the results of a survey of academics teaching business related subjects in Belarus and Kyrgyzstan. In over half of respondents in Belarus and nearly two-thirds in Kyrgyzstan were educated during the Soviet period. Only very few were exposed to Western methods of education. Interestingly, in both countries only 10 per cent of respondents revealed any sort of resistance or contempt to Western knowledge, but as many as 28 per cent in Belarus and 39 per cent in Kyrgyzstan considered Western knowledge not relevant to the situation in their economy.
5 Translations from Russian have been made by N. J. Holden and O. Kuznetsova; from German by N. J. Holden.

9 Language and careers in multinational corporations

Rebecca Piekkari

Introduction

The requirements for foreign-language skills are on the rise in the corporate world. For example, a recent report commissioned by the City of London suggests that investments banks are looking further a field for staff, particularly for graduates from abroad. According to the report 'these foreign graduates are more suited to a career in the city as they have superior language skills and tend to be more mature' (*International Financial Review* 2006: 6). Competitive pressures force investment banks and companies alike to improve their services by attending customers in their native tongue. International mergers and acquisitions constantly restructure businesses and increase the demand for high-level personnel equipped with the requisite language skills as well as a university degree in business or engineering. Multinational corporations also continue to send expatriates to foreign offices in order to ensure continued business succeed in the global environment. Thus, despite the rise of English as the lingua franca for international business, the demands for multilingual employees has not declined. Therefore, both in terms of external and internal organizational communication, knowing a foreign language is an individual asset and part of a person's career capital (Terjesen 2005).

Research on careers in general and global careers in particular shows that foreign-language competence is one of the key capabilities individuals should possess when striving for an international career (e.g. Suutari and Brewster 2000). Language skills of expatriates are often assessed and evaluated prior to sending them on foreign assignments (Dowling and Welch 2004). However, the requirement to effectively operate in a multilingual workplace is not only limited to a small group of employees who physically relocate from one country to another. On the contrary, an increasing number of personnel who work on teams spanning many different countries and cultures use foreign languages in the daily work. This applies not only to the top echelons of the organization but also further down the hierarchy (Charles and Marschan-Piekkari 2002). Therefore, many managers and employees, who are based nationally, experience the psychological aspects of working and adjusting to foreign colleagues, customers and partners

(Baruch 2006). The requirements for being able and willing to operate in foreign languages have thus deeply penetrated the multinational corporation.

It takes substantial time for a person to reach operational fluency in another language. For some individuals, learning a foreign language may be instrumental in becoming employable and pursuing an international career (Bloch 1995; Kordsmeier *et al.* 2000). For others, it may be a vehicle of self-development and studying a related culture. Companies face the question of whether to invest in language training of existing staff or whether to hire new staff with the appropriate language skills, assuming that such employees are readily available. Either way, the company faces additional costs as well as the time constraint in achieving the necessary skills base (Marschan-Piekkari *et al.* 1999a).

Until recently, the effect of foreign-language competence on careers in multinational corporations has received limited scholarly attention; in part this may be due to the relative lack of rigorous research into career paths *per se* within multinationals as well as the effect of global assignments on individual careers. In addition, the issue of language competence within the multinational has only recently come to the fore of international business research. In their suggestions for future research, Luo and Shenkar (2006: 336) propose that 'language proficiency is not only a key organizational capability but also a strategic career asset'. While it is sometimes acknowledged in previous research that foreign-language competence may open up career opportunities that would not otherwise exist (e.g. Bloch 1995), the view of language tends to be rather narrow in that it is seen as instrumental in the initial securing of a job. From this perspective, language is regarded as a technical skill which can easily be learned through appropriate training or acquired when needed. However, the present chapter explores the effect of foreign-language skills on careers that are pursued in multinational corporations. Particularly, attention is paid to changes in the corporate language environment due to an international merger or acquisition, for example when a new common corporate language is imposed on staff. Based on a review of the literature and insights from empirical research I argue that foreign-language competence may have broader career implications by shaping, steering or even diverting individual career paths. Many of these effects tend to remain invisible to top management who is likely to be competent in the key foreign languages commonly used within the firm.

The remainder of this chapter is organized as follows. First, language competence in the context of the multinational corporation is problematized. The multinational corporation is defined as a multilingual organization in which the necessary language competence needs to be broadly assessed. The discussion aims to show that competence in English only is not likely to be sufficient for making an international career. Second, the potential language effects on careers, both positive and negative, are discussed by referring to empirical evidence from my own and others' research. The concluding section draws the discussion together. It should be noted that isolating the language effect on careers is very difficult as final career outcomes are intertwined with a number of other personal and contextual issues. Yet, for analytical purposes this chapter discusses separately the potential effects of language on careers.

Language competence in the corporate-language environment

Recently, the multinational corporation has been conceptualized as a multilingual organization (Barner-Rasmussen and Björkman 2007) or a multilingual community (Luo and Shenkar 2006). Staff in these firms often operate at the interface between several languages including those of the parent country, the common corporate language and the various subsidiary languages (Marschan-Piekkari *et al.* 1999a). Therefore, the answer to the question which language matters is not straightforward.

Several multinational corporations such as ABB, Electrolux, General Electric, Nokia and Phillips have adopted a common corporate language to facilitate in-house communication. While this decision often falls on English, it does not necessarily become an overruling language within the firm. First, the level of proficiency in the common corporate language is likely to vary resulting in different kinds of 'Englishes' and causing comprehension problems (Charles and Marschan-Piekkari 2002). Second, lower-level employees in foreign subsidiaries are inclined to speak only their local language. Consequently, English is used more generally as an intermediary language between various parallel subsidiary or parent-country languages (Sørensen 2005). For example, once documents in English arrive at subsidiaries, they are likely to be translated into the respective local languages. In particular, much of the informal communication often occurs in native languages, as will be discussed later in the chapter.

Multinational corporations are likely to follow different language strategies. While some multinational corporations may choose one common corporate language and prioritize it in their internal communication, other companies may consciously or unconsciously avoid making this decision. Consider the following two examples. Scandinavian Airlines (SAS), which is a pan-Scandinavian organization originating from Sweden, Denmark and Norway, did not formally select a common corporate language partly due to an attempt to maintain the power balance between the three nations (Bruntse 2003). Therefore English as well as Scandinavian languages were extensively used within SAS for purposes of its internal communication.

The German-based Siemens Corporation is another example of a company which does not follow an English-only approach. Siemens is a globally operating electronics and electrical-engineering company with some 434,000 employees and a presence in over 190 countries. Most of the employees are located in Germany (almost 40 per cent) with 26 per cent in the rest of Europe. Siemens uses predominantly English and German – the parent-country language – in its internal communication. However, the case study of Siemens shows that neither English nor German held unambiguously the position of a common corporate language although there was a strong trend of convergence toward English in many parts of the organization. One may speculate that, in order to avoid provoking emotional reactions from either the 'German' or the 'non-German' parts of Siemens, the issue of a common corporate language was intentionally left ambiguous and allowed to solve itself in an emergent manner, inviting different parties to make their own interpretations (Fredriksson *et al.* 2006).

Furthermore, language competence in the organizational context needs to be defined broadly to include also 'company speak' and professional jargon (Welch *et al.* 2005). 'Company speak' refers to acronyms, special terms and abbreviations that are specific to the company. For example, General Electric uses abbreviations such as N-1 and N-2 to indicate the person's status in the organizational hierarchy. Newly recruited staff may easily find themselves excluded from communication exchanges and social interaction because they do not master this form of language. On the other hand, once a person becomes competent in the professional jargon associated with the job communication is facilitated. For example, engineers, who have a fairly similar professional training worldwide and who therefore share a common terminology, belong to the same professional community. They all speak 'the same language' when it comes to their jobs. Although these engineers may be located in different foreign subsidiaries of the multinational corporations and speak different mother tongues, they are still likely to communicate with relative ease.

Thus, despite the use of a common corporate language such as English, communicating within the multinational corporation is rarely a mono-lingual event. In reality, internal communication frequently crosses language boundaries and is carried out in a mixture of languages. Therefore, the appropriate type and level of language competence in the context of the multi-national corporation needs to be broadly assessed by considering the requirements to use the common corporate language, parent-country language, 'company speak', professional jargon and various host-country languages.

Language effects on careers

In the following, language effects on careers are discussed. It shows that depending on the person and situation in question, language may advance or hamper a person's career, create a glass ceiling, divert career paths and influence the overall image of the firm as a potential employer. The analysis aims to be broad in order to cover career implications of both expatriates and domestic-based employees.

Expatriate selection

One of the main reasons for expatriates to accept a foreign assignment is career advancement (Dowling and Welch 2004). Foreign work experience may be regarded as a 'must' within the firm in order to climb up the corporate ladder. Multinational corporations frequently use foreign assignments as a vehicle of developing management talent for cadre positions. Therefore, being sent on a foreign assignment tends to raise career expectations.

Some multinational corporations value foreign-language competence to the extent that it is used as an explicit criterion in expatriate selection, recruitment and performance appraisal. More specifically, Dowling and Welch (2004) refer to the expatriate's skills in the local language of the host country as well as in the common corporate language of the multinational corporation. In a study of the Finnish multinational corporation Kone, the expatriates were primarily selected among Finnish staff, who represented parent-country nationals, and staff from English-speaking subsidiaries in the UK, Australia, Canada and the USA who were fluent in the common corporate language (Marschan-Piekkari *et al.* 1999a). In many recruitment and selection decisions, however, more emphasis tends to be placed on professional competence rather than language competence *per se*. Foreign-language skills tend to work best in tandem with business or engineering skills (Bloch 1995).

International projects are a good example of foreign operations that require highly specialised skills and competences (Welch *et al.* forthcoming). Many project workers have a solid base of technological or commercial expertise but may not possess the necessary language skills to transfer this expertise across language boundaries. Yet, in the face of scarce human resources these troubleshooters are sent on the spot despite their often less than adequate fluency in the local language.

Foreign-language competence may initially contribute to selecting a person for a foreign assignment or providing a person with opportunities to travel internationally. On the other hand, the motivation to learn a foreign language may be triggered by experiences of working in a foreign location. Either way, language competence is likely to facilitate the process of gaining foreign work experience but is not a necessary requirement.

Expatriate job performance

Expatriates are sent on foreign assignments for various reasons such as to fill a skills gap locally, gain valuable training overseas or assist in the development of common corporate values (Dowling and Welch 2004). In order to perform their work roles, expatriates need to communicate effectively with the local subsidiary personnel and business environment and this often requires proficiency in the local language.

Communication between expatriates and local employees has received some attention in previous research. Japanese multinationals are a case in point as they are largely managed in Japanese by staffing key subsidiary positions with Japanese expatriates (e.g. Lincoln *et al.* 1995; Yoshihara 2001). Previous research reveals the magnitude of communication problems between Japanese expatriates and local subsidiary staff. For example, in an interview study of 31 Japanese-owned subsidiaries in Germany, Lincoln *et al.* (1995) observed that English was used as a common language although it was not the native language of neither the locals nor the expatriates. The English spoken by the Japanese was often mediocre at best and the Western staff spoke no Japanese at all. In another study, workforce interviewed in seven Japanese-owned subsidiaries in Scotland, 'broken English' or 'pidgin English' was used in the communication between the Japanese and local Scottish management (Wright *et al.* 2001). Since Japanese expatriates tend to spend three–five years on foreign assignments before they return to the Japanese-speaking headquarters there are few incentives for them to learn the local subsidiary language.

Similarly, in a survey of US-owned subsidiaries in South Korea Park, Park *et al.* (1996) investigated the communication between American expatriates and local Korean managers. English was mostly used as the common language since the American managers were not able to fully understand the Korean language. To the surprise of the researchers, the US managers reported greater frustration, feelings of alienation, hostility, peripherality and mistrust compared with their Korean counterparts. Korean managers, on the other hand, had a greater likelihood of understanding and penetrating the corporate communication network due to their skills in English. The communication problems negatively influenced the personal adjustment, interpersonal relationships and job performance of the American managers at the workplace.

Thus, previous research demonstrates that failing to speak the native language of the local subsidiary staff may undermine the expatriate's job performance during foreign assignment. However, the extent to which limited language skills actually hampers managers' career advancement is open to speculation, given the lack of evidence of the impact of language on career paths. Earlier work on the effects of foreign assignments on careers is inconclusive as many expatriates leave their companies and change jobs upon return (Stahl *et al.* 2002). We shall now broaden the discussion and explore the effect of language on careers of other groups of personnel beyond expatriates.

Local subsidiary staff

Turning the attention to local subsidiary staff, the ones who are able to speak the native language of the parent company (and the common corporate language) are likely to have better career opportunities than those who lack this proficiency. For example, in her ethnographic research of an American company in Japan, SanAntonio (1987) singles out the English fluent Japanese as a special group of local employees. Since the American company was following an English-only policy these Japanese employees were positively evaluated by the American managers and judged as intelligent, ambitious and interested. SanAntonio describes a situation in which an English-fluent Japanese was promoted on the recommendation of the American manager based on the successful interaction between the two.

Furthermore, SanAntonio (1987) observes that only selected Japanese employees were able to communicate easily in English and they were the ones who interacted with the Americans. The English policy of the firm circumvented the indigenous Japanese hierarchy and created its own American communication-based hierarchy. The study shows how the status and roles of Japanese employees in the American company evolved from language ability in interaction. While the language-based roles such as interpreter and mediator were not formally designated they were used as stepping stones to higher positions in the company.

In the above example, language sets the boundaries between the various groups at the workplace and marks the limits of social inclusion and exclusion. Building on Wright *et al.* (2001), the workplace hierarchy in foreign subsidiaries can be expressed in terms of language competence: Expatriates tend to be native speakers of the parent-country language and competent in the common corporate language, local managers speak the local language and the common corporate language, the workforce speaks the local language and may at best comprehend the common corporate language. Such an informal language-based hierarchy mirrors the unequal career opportunities between various groups of employees within the multinational corporation.

Glass-ceiling effect

In earlier research on careers there is seldom mention of a common corporate language as an imposed factor influencing career paths. The introduction of a common corporate language may operate as a glass ceiling preventing promising individuals with management talent from advancing in their careers and reaching the top echelons of the organization. The term 'glass ceiling' is used here to denote that promotion above a certain level in the multinational corporation depends on proficiency in a particular language. While the term was originally applied to female managers it is a valid concept for any disadvantaged group of personnel.

My own research with some Finnish colleagues was an ethnographic case study of MeritaNordbanken – a Finnish–Swedish merger of a financial institution which was later renamed to Nordea. After the merger, Swedish was introduced as the common corporate language (Piekkari *et al.* 2005). Imposing Swedish as the common corporate language meant that many Finns had to operate professionally without adequate skills in the common corporate language. These otherwise capable employees felt that speaking Swedish affected the way they were perceived as less intelligent and able. Consequently, they often remained silent although professionalism would have required active participation. It seemed that their professional competence was hidden behind the language barrier causing sentiments of under-performance. The case study shows how limited skills in the common corporate language negatively affected perceptions of professional competence and identity ((Piekkari *et al.* 2005).

From a career perspective, the new common corporate language in MeritaNordbanken introduced a situation in which language skills of those applying for promotion attracted considerable attention. It was not uncommon to hear Finnish-speaking staff blaming their Swedish-speaking colleagues for unearned career advancement. These comments revealed concerns about whether colleagues with the requisite language skills were promoted 'just' because of their language proficiency. The case study of MeritaNordbanken shows that the Swedish language operated as a 'glass ceiling' effectively excluding non-Swedish-speaking individuals from career advancement (Piekkari *et al.* 2005).

Consider another example of Siemens, the German-based multinational, in which both English and German are used in internal communication. Fredriksson's (2005) study of language diversity in Siemens shows that skills in both languages are needed for top-level positions. However, while the interviewees' described the proficiency in German in a more subtle way, the importance of English skills for career advancement was made very explicit. As one interviewee put it (Fredriksson 2005: 102): 'You have to know English in order to be promoted ... so you can't seriously get very far in Siemens if you don't speak English.'

Research on Japanese-owned subsidiaries also shows that Japanese as the language of top management creates a 'glass ceiling' restricting the upward mobility of non-Japanese staff and making them pursue different career paths (e.g. Wright *et al.* 2001). Obviously, the preference for Japanese nationals over others in key staffing decisions is likely to result in selective recruitment and promotion practices. However, this may be problematic due to recent calls for diversity management and equal opportunity policies in multinational corporations.

Diversion of career paths

Alongside the glass-ceiling effect which limits upward mobility of staff, empirical evidence suggests that the imposed corporate language may also influence staff mobility and rotation horizontally within the firm. Our case study of MeritaNordbanken shows that the career paths of some Finnish-speaking employees were diverted as they sought to escape the Swedish language through internal mobility. Such 'Finnish-speaking havens', as the interviewees described them, could be found, for example, within the domestic Finnish branch network where Finnish was the main medium of communication. In this way, they could avoid the use of the newly imposed corporate language, Swedish, by staying local and avoiding direct contacts with their counterparts in Sweden (Piekkari *et al.* 2005).

During the turmoil of the MeritaNordbanken merger, some employees left the bank. We interviewed nine of them in order to ask whether the choice of Swedish as a common corporate language had directly affected their decision to leave the organization or altered their career in some way. This was not confirmed in the interview data. Many of them had worked in international positions within the bank and primarily used English in their everyday communication. In addition, most of them regarded themselves as competent speakers of Swedish and were eager to use their skills. Yet, the common corporate language decision did matter, as one interviewee commented (Piekkari *et al.* 2005: 339–40): 'Indirectly, language might have influenced [my decision to change jobs], because [the bank] seemed to lose some of its international appeal when becoming more Swedish-speaking.' From this perspective, the common corporate language may affect the organization's ability to retain professionals and provide them with meaningful career opportunities (Piekkari *et al.* 2005). As Bloch (1995: 25) argues, 'foreign language skills offer a variety of direct and indirect benefits including cultural awareness and sophistication, general intellectual growth and for the company itself, an improved overseas image'.

Career capital

Language competence is part of a person's career capital (Terjesen 2005), which complements general human capital. DeFillippi and Arhur (1994) divide career competences into know-why competences such as career motivation, personal meaning and identity; know-how competences including various job-related skills, abilities and knowledge; and know-whom competencies reflecting relevant networks for career purposes. Language skills fall into the categories of know-how and know-whom and can be regarded as an important element in building an international career.

In the case study of MeritaNordbanken, many Swedish-speaking Finns benefited considerably from the new Swedish-language policy, finding themselves in influential positions within the merged organization (Piekkari *et al.* 2005). Given their language skills, they became important gatekeepers and liaisons between various groups of individuals. In addition, their access to corporate information was far better than that of those who only spoke Finnish. Moreover, they tended to act as translators and intermediaries for their colleagues. The Swedish-speaking employees became 'language nodes' (Marschan-Piekkari *et al.* 1999a: 386) because they operated as interfaces, through language, between various groups of the merged organization. Overall, proficiency in Swedish extended personal-ommunication relationships and enhanced career opportunities within the bank (Piekkari *et al.* 2005).

The positive effect of foreign-language competence on the breadth and depth of personal-communication networks is likely to influence a person's career opportunities both within the firm as well as outside it. This is in line with recent conceptualizations of the boundaryless career (DeFillippi and

Arthur 1994) according to which people have a variety of career options and paths and they navigate their careers beyond the constraints of a single organization.

Conclusion

This chapter has discussed the effect of language competence – primarily in the common corporate language, parent-country language, or local sub-sidiary language – on careers in multinational corporations. Some employ-ees will master the key languages of the firm while others will have to decide whether to invest the time and energy in order to learn a new language. For outsiders, the choice of the common corporate language may also shape the company image among potential recruits in terms of its attractiveness as a potential employer. Once a common corporate language is in place, it becomes a requirement for being admitted to corporate training and man-agement development programmes, potential international assignments and promotion thus affecting individual career opportunities (Marschan-Piek-kari *et al.* 1999a).

Depending on the particular situation, language competence may advance career development and allow a person to climb up the corporate ladder or even penetrate the glass ceiling created by the common corporate language in use. Conversely, lack of language competence may limit career opportunities, hamper career advancement or divert career paths from international to more local. Career paths are influenced and transformed through self-selection. They are also shaped by explicit top-management measures to move staff with the purpose of developing a better fit between job requirements and foreign-language competence of staff. In the light of the empirical examples, it is clear that language training should be a high priority in multinational corporations.

Thus, it is concluded that the effect of foreign-language competence on career paths goes far beyond mere technical considerations which is worthy of greater attention by scholars in the field.

10 The business-unit concept at AKZO and the interpreting role of the CEO

Luchien Karsten and Luc-Jan Wolpert

Introduction

In 1985 a Dutch book 'The style of the leader' (Dijk *et al.* 1985) was published. It contained 26 interviews with leading Dutch businessmen and top managers. The contributions were inspired by the ideas of Peters and Waterman work *In Search of Excellence* (1982) which had popularized the view that company cultures, close linkages with customers and new leadership had a significant impact on effectiveness. Amongst the 'tableau de troupe' was a depiction of Esquire A. A. Loudon, who had become chairman of the board of the Dutch chemical multinational AKZO. He reduced the board membership from ten to four members to improve decisiveness, build team spirit and take joint decisions. The corporation, however, was still a strongly decentralized federation of powerful divisions and autonomously operating divisional presidents. For the company he wished to become the conductor of a newly structured orchestra as he retorted to the interviewers (Dijk *et al.* 1985: 95). To that end he was guiding a transition towards business units and initiated strategic control, a hybrid style, which involves both the promotion of overall corporate interests and business unit autonomy. The end result was the disappearance of the divisions.

This chapter explains the style Loudon developed which combined 'dialogues' and 'monologues' to establish a new discourse about AKZO's excellence. Within that discourse he played an interpreting role and facilitated the transition to an AKZO structure within which business unit managers could excel. Traditionally headquarters design plans and budgets, and monitor business performance against strategic milestones such as market share and budgets (Mintzberg *et al.* 1998). However, with decentralized business units put in place a CEO can only conduct management 'from a distance' and has to rely on commitment as a means to achieve communality of effort. To reach a sense of communality (Kogut and Zander 1996) amongst managers operating at distinct levels in the corporation, Loudon favoured dialogues with his board members and he also stimulated a discourse with the top 100 managers moulding conversations, debates, conflicts and diverse communication into a commonly shared language.

Whereas the object of debate is to overwhelm and obliterate one's opponent, 'the object of conversation is to keep it going: to plant, nurture and cultivate' (van Maanen 1995: 140). Through a chain of texts and talks Loudon tried to introduce a new and flexible organizational structure with business units. Before doing so, though, he had to elaborate a company identity and logo which could subsequently assist in the large-scale restructuring and decentralizing of the organization.

This organizational change, however, had to cope with the hegemonic internal structure of AKZO which reproduced particular power relations between (groups of) social actors (the dominant coalition). Only when this structure had been unravelled could a change in the discourse lead to a change of the existing organizational structure. We will stress the relationship between change as an inherent feature of organizational processes and change in organizational structures. 'With respect to organizational change, both organizational structures and the agency of members of organizations in organizational action and communication have causal effects on how organizations change' (Fairclough 2006: 918).

As will become clear Loudon quite often required the support of several different consultancy firms with approaches to introduce and translate the concept of corporate identity and business units to finally change the company. Throughout the period of 1982–94 consultants produced texts containing particular knowledge about the structuring of an organization which guided that transition.

Translation of management knowledge

Over the last 25 years *In Search of Excellence* has been one of the most influential management books, stressing the importance of corporate culture for the establishment of 'excellent companies'. It pointed out that excellent corporations have coherently composed shared values and a clear set of entrepreneurial competencies. The authors made frequent reference to language and the role leaders play in creating a particular language. Leaders call for a new language to change a company while adding new terms to the management vocabulary. Peter and Waterman's study propagated a vision about language as a feature of the corporate culture and a product of cooperation which employees identify with and find motivating.

However, due to its proliferation the management vocabulary became saturated with a wide range of popular management concepts. The question was raised as to what managers actually do when they introduce new concepts into their organizations to change specific company practices. Eccles and Nohria expressed their worries about the plethora of concepts that came to the market in *Beyond the Hype* (1992: 8): 'The time has come to get off the verbal merry-go-round which the search for the newest management ideas has become.' They pointed out that management is a practising art and that mastering rhetoric is a key feature in becoming a successful business leader. The essence of management is the effective use of language to get things done. 'Yet because these messages are typically very general, managers have a lot of leeway in interpreting them' (Eccles and Nohria 1992: 30). The interactive nature of management means that most managerial work is conversational and should facilitate 'an agora for creating social knowledge' (Krogh *et al.* 2000 126). Conversations require openness, patience, the ability to listen, experiment with words and concepts and the formation of persuasive arguments. While the exact meaning of concepts like 'excellence' may vary from company to company, often even within one company, conversations are needed to explore the meaning of concepts to induce an organizational change. They are part of a discourse within which the meaning of a label like 'business units' will condensate. Companies generate discourses through texts.

> Organizational texts are ongoing constructions of meaning, constantly changing from one situation to another, from one participant to another and one context to another. From this perspective, narratives do not possess a meaning, represented in a text; instead, their meanings are supported and contested through the production and reproduction of texts within a context.
>
> (Barry *et al.* 2006: 1094)

The way people share knowledge within a discourse can take different forms. Knowledge can be transmitted in an instrumental way like a monologue (i.e. strategic action to influence the listeners). Speakers do not discuss their insights but try to impose it onto others. A monologue delivers a coherent narrative of the speaker which usually represents the perspective of the author self. Monologues usually contain some kind of exhortation, a warning for a disaster and feed fear (Mueller and Carter 2005). A dialogue, like a conversation, rests on the foundation of the intersubjectivity of subjects interacting with each other in a symmetrical way (Arens 1994; Hardy 2004). 'Meanings are then created in the spontaneously coordinated interplay of people's responsive relations to each other' (Shotter and Cunliffe 2003: 17). The interaction itself is governed by binding consensual valid norms which define the reciprocal expectations about the people involved in the interaction. Moving from monologues to dialogues shifts the focus of analysis.

'Whilst monologism assumes individuals to be analytical primes, dialogism takes actions and interactions e.g. the discursive practices in their context as basic units' (Linnell 1998: 7). Such kind of interaction is symbolically mediated and its realization depends on the speaking of an intersubjectively shared language. In situations of organizational change, however, the existing and shared language is challenged and the meaning of particular words and terms are reassessed in a dialogue to reach an agreement on the becoming of future company practices. The dialogical perspective explicitly acknowledges that within an organization plurivocality exists and may reflect an overt or covert struggle for discursive dominance and may provoke distorted communication. A dialogue requires egalitarianism, reciprocity, consensus and agreement while suppressing negotiations of meaning, vagueness and ambiguity. When top management intends to avoid a strategic debate and struggle which prevent the dialogue to gain its own right, it better provides a lens on the corporation and build a 'social community specializing in the speed and efficiency in the creation and transfer of knowledge' (Kogut and Zander 1996: 503).

The newly appointed chairman of the board of AKZO set the goal to shape such a sense of community, craft a discourse which improves coordination and create identity amongst top management.

Method and data collection

This research was designed to investigate how in the late 1980s and early 1990s the implementation of the BU concept in AKZO unfolded. A qualitative case-based inquiry was adopted, underpinned by a close understanding of the industry's context. For that matter newsletters like 'AKZO berichten' (1969–86) and 'News and Views' (1987–94) were consulted to draw time-lines in the development of the corporation.

The study focused mainly at the boardroom level to examine how the members of the board and presidents of divisions have interpreted different proposals and ideas about reorganising the company. Boardroom minutes over the period 1982–1994 were studied for the conversations that took place at board-room level as well as with the group council. We applied Pettigrew and Whipp's framework (1995) that made a distinction between context, process and content of change. This framework provides the possibility to understand change while focusing on organizational discourse. Fifty key players from board and division level were selected for interviews as they directly contributed to the transition towards business units and the implementation of the new organizational structure. The interviews lasted on average for two hours, were tape-recorded, transcribed, coded and analysed using software to search for broad categories to structure the translation processes.

The researchers had a particular interest in the organization of the dialogues and the processes which changed the character of the discourse within AKZO. The consultancy firm Rijnconsult (outsourced in 1979 through a management buyout) was an important part of the change process and provided internal management consultancy and training services and was deeply involved in the processes leading to the implementation of the BU-concept and a new top structure. In this chapter this consultancy firm is considered as operating in a semi-internal way and therefore two key consultants were interviewed several times. The archives of that firm were made available to put our views in a broader perspective (Wolpert 2002).

Research context

Chemical fibres like rayon (artificial silk) and nylon (a synthetic fibre) have become emblems of modern industry's potential to substitute natural with artificial and synthetic materials. These products were manufactured by two different generations of companies. The first generation was made up of highly specialized companies like the German firm Glanzstoff, and was usually linked to the textile industry. Artificial fibres very soon replaced natural ones like cotton and wool. Due to its success some of the pioneers formed large groups like the British Courtaulds, and the Dutch Algemene Kunstzijde Unie (General Synthetic Fibre Union) AKU. The second generation with firms like the American DuPont produced nylon which was based on the advances of the organic chemical industry like polymers (Puig 2004). The dynamism of the field also pulled petrochemical companies in the business of synthetic fibres.

AKU launched an internationalization strategy based on acquisitions and incorporated Glanzstoff in 1969, which was allowed to keep an independent position (Klaverstijn 1986). It was still looking around for other partners. While the Dutch chemical Royal Salt-Organon KZO was also expanding into pharmaceuticals and chemical products to enter the American market, both companies noticed joint growth potential. AKU and KZO merged into AKZO, which was established in November 1969 with almost 100,000 employees. Top management was inclined to put in place a divisional company structure to combine 'the virtues of centralised control with those of decentralised decision making' (McCraw 1997: 287). In the late 1960s Mckinsey had transferred this concept to Europe (Kipping 1999) and AKZO was one of the companies which implemented it. All previous Dutch activities of AKU became grouped under a new umbrella ENKA, rejuvenating the original name of the Nederlandsche Kunstzijdefabriek of 1911 being a predecessor of AKU. The links with Glanzstoff were redefined and a joint board of management was put in place. Over the years ENKA-Glanzstoff kept, however, an autonomous position within the conglomerate. The previous KZO companies were divided in six divisions: salt, chemicals, coatings, pharmaceuticals, food products and domestic (household) products. AKZO kept the characteristics of a holding with decentralized operations and a decentralized strategy (cf. Whittington and Mayer 2000). In 1971 the corporation designed a common house style and logo (a blue triangle) but some of the divisions kept their own company name and logo. Overcapacity in the fibre production forced AKZO to restructure. McKinsey was commissioned twice to propose organizational changes. In 1977 a presidium of one chairman and two deputy chairmen was put in place which together with a corporate council of five division presidents and two members of corporate staff responsible for research and technology as well as financial and administrative policy had to run the corporation. Although the council meetings of ten people were meant to facilitate communication and create a learning platform that monitors and stimulates the advancement of the company, the presidium concluded that after ten years the new roadmap had been disappointing. The organizational structure had become ossified and reproduced particular power relations between groups of social actors. More focus on core activities as well as generation of synergy was urgently needed.

Unit management

Unit management describes the move away from a dominating technical focus, central bureaucratic management and a closed culture towards a customer-oriented focus, decentralized management and an open culture. With management operating more autonomously as entrepreneurs, corporations still had to strive for synergy. Nevertheless, the transition from a centralized overly bureaucratic management approach towards a more flexible structure with BUs and an entrepreneurial spirit became popular. Unit management is 'a management style and an organisational form geared to decentralisation of entrepreneurship within an organisation, while optimising corporate synergy' (Wissema 1992: 4). Business units are assigned integral business responsibility for certain product/market combinations (PMCs) and report directly to top management. The concept propagates a customer-based organizational design and contract management to regulate internal relations.

Findings

In 1982 the lawyer A. A. Loudon became chairman of the board of AKZO. After an initial career as a banker, head of the financial department of KZO in 1969 and financial manager at a paint plant in Paris, he became president of AKZO Brazil. There he had noticed how difficult it was to imagine the corporation as one integrated firm. In 1977 he joined the board of management responsible for human resources and later on became deputy chairman of the new presidium. AKZO still was a federation of divisions in which ENKA kept a powerful and autonomous position.

Loudon took the initiative to shape AKZO into an integrated corporation by strengthening the position of the board of management. To this end he replaced the presidium and the corporate council by a board of management composed of four members and a group council. He introduced the strategic planning procedure (SPP) as a technical management concept to build the corporation into a financial holding (H form). For that purpose 40 Group Planning Units (GPU) were designed to facilitate a more coherent organizational overview. The new structure 'enhanced the possibilities of a more integrated management without affecting the principle of delegation of powers to the management of divisions and operating companies' (AKZO *Annual Report* 1982: 5). The severe discussions within the group council about the new planning technique demonstrated that the board had no grip on the divisions. Although full integration had still 'great priority' (AKZO *Annual Report* 1982: 5) the new organizational structure 'only ponderously arrived at collective decision making .... A number of people primarily or solely monitor their own divisional interests and as a result of this, manoeuvre very cautiously' (Corporate History AKZO: 53). Some group members of the top had difficulty conceding their scepticism. In 1984 Loudon stated that in the coming years

> We will have to place particular emphasis on opportunities for intra-group synergism, not only with respect to the development of management potential but also with respect to the development and application of new products and processes the knowledge of which is shared among several divisions.
>
> (AZZO *Annual Report* 1984: 3)

The positive financial results of 1984 and 1985 – the best result over the first 15 years of AKZO – were used as a favourable external context to legitimize the strengthening of the board's position. Loudon noticed that the lack of willingness to cooperate between divisions was the negative side of a divisional structure and tried to persuade the divisional presidents of the relevance of attaining more vertical synergy.

New logo – new identity

At an annual New Year's speech for the top of the corporation Loudon introduced a new policy to communicate. His monologues became an instrument to inform the staff about the urgency to change. One of the key issues was the creation of a shared image amongst the staff of the conglomerate. For that purpose G. J. Nightingale of British Synergenics/Burson Marsteller was commissioned to design a mission statement which would reflect corporate thinking at AKZO even to the outsiders who still perceived it as 'a conglomerate little known outside of its own industry' (Chandler 1994). Although the group council – guided by Loudon – soon attained consensus about the values of the corporation and potential synergies, resistance rested about a common identity as ENKA, Coatings, and Pharma portrayed themselves as independent divisions. Nightingale's report (AKZO 1986) did not solve the issue. Each division kept its own name and simply added 'division of AKZO'. ENKA refused even that proposal and kept its own tile logo which at some earlier time had been designed by the British PR company Olins.

Loudon's New Year speech of 1986 pointed at the inherent tensions within AKZO and the slow development of human-resource policies to unite the staff. Despite the fact that the decentralized structure made the corporation operate close to the market, customers did not recognize its corporate identity. He recognized that implementing the mission needed a different narrative based on a different management attitude or habitus (Bourdieu 1990). This allowed him stimulate the process of 'languaging':

> As organisational members observe events and situations, and as they engage in languaging, that is, apply and invent distinctions, phrases, sentences etc., they participate in developing organisational knowledge. Agreement and disagreement are apparent at many levels of the organisation at all times, and as organisational members strive towards agreement (or settle for disagreement) they continue to develop organisational knowledge, enabling finer and finer distinctions.
>
> (Krogh and Roos 1994: 62)

In order to create a dialogue about the future identity of the corporation, Loudon decided to commission Olins to explore how AKZO perceives itself. A team consisting of Loudon himself, two division presidents (Chemicals and Pharmaceuticals) and the director of corporate communications were asked to investigate the matter. An agreement was reached to retain the name AKZO for the conglomerate but for marketing purposes some companies were still allowed to continue and carry their initial brand names like Organon for pharmaceutical products. Whereas Pharma obtained an endorsed identity, Chemicals and Salt accepted a monolithic identity. Olins drew the conclusion that the identity of AKZO was still invisible and that a new common house style on all their printed material would be the best method to convey a common identity. The new corporate mark was inspired by a sculpture dating from 450 BC which was found on the Greek island of Samos. The sculpture shows a life-size representation of a human figure which stretches out its arms and is called a meteorological relief, which is currently in the Ashmolean Museum in Oxford, Britain. It symbolized a new, more 'humane' image for AKZO and this certainly pleased Loudon while it indicated an embodied overarching unity and it put a clear emphasis on the human side of this chemical conglomerate. In March 1987 the new logo was revealed at a gathering of 300 managers as 'AKZO, a new spirit'. However, the discourse about the new mission of AKZO and concomitant corporate identity did not yet end the autonomous position of the ENKA division. That only happened in May 1987 when the divisional president of the ENKA-group retired.

Business units

While addressing the AKZO top, Loudon's New Year's speech (7 January 1987) stressed again and again the importance of decentralization. The monologue was widely distributed through the summer issue of the corporation's newsletter but Loudon did not wait until the monologue had been read by all staff members. He launched a 'strategic plan' stressing that competitive advantage is only created at the business unit level. It was not clear what was meant by this label but AKZO should henceforward compete at product level. The overall organizational structure, however, did not yet reflect that plan.

Soon thereafter the new president of the ENKA group, J.R. Hutter, announced that his division would introduce the business-unit concept. He had come across this label in the early 1980s during his visits to DuPont in America to discuss the aramid patent conflict. 'It had become clear to me that in America the concept of BUs had already become obvious' (interview Hutter 15 April 1996). The AKZO setting, however, was too complex to implement it in a straightforward manner. 'We are convinced that the solution for an attractive and appropriate organizational structure can be found in the BU concept. We feel that it is necessary to decentralize further and to form more independent units with largely integrated decision authority' (First Management Letter BU organization no. 1 December 1987). Although there was some willingness to follow the new fashion, within the conglomerate only a few managers were familiar with the label and used it interchangeably with Portfolio Planning Unit (PPU), Group Planning Unit (GPU), and Strategic Business Unit (SBU) or management unit.

Loudon had understood the initiative and his New Year's speech of 1988 underlined once more that the corporation had a strong desire for renewal and potential for cooperation. The board decided that the recruitment of high potentials and the arrangement of their labour contracts would no longer be the prerogative of the divisions but that AKZO Human Resource Management (AHRM) at headquarters would be involved in their recruitment to promote cooperation and synergy potential. This intervention caused some distorted communication with the division presidents. Some members of the group council pointed out that recruitment policy at headquarters, divisional level, and country level as well as at company level lacked efficiency. Within the ensuing debate the board referred to the logo to justify its intervention.

External consultants

In April 1988 Loudon introduced to the council a document 'about synergy potential and decentralization within AKZO' to explore the new spirit, but it received a lukewarm response. During the next meeting in August 'Europe 1992' was put on the agenda. Both topics were a contingent trauma, an intrusion of certain non-symbolized entities. For a while ambiguity reigned. Loudon realised that only a generally accepted definition and through continuous repetition these topics could become recognized in their symbolic necessity and find their appropriate place in the discourse of the corporation. He decided to engage different consultancy firms to achieve a dialogue about the required organizational change. Mckinsey was commissioned to identify challenges and threats for the corporation and provide a rational justification for an intervention in the actual organizational structure. Based on talks with the top, their report contained a general analysis of the market development after the dissolution of the internal borders of Europe. Loudon used this document as a kind of exhortation to claim urgency for the corporation to change and become more flexible.

Two consultants of Horringa and De Koning, later to become partner of the Boston Consultancy Group BCG, analysed the internal functioning of the group council to enhance the learning process. Their role was one of exchange of experience with the purpose of translating proposals into adequate policies. Their report was legitimating change in terms of new norms and mores. Apparently the members did not know what their role should be and needed a moral legitimacy which Green (2004) labels as an ethos justification. To reach that goal Loudon with the consultants pressed for a dialogue amongst the members to reach an agreement on the organisational change. He pointed how the Fibres and Polymer division – previously the ENKA-group – had recently introduced the BU concept. However, the ground was not yet sufficiently prepared to reach a general agreement and moral approval. Loudon gave the divisions some room for reflection and explore their own situation in terms of business units.

A conference

Loudon sensed that the transition of the Fibres and Polymer division into BUs could be taken as an example for AKZO at large. During one of his conversations with De Ruijter, chairman of Rijnconsult, the issue about the ideal organizational concept for AKZO was raised. Loudon was not sure whether the central steering of the corporation should have the same shape and content for all five divisions. In a letter to Loudon (5 April 1989) De Ruijter evoked that a BU organization is characterized by integral management at a lower level having responsibilities for all functions. Loudon brought the issue to the fore during a group council meeting and boiled the subsequent conversations about decentralization down to a new strategic plan of AKZO. It estimated some 20 BUs but was not clear about the cooperation between board and divisions. A conference should settle the matter which was held in June in Anholt (Germany) with 120 participants. The presidents of the divisions were offered the opportunity to clarify their own situation. Hutter propagated the switch to BUs whereas the president of the Salt division was very moderate and said that his organization was still in a process of considering a change towards BUs. Coatings said to cling to their own matrix structure. The conference was the first time a large part of top management heard in a more official manner about BUs, but it did not provide the expected breakthrough. Although it had created a positive atmosphere, the board was not sure the division presidents were all willing to introduce an extended decentralization within the divisions.

A new dominant coalition

Out of fear for a congestive bureaucracy if the divisions continued to operate as they did, Loudon expressed an urgency to switch to business units. To
achieve this goal he needed a new dominant coalition amongst the top
managers (cf. Prahalad and Bettis 1986). Loudon used his formal authority
to do so and presented a new dominant coalition at the council meeting on
26 October 1989. Three new non-executive officers' positions (strategic
planning, corporate control and human resources) were added to the group
council having the same rights as the divisional presidents. The coalition
was now composed of four board members, five divisional presidents, five
functional members and two geographical members (AKZO America and
AKZO Nederland). Loudon pointed out that the functional and divisional
members should jointly decide about corporate issues; only in case of a
conflict would the board intervene. Loudon realized that with the new team
partnership ties had still to be established.

The new Management Committee showed an initial willingness to cooperate and commissioned De Ruijter and Harmsen, who within AKZO
operated as a project manager and favoured a BU structure, to write a plan
for an adequate composition of the new staff structure. While some of the
divisional presidents were still hesitant Loudon asked during subsequent
meetings in December and January 1990 for guidance and demonstrated a
preparedness to share all relevant information and to promote an open cli-
mate of communication. He finally was able to persuade the division presidents of the relevance of a new approach and justify the advantage of a
different organizational structure. His New Year's speech (4 January 1990)
disseminated the information about the changes within the top structure of
the corporation and established the relevance of a decentralized organization with short decision lines, leaving 'the marketplace to small units for
homogeneous market/product combinations which have integral decision-
making power for all sub segments and disciplines – in other words business
units'. Loudon presupposed that the set-up of the business units might
differ from division to division but that overall the divisional boards played
an indispensable linking role between the operations (BUs) and the board of
management. His monologue was again published in a special edition of
News and Views (June 1990) to reach the corporation at large. Although the
position of the BUs in relation to the corporate centre as well as to the divisional
president were explicitly mentioned, their roles were still not crystal clear.

A new staff structure

The Management Committee approved the proposal of the board to further
clarify the structure of the staff. Rijnconsult and Harmsen were again
commissioned to study the optimal organizational design. Rijnconsult was
striving after a dialogue to draft an adequate meaning of the BU concept.

They interviewed 114 managers of all divisions and asked them to describe the images they had about the layout of the organizational structure which led to the 'norm organization'. The norm organization is an organizational concept and served as a frame of reference for definitions of strategy as well as, control, administrative and service activities. It set the required size of the staff departments and defined the roles of different actors within the conglomerate, the relations between these actors, as well as a description of the desired planning and control process. It drew the conclusion that the divisional presidents still played a key role for the implementation of the organizational change. Their report was a catalyst and stimulated an intellectual exchange about the necessary changes to be induced. Some of the presidents, however, reproached that the suggested changes were a threat to their own positions. The consultants insisted that the goal of the investigation was not the implementation of BUs as such but only served to explore the common sharing of emergent images about the future organizational structure of the corporation. In several letters to Loudon De Ruijter stressed the importance of constructing a common lens to reach a shared meaning about the new organizational structure.

The investigation accelerated a dialogue about the new structure. For the first time the issue of service units (SUs) was raised as an emulation of the BU concept. Service units have a hierarchical relationship with the site manager, who himself reports to the divisional board. It stayed unclear if country organizations would be called service units. Subsequent meetings took place in an open atmosphere and much time was devoted to the role of HRM. Consensus was reached with regard to the principles behind the norm organization which distinguished five parties: BUs, SUs, divisions, staff units and a board but the meaning of the corporate centre stayed ambiguous. A new label 'management holding' was launched which included human resources, strategy and operational control. Loudon appreciated the new label:

> We all knew that headquarters did not represent a financial holding, but we did not know either what we actually were. We did not have words for it yet. I do not even know who introduced this concept. Anyway, it was a concept we were not familiar with, but the moment it had been introduced it immediately called for recognition.
>
> (Interview with Loudon, March 1996)

However, the Management Committee (28 June 1990) struggled with its meaning. The consultants were asked to develop a 'unifying philosophy' (cf. Pettigrew 1985) and the subsequent translation process carried the concept forward, modified it and adapted it to prevailing interests (cf. Gherardi and Nicolini 2000). Finally the process toward an extended decentralisation within the divisions gained momentum and eventually a moral justification was obtained. However, no one had as yet defined the necessary number of BUs and estimates varied between 60 to 90.

Changes in the dominant coalition

Loudon used his New Year speech of 8 January 1991 to announce that three members of the board retired. C. J. A. van Lede, previously chairman of the Dutch employers' association and very familiar with Dutch consensus politics (cf. Karsten *et al.* 2007) was appointed as a new member with the perspective to become the future CEO. The appointment of new members who favoured the BU approach provided Loudon with more latitude to strengthen the role of the management holding.

On 28 February Loudon gave a winter lecture to the top 100 managers of the corporation. The lecture had been prepared by De Ruijter, was recorded and formed the basis for 'Business Units – the basis of the AKZO organization' which appeared in May. This 'blue book' contained an elaborate description of the organization. It stated that many other companies had adopted the BU concept. 'However, at AKZO we needed to translate this general concept to suit our own particular needs .... No matter how good the concept is, it remains a tool ... The introduction of the business units calls for a new management style throughout the organization' (AKZO Business Units 1991).

Despite the translation process of new concepts like the BU and 'holding' leading to the 'blue book', the text was obsolete the moment it appeared. Although it had kept an important role for the divisions, in practice things worked out differently. Loudon noticed 'that more BU managers started to take up contact directly with the board neglecting the division' (interview Loudon, June 1996). The position of the divisions itself was at stake. Rijnconsult offered two options: merging the divisions with the corporate centre into a president's office or keep them as a separate middle layer. Neither proposition satisfied. Thereupon Loudon and Van Lede commissioned McKinsey to interview members of the Management Committee. Some of them proposed a hybrid form for the corporate centre, others preferred a financial holding, and others again favoured a management holding. Eventually Loudon was able to guide the dialogue about this issue towards a remarkable decision.

The disappearance of divisions

Loudon proposed to replace the existing terminology of divisions by introducing the label 'group'. The board of management now comprised other than himself and the vice chairman four members supervising one of the four BU-groups (Salt and Chemicals being integrated into one group). There was an urgent need to implement these decisions as negative financial results made Richards (1991) of Credit Suisse First Boston conclude that AKZO was the worst performing corporation in the chemical sector. The Management Committee asked Loudon to use his New Year's speech of 1992 to inform the corporation about the latest changes which should be achieved by 1 May 1993. Although this implementation took an 'unimaginable speed' (interview vice chairman Westerman, 15 April 1996), the new labels still required a lot of further clarification. Van Lede tried to solve the lack of clarity by publishing 'AKZO topstructure'. Each group nominated an implementation manager to facilitate the change in which Rijnconsult assisted. But a second large conference was deemed necessary in April 1993 to address critical comments about the transfer from division to group. De Ruijter advised Loudon to use clear language and avoid talking about the 'management team of the group', because that would imply that each group could take decisions autonomously and revive the divisional structure. He should only talk about the board as carrying joint responsibility for all the BUs. Loudon invited all participants to join the conversation and clarify the impact of the new top structure. Once more he demonstrated his capability to raise a key issue at the right moment and thus stimulate the conversation. Loudon used his last New Year speech on 6 January 1994 to point out that 'a management holding' balances the main responsibilities of BUs, SUs and board, but that the Management Committee takes decisions. His most remarkable statement in this context was that from now on it was 'absolutely forbidden' to return to divisional tasks and responsibilities which might otherwise reiterate the traditional lines of the divisions. He no longer wanted to hear managers talk about divisions. No clearer distinction could have been made. Looking back at what had been established, Loudon concluded that

> Business units are now in fashion. Of course the concept has its proponents and opponents, and the business unit organization is not the right answer for every type of company. At the time, we asked ourselves whether it would be right for us. AKZO already had a division whose organization was based on the business unit concept, but there were also other divisions where management was primarily functional. Talking with colleagues, you discover that different interpretations exist of the business unit concept. The distinguishing features of a business unit organization are integrated management, short reporting lines and no layers between higher management and the business unit. At AKZO we have had to introduce far reaching reorganizations on the road toward this concept.
>
> (AKZO News and Views January 1993: 65).

The corporation had become sensitive to a popular management concept that at some time certainly could have been described as a 'mere fashion', but Loudon has paved the discourse to a translation of the concept which fitted the firm and balanced out tensions between decentralization and centralization. However, the plan to design a new mission statement which would comply with the new organizational structure was overruled by the sudden takeover of the Swedish corporation Nobel Industries.

Conclusion

AKZO concluded its 25 years of existence and Loudon his 12 years of chairmanship with a take-over of Nobel in the spring of 1994. In May of the same year Van Lede became CEO and continued a policy of expansion through mergers and acquisitions.

Loudon's actions certainly facilitated communication about the future excellence of the corporation. His preference for dialogue accorded him agency and made him a social actor promoting a particular discourse. Regardless of the fact that he was not in all cases the author of specific texts, he certainly used his formal power to produce and disseminate certain kind of texts and messages. He used them to enact particular organizational processes and interfered wherever necessary to promote, advance and stimulate the dialogue. To build a common sense concerning the proposed transformation Loudon frequently required consultants to assist the process of organizational change and explore the validity of concepts like BU and management holding. He sometimes minimized the significance that should be accorded to his role and frequently asked consultants for guidance. With their assistance intelligible formulations were created of what sometimes seemed a chaotic welter of impressions. As CEO he developed a participative management style and enacted a new discourse which became institutionalized at AKZO.

Loudon's languaging activities can be likened to those of the conductor of an orchestra with one common score, with clear-cut and well-defined roles and expectations for each musician. He had to struggle with division presidents who liked to be solo performers, free to select and interpret their own pieces of music according to their own preferences. What came out of the process was a jazz ensemble, with each performer having a certain amount of freedom within a general but loosely defined framework. Loudon had become a mediator by which new compositions could be developed. Due to his involvement the translation and implementation of the BU concept and the top structure became a success.

As an actor in the discourse on an organizational change of AKZO he demonstrated what we like to call a 'consensus habitus', an embodied disposition to engage in dialogues to resolve social issues. His formal power, access to resources, links to particular actors and discursive legitimacy helped him to coordinate textual production and dissemination. The structural renewal of AKZO culminated in 1992 and permitted a greater unity of the corporation with four groups (Chemicals, Coatings, Fibres and Pharmaceuticals). AKZO had eliminated one complete structural layer with the purpose of becoming more efficient and excellent. Loudon had coordinated the interactions and promoted among all concerned a shared common sense and a shared responsiveness to events within the corporation. He mastered the art of framing events and insisted on the important role of 'languaging'. In concert with those around him, Loudon explored new possibilities within which both they and others could live and work

During the period of Van Lede the corporation has become a strategic holding with three groups – coatings, chemicals and pharmaceuticals – and consolidated into 23 BUs. In 2003 G. J. Wijers became CEO. As a former consultant of the Boston Consulting Group he had published about horizontal synergy and as minister of Economic Affairs in the Kok cabinet (1994–98) he, too, had become very familiar with the Dutch consensus model, redefining it as 'the Delta model' – respiring with the ebbs and flow of the economic tides. AKZO is now operating 17 BUs which still report directly to the board as Loudon shaped it. The BU structure with its product specific operational management is still the backbone of the corporation.

11 Communication strategies and cultural assumptions

An analysis of French–Japanese business meetings

Hiromasa Tanaka

Introduction

The aim of this chapter is to provide an East Asian local perspective of English use in international business interaction involving Asian and European managers. The context of the research site reflects two critical emergent effects of globalization. One of them is an increasing presence of Asian countries of which Japan will remain an important player (Davis 2004). The other effect is the global expansion of English as the lingua franca and emergence of World Englishes. English is currently the preferred language to choose as the business language even where native English speakers are a minority (Graddol 2004).

The case study intends to depict the effects and a consequence of use of English as the business language among employees of two of the world's largest automotive manufactures, namely Nissan Motors and Renault SA. I analysed video-recorded data obtained from three cross-cultural meetings that involved Nissan sales managers and marketing in-chargers of their alliance partner, Renault.

The meeting data show the complexity of the cross-cultural meetings. The data also indicate that the employees from each company are diverse in their use of strategies, socio-cultural behaviour, and linguistic competence. The analysis reveals that the decision made at the end of the meeting may have been influenced by participants' cultural assumptions and their use of language and silence.

Use of English in the Japanese workplace

The expansion process of English use for business in Japanese corporations has been less straightforward than is generally assumed. In the 1980s, the significant appreciation of the Japanese currency, yen, and burgeoning growth of investment by Japanese companies highlighted the need for English-speaking Japanese managers to be sent to overseas business sites where Japanese companies made investments. These English-speaking expatriates were a trained or educated elite. Most Japanese business people, at that time, only used Japanese in their daily business activities. Domestic Japanese business communities were relatively isolated from globalization up until the early 1990s (Cabinet Office 2001).

Accelerated globalization has required Japanese companies to be integrated into the global business fabric at the beginning of the twenty-first century. The need for using English at work dramatically increased among business people as a result of many international mergers and acquisitions or formation of alliances involving Japanese companies. Consequently, shifts of corporate language policies followed this fundamental change (see Yoshihara *et al.* 2000).

Business discourse studies involving Japanese

Considering the size of Japan's economy, the number of studies investigating English language use within Japan has been small. In particular, research into the spoken mode of business interaction has been neglected. Past studies emphasize the linguistic component, such as lexicon (see Nakasako 1998). This was because Japanese business people's exposure to business discourse in English was mostly limited to written trading documents. As globalization ripened, quite a few studies that focused on interaction between Japanese and non-Japanese were carried out (for example, Kleinberg 1999; Marriott 1995, 1997; Yamada 1992, 1997). These studies used business interaction data in English involving Japanese and native speakers of English. Data was obtained outside Japan since one early effect of globalization on Japanese business was to increase the number of Japanese expatriates staying overseas. The studies, therefore, investigated contact situations involving Japanese expatriates. These studies concluded that the complexity of business discourse cannot be analysed by only looking at the surface linguistic aspects. They emphasized that cultural assumptions and socio-economic behaviours based on business and management ideologies needed to be taken into account.

For example, using the framework developed by Neustupny (1985), Marriott (1997) examined Australian–Japanese interaction in two dimensions, communication and socio-cultural behaviour. She views interaction as constituted by communication and socio-cultural behaviour. Communication is based on linguistic components such as grammar, lexicon, and phonology, and socio-linguistic component such as strategies, frame, and channel. Socio-cultural behaviour consists of con-communicative features including socio-economic aspects such as the specialized set of knowledge required for a certain workplace. She demonstrated the diversity of communication problems caused by these different layers of components. Marriott's data shows that each of these components does not affect communication independently; rather interrelations influence interaction.

In the light of previous business discourse studies, I take a position that views the use of English for business as not a standardization of the global business language, but as a comprehensive approach to creating a hybrid business discourse. This study will pay attention to socio-linguistic aspects of communication, strategies, as well as socio-cultural behaviours, in particular the socio-economic behaviour of speakers, which is influenced by business ideologies. I hope that this case study will shed light on the less explored part of business communication, i.e. spoken business discourse between Japanese and French speakers.

In the following sections, I will review research that investigated socio-cultural and socio-economic behaviour in business discourse and communication strategies in contact situations involving Japanese.

Cultural assumptions and business ideologies

When a person is being integrated in a certain discourse, this person acquires taken-for-granted behaviours of the discourse. In other word, socio-cultural behaviour is a result of people being disciplined and normalized in a certain discourse. Different business settings have different discourses, each of which includes a set of social practices, beliefs, language and values (Gee 1996).

English used in cross-cultural business settings can be imbued with various cultural assumptions that interlocutors bring from their home business discourses. Thus, business interaction with participants holding conflicting cultural assumptions can become problematic. A great deal of past studies emphasized cultural assumptions as a cause of communication breakdown. Some of such studies draw arguments from *nihonjinron* (theory on Japan and Japanese) which highlights the uniqueness of Japan and Japanese. Yamada (1992), for example, applied Japanese harmony-orientation or group-orientation (Nakane 1986) to explain the equally distributed turns in a meeting held by Japanese speakers while applying individual orientation to explain frequent turns taken by in-chargers of each topic. Harmony orientation is also found in Jones' study (1995) of Australian–Japanese negotiation. Her data shows that Japanese speaker put high value on interpersonal relations avoiding confrontation.

Socio-economic behaviour, positioned as a sub-category of socio-cultural behaviour in Marriott's study, consists of a certain set of business practices in a business discourse. In this study socio-economic behaviour is viewed as particularly critical because a number of researchers address the 'otherness' of Japanese management ideology by pointing out several characteristics of the Japanese business management model. Such studies often argue that the geographical and cultural distance between Japan and Western countries caused the management ideology in Japan to develop several 'unique' systems such as lifetime employment, participative decision making, and harmony-oriented management (Mendenhall and Oddou 1986).

Business-discourse researchers use such socio-economic behaviour as a framework of analysis. In order to account for Japanese speakers' prioritization of relationship among colleagues during the meeting, Yamada (1997) uses the notion of interdependence, which was fostered by long-lasting relationship between employees. One of Japanese-style management systems, lifetime employment is believed to increase the value of intra-organizational harmony among Japanese.

Marriott (1995) investigated Australian seller–Japanese buyer negotiations, and found that each participant's lack of knowledge regarding the difference of decision-making process between Australian and Japanese caused problematic situations. During the negotiation the Japanese manager did not make any commitment since he needed to bring back his Australian counterpart's proposal to his company in order to make a participatory decision with his team members. The Australian company owner interpreted the Japanese manager's vague response as lack of interest. Marriott emphasized the importance of socio-economic knowledge of one's own business as well as of overseas business.

The studies of Kleinberg (1999) and Sumihara (1993) found that the Japanese participatory decision making system slowed down business process and consequently frustrated non-Japanese counterparts. Since the decision was not delegated to the Japanese speakers in these studies, they sounded indecisive or negative. Sumihara explains the cost and benefit of this participatory decision making style. Although it takes time, this way of making a decision has the advantage of more people feeling responsibility and 'owning' the decision (see also JETRO 1999: 12–13).

Japanese socio-economic behaviour in contact situations based on their 'unique' business ideologies, such as participatory decision or non-confrontation, are generally not the preferred way of Western managers. Although there are strength and shortcomings in Japanese management styles, their socio-economic behaviour is not seen as the correct way of doing business by Westerners. Thus management researchers point out the difficulties of 'translating' Japanese management ideologies that developed in an isolated environment (Keeley 2001).

In fact, there have been numerous studies that investigate Japanese management ideology in the management science field; however, the accumulated knowledge seems to be shared by few linguistic researchers. One of the reasons that business discourse researchers pay less attention to such discussion among Japanese management researchers might be the diversity of speakers within a cultural group in regard to their language use. Second-language speakers of business English often vary in vocabulary, grammatical knowledge and use of communication strategies. The same argument can be applied to the typified Japanese culture described in *nihonjinron* (see Kubota 2002). Thus, I am not arguing that there are two monolithic business ideologies, Japanese and Western. Rather I recognize diversity among Japanese and among the Westerners, and variation between Japanese participants plays a critical role in negotiation which will be described later.

In this study I attempt to demonstrate that language and management ideology are often interrelated and that their interrelations potentially influence business results. At the same time individual differences within a cultural group is taken into account. I will pay attention to speakers' use of communication strategies and their anxiety caused by their limited linguistic competence. Acquisition of strategies and anxiety are often related to individuals' specific experiences more than cultural characteristics that people in a same culture might share. In the following section, I will discuss such variety within a cultural group.

Anxiety and communication strategies

While speakers' socio-cultural assumptions are hardly observable in the video-recorded interaction, communication strategies that speakers employ and their lexical or grammatical knowledge are relatively easy to recognize. In this section, I will review research that investigated linguistic anxiety, silence, and communication strategies.

Silence and anxiety

There are studies that indicate Asian speakers are quiet in general. Sato's research (1982) that investigated turn taking frequency in second-language classroom interaction provided evidence of taciturn Asians. Yamada (1992), in her study of business interaction, shows strategic use of silence by Japanese. For example, when a speaker is silent for a moment, it can be a signal for the other person to take a turn in a conversation held by Japanese. However, if the speaker wishes to hold his turn, he may look away from his partner; typically the partner will recognize this cue and wait. Since Yamada's study suggests silence in Japanese conversation has a pragmatic function, it is arguable that silence in a meeting is socio-cultural behaviour. Thus silence of Japanese meeting participants can be a consequence of both insufficient linguistic competence and socio-economic behaviour.

Tanaka's study (2006) showed fewer turns taken by Japanese participants of a business meeting. Tanaka identified combined effects of Japanese participants' assumption of how a decision would be made and their linguistic limitation, which made Japanese participants take fewer turns during the meeting. From the participants' interview Tanaka found that the Japanese participants believed that the final decision would be made later applying their participatory decision making system to the intercultural setting.

In regard to the difference between the first language and the second language, there is certainly larger distance between English and Japanese than, say, between English and other European languages, many of which use Roman alphabet and belong to Indo-European language family. Thus Japanese speakers of English can face more difficulties in terms of transfer issues than Indo-European language speakers. Tanaka (in press) showed how such anxiety might make Japanese second-language speakers sound less confident in a business meeting through his analysis of a business meeting and exchanged emails from the Japanese participants in his study. The research reveals that talking in broken English in front of native speakers of English is face threatening for some managers.

Communication strategies

Communication strategies help speakers communicate in their second language despite gaps in target language knowledge. Communication strategies include paraphrasing, mime, transfer, avoidance, and appeal for assistance (Tarone 1980: 429). Communication strategies can play a critical role in second language speakers' speech in business settings. Tanaka (2006) suggests that speakers' mastery of communication strategies relates to turn-taking frequency. Among the participants of his study, the one who acquired strategies to take turns through working in American companies took a dominant role and impressed the president. Tanaka extends his discussion to power-relation of the speakers and argues the uneven turn-taking among Japanese and American participants in the business meeting led to dominating and dominated business relationships. Tanaka pointed out that Japanese participants' fewer turns and delayed initiation gave the president the impression that they were incompetent and finally disempowered the Japanese participants.

Cameron (2002) argues that communication strategies are not culture free or power free. She notes that recommended type of communication strategies by communication consultants is similar to preferred speech habits of educated white Americans. Her argument indicates that adopting such communication strategies can produce and reproduce the dominating-dominated relationship in business.

In the next section, I will discuss socio-linguistic aspects of communication, in particular co-construction, which is of particular relevance in this study.

Co-construction

It is generally assumed that there is a one-way model of communication in which a speaker has an idea that is formulated into some form that is then expressed to a listener. Then the listener receives and interprets the message. However, according to Sonnenmeier (1993), throughout conversation between natural speakers, each speaker effects and influences the communications of the other. She argues that conversational exchanges between natural speakers are frequently co-constructed in a collaborative way (see also Goodwin 1981).

Foster and Ohta's study (2005: 425) presents data that learners benefit from sharing their meaning while monitoring each other's utterances, minimizing communication breakdown. When co-construction is employed by second language speakers strategically, it might facilitate their communication and possibly decrease their anxiety by releasing them from their assumed responsibility to create a grammatically and pragmatically comprehensive message all by themselves. Foster and Ohta (2005) suggest that in order for learners to negotiate for meaning, the learners need to signal communication problems to each other and seek to resolve communication breakdown. Such a signal may initiate co-construction.

Asking another person for information or language that the speaker has forgotten is included in communication strategies. In this way, learners might be able to form a comprehensible message by asking other speakers to tell them the language they cannot recall. She notes that the reciprocal nature of the interaction facilitates communication as both speaker and listener co-operate to ensure mutual understanding.

Awareness of the notion of co-construction as a communication strategy can liberate second language speakers from the sense of responsibility that they have to form a comprehensible message all by themselves and eventually decrease their anxiety. Although the need of making learners' aware of communication strategies was highlighted by linguists (Bygate 1987), co-construction of messages has not been emphasized in English classrooms in Japan. In order to acquire it, one needs to be integrated in English speaking business discourse.

Background of the study

This case study is situated in this early stage of English permeation of Japanese domestic workplaces. Nissan Motors, a Japanese automotive manufacturer, recorded the biggest deficit in its history in the fiscal year 1999. In order to break through the stagnation, the company chose to strengthen its international collaboration with its French partner, Renault SA. When the alliance agreement was signed, their Chief Operating Officer (COO) at the time, Carlos Ghosn, announced a restructuring plan which included a change in its language policy. English was chosen as a working language, although it was a foreign language for most of the employees of the two companies. Nissan employees started to use English as one of their official language along with Japanese.

Among researchers of Japanese management there was a strong interest in the future of the alliance. Those interests were transformed into questions such as, 'how should the senior management addresses issues that had surfaced as employees of the two firms worked together across corporate and national cultures, functions, and geographies?' or 'whether or not the two firms would be able to strike a balance between deepening their alliance while respecting the identity and culture of each company and not interfering in operations?' (Yoshino & Fagan 2003).

The meetings analysed in this study were recorded in 2000, in the early stage of their alliance, right after the announcement of the alliance formation.

Method

The data presented here are from a documentary film entitled *Eigo ga kaisha ni yatte kita* ('English has come to our company'). The video-recorded meetings were broadcast on TV by NHK (the national broadcasting company of Japan) on 28 October 2000. I obtained permission from NHK to use the data for the present research.

The Nissan–Renault portion of the programme is 28 minutes and 10 seconds in length including 8 minutes and 38 seconds of meetings and 2 minutes and 57 seconds of interview data which were recorded immediately after the meetings and before the meetings.

In the analysis I attempted to retrieve participants' linguistic constraints and cultural assumptions. However, interpretive analyses of such underlying elements can be subjective and possibly lack validity. In order to increase the validity of the analysis, this study uses data from critical viewers' debriefings. I had three debriefing sessions with business people who viewed the recorded data carefully. The viewers consisted of 36 Japanese speakers and twelve non-Japanese expatriates working in Japan. All of them had experience using English for business inside and outside of Japan. In the debriefing sessions, I first asked the viewers to fill out a questionnaire with six open-ended questions and then to discuss their reactions based on my analysis of the data. It should be noted that the questionnaire was not used in the earliest session with non-Japanese viewers for operational reasons. Through the debriefing I confirmed my analysis and received some additional voices from these viewers who faced the reality of business where English is used.

The meetings

In this section, I will present the flow of the meetings that leads to their final decision. The programme showed three segments of the meetings held between the Renault senior managers and employees of the Renault Sales Department of Nissan. The narration of the meeting and NHK website provided the following data (NHK 2000, 2007). The meeting was held in order to determine their marketing strategy for the new product model that was going to be released for the Japanese market. The three segments were recorded in their initial meeting, a meeting with a smaller number of key participants that followed the first meeting on the same day, and a meeting in which the final decision was made on a separate day.

Although I recognized at least six Nissan participants and three Renault participants in the meeting, the number of the Nissan participants who talked during the recorded meeting were three. Therefore in my analysis I focused on the six participants. The background of some of the meeting participants was described by the narrator as the following.

Meeting participants

Nissan participants (Renault sales team of Nissan)
K: Newly assigned Chief. Previously he stayed in Europe for about 12 years as an expatriate.
T: Sales manager. All through his career he devoted himself to car sales. He had never been in the position where English was used on the job until he was assigned to take part in the Renault Sales Team.
J: A member of the Renault Sales Team. No further information was given in the programme.
Renault Participants (Renault, Japon)
P: President of Renault, Japon.
D: General Manager. According to the NHK Website, neither P nor D had worked in Japan previously.
F: An expatriate of Renault, Japon. No further information was given in the program.

Most of the meeting interaction was related to whether the commercial film would emphasize Renault technology to manufacture utility cars or 'refined French style' of the model. The Renault participants stressed the need to emphasize their technology based on their past commercial success in European market. On the other hand, the Nissan participants argued that emphasis should be on 'French style' because of Japanese customers' preference for refined French tastes.

   After examining the commercial film, excerpts 1 and 2 show that K (Nissan participant) argued against using a picture of the rear gate of the car, and said that stressing 'utility' too much does not appeal to Japanese customers. (Transcription conventions are listed at the end of this chapter.)

Excerpt 1

K: Design might be style (.) might be stylish but er showing this it reminds you that the er (1.0) this is (.) wagon type.

Excerpt 2

K: = Less stress on the utility. Then what we have (?) now... is the ... er..if we look at the er the original. This is the original. So you can see that two ... two time ... two times of the er the rear gate. Maybe er might be too much..

   On the other hand, D and F from Renault answered back by stating that car users are always interested in functions of a car as seen in Excerpt 3.

Excerpt 3

D: = Yes. Yes. For this reason I say (.) that (.) when you buy..er..special picture or special (1.0) er..(1.5) statue..er..You are should =
K: = Yeh..
D: fascinated =
F: = Yes.
D: and when you < < f > put > in the car. (.) er (.) You should the (.) functionality of the car. But it's very different =
F: = yes.

While the meeting participants were talking about the narration of the commercial film, K strongly insisted that Japanese customers favour 'refined French taste' (excerpt 4), and recommended using a French looking actor and French narration (excerpt 5).

Excerpt 4

K: We..we could try rather than Japanese er French and put the er superimpose
P: rather than [English]
F: [superimpose]
D: rather than French French [language]?
K: [French French] voice over
D: French voice

Excerpt 5

K: In ... Japanese has er more broader view. un..fortunately or unfortunately I don't know. but from the Japanese point of view (.) still er.. when when they think of the..er..the..France. it's er ano er Paris maybe baguette or cheese or wine such simple things from Japanese point of view but I I'm not saying er I'm not saying that we should u u er we er we er show the er wine or baguette and cheese on our films. But I'm talking about the er image of French. image of the country of the French from the Japanese point of view should be into the er the taste of the commercial films. (3.0) Change the nationality (of the actor) but they try to(?)

D attacked K's stereo type of culture (Excerpt 6).

Excerpt 6

D: The French touch. It's not only baguette salads or er Vuiton of the [fashion or]

K: [You're right] but from your point of view. When you (.) when you uh think about Japan. (1.0) what do you think? (2.0) Geisha Harakiri, [Mount Fuji]?
D: [Oh. no.](shakes head) No (.) absolutely no. I think technology.
K: What..
D: think..Uh … e..a very good organization. this (?) Not not..uh … not [Sumo..or] …
K: [what] [but what..what..]
D: Geisha not not It's old old

After three meetings with the same debate recurring, the final decision was made: the Renault president decided to promote the model emphasizing their technology and using a Japanese looking actor in the commercial film (Excerpt 7).

Excerpt 7

P: Would it be non-sense to have a Japanese looking guy. So that people identify to the customers As er watching TV if you want to identify your self at some stage say possibly like it could be me driving this car. You see he is a Japanese model. He is wearing a target He is stylish he is modern he is someone (.) we (.) you as a Japanese guy want to be identify yourself. someone that you really see driving you think.

In the following section, I will discuss how the participants' cultural assumptions and communication strategies the participants used influenced the decision. The data shows that the use of particular communication strategies was found to empower certain participants who had been 'normalized' in an English-speaking business discourse. Some participants' lack of awareness of different communication strategies resulted in potential misinterpretation and communication breakdown.

Data analysis

At the first glance, there is clear contrast in participation styles between Renault and Nissan participants. While Renault participants talked frequently and alternatively, deviation among the Nissan participants' turn-taking frequency is large. Although the similar number of the turns were taken by each of Renault participants, it is quite obvious that among Nissan participants only K talked. Table 11.1 shows the number of turns taken by the six meeting participants and the number of words by turn. As described in the previous section, in the meeting there are a few more Nissan participants who did not talk at all. This indicates that Japanese do not follow a monolithic, pre-described communication strategy.

Silence and nodding as acknowledgement

Critical viewers' responses to my initial question, whether the decision was reasonable or not were clearly separated into two. Five Western and three Japanese critical viewers expressed that the decision was quite adequate:

> I assume that was a sound decision. You know, listening to everybody, and then a decision. (Western critical viewer 3)
>
> Other Japanese: ga K-san no iken ni sandou wo shimesite inai to handan shita kara [The president must have judged that other Japanese did not support K's argument].

Critical viewers with this line of opinions pointed out that they thought the decision was based on the agreement of most participants among whom only K insisted on using a French actor and emphasize 'French taste' but his argument was not strong enough to change others' opinion.

On the other hand, two Western viewers and 12 Japanese viewers told that the decision was made on misinterpretation of the intention of Nissan participants. According to this group of viewers, Nissan participants other than K did not voice their opinion because they had the same opinion as K. For them, they did not need to open their mouth since K is giving his opinion as a representative of his team. Silence in this case was interpreted as support to K by the majority of the Japanese critical viewers. They assumed that Nissan participants had already reached their consensus by taking a participatory decision making approach and are aligned in their thought.

27 out of 35 Japanese viewers answered that they would also be quiet in the context of this case. Their suggested reasons of their possible taciturnity are categorized into two categories. The first category of the reasons is anxiety that derives from their insufficient English competence.

> Hatsugen deki nai to omou. Jibun no iitai koto wo eigo de tadashi ku iwa nakute wa to iu ishiki ga doushitemo nokotte shimau node [It is possible that I would remain quiet. I might think that I need to say my opinion in correct English]. (Japanese critical viewer 16)

Table 11.1 Turn-taking frequency

Renault Participants	Turns (words per turn)	Nissan participants	Turns (words per turn)
P	18 (8.7)	K	27 (18.3)
D	4 (25.8.)	T	1 (1.0)
F	10 (4.2)	J	1 (3.0)

Hatsugen no taimingu to eigo de umaku aite ni tsutaeru koto no muzu-kashisa. [Difficulties to capture the timing of speaking out in a meeting and to convey my message accurately]. (Japanese critical viewer 1)

The second category can be labelled as 'dependency on competent and powerful speakers in their team'.

Nissan gawa no shuchou de kyoutsu no ninshiki matawa kangae kata wo motte inai to muzukasii. [It will be difficult unless I have exactly aligned understanding and thoughts.].

Joshi ga iru baai wa enryo gachi ni naru kamo. [I might be hesitant to speak out when my boss is present].

The above comments can be also interpreted that the participants' identity as Nissan employees made them think that they needed to be aligned as a team.

The meeting interviews of the Nissan participants, K and T, revealed that the Nissan participants did not feel that they successfully conveyed Nissan's opinion to the Renault decision makers. K and T realized they have to repeat the same thing for many times to have Renault management understand what they claimed. K said:

Karera wa, tokuni furansu jin toka yooroppa no hitatachi tte tonikaku hyakuman kai iwa nakerdeba dame desu kara [To have them (Renault managers) understand what we want to say, we need to repeat a million times.].

T echoed K and said:

Sore koso Hyakuman kai iu n desu yo. Hyakuman kai yuu shika nain de sho Kodomo mitai na koto iu kedo. [There is no alternatives. I say that I need to tell them a million times although I might sound childish.].

The interview data indicate that T also had the same opinion as K but was not able to say his opinion. T's silence meant his trust and support to K. T and K seemed to think that the decision was not based on the majority of the participants' opinions.

One of the reasons of this communication breakdown could be mis-interpretation of T's non-verbal cue. While the Renault participant was talking, T nodded, as shown in excerpt 8.

Excerpt 8

P: No. Advertising.(.) we focus on inter(not audible)..we say.
T: Say =
P = it's non-sense whereasT: (nods)

P: if you < < f > say > because in the end I mean ...

Mulholland (1997: 101) noted that Asian's saying 'Yes' or 'OK' followed by silence means acknowledgement but not agreement. According to Mulholland, acknowledgements are signals by hearers that they have heard the request and they do not necessarily mean the request will be complied with. Likewise T looked as if he had agreed with what Renault manager was saying to Westerners but in fact he only showed that he heard the message. As I discussed, the silence of Nissan's participants is socio-economic behaviour which could be interpreted differently by hearers from various backgrounds. In the following section, I will explore the variation among Nissan participants in regard to their turn-taking frequency.

Socio-cultural behaviour acquired in Europe

K is the only one of Nissan participants who took turns frequently during the meeting. Nevertheless, it does not mean that K's linguistic competence is higher than other Nissan participants. Interview in the programme revealed that K has not received formal English training. The critical viewers' questionnaire result shows that 30 out of 35 viewers do not suppose that K has markedly higher linguistic competence.

The analysis of data informed that use of co-construction of message enabled him to take frequent turns in the meeting. In fact there were moments when K struggled to find the very words to express his opinion. However, unlike other speakers, insufficient vocabulary did not stop him from expressing his opinion. Instead, K tried to co-construct his message with help of other participants.

Excerpt 9

9–1. K: To minimize. ... =
9–2. F: = Yes.
9–3. K: To minimize ... the ... er ... what can I say(.).er ... special
9–4. F: = Special impression.
9–5. K: [Impression of being a utility car ...] That's number one. (.) Number two. We should enhance..er..more dynamic ... er ... more ... we should allocate more time.

In 9–3, K overtly expressed his difficulty to identify the best word to convey his message. F guessed the word that K wanted to say, and suggested to use the word in 9–4. Immediately K used the word and continued his talked in 9–5. It is reasonable to assume that because K co-constructed his message, he had less anxiety.

In excerpt 10, K did not show his struggle verbally. Instead, his non-verbal expression signalled his trouble.

Excerpt 10

10–1. K: We should er we should make it more weaker. Er make the (hhh) er. weak er (scratches his nose) =
10–2. J: = Less stress =
10–3. K: = Less stress on the utility.

After J's support, K again immediately used the offered word and completed his speech. K did not ask for help to only French participants. In excerpt 11, K asked his Japanese colleague for help.

Excerpt 11

11–1. K: French voice over and then er Japanese superimpose. (.) by using French words which will match or enhance more on the visual. This could be regarded as er their ano lady or guys ano nanda..hitorigoto tte nante takke.
11–2. S: talk to himself
11–3. K: talk to himself.

In the end of 11–1, K realized the exact translation of the Japanese phrase *hitorigoto* is 'talking to himself', and murmured, '*ano nanda..hitorigototte nante takke*' ('Well, how do you say hitorigoto in English?') in Japanese.

English teachers in Japan have not paid much attention to explicit teaching of co-construction as a communication strategy. Thus someone like K who is aware of the notion of co-construction as a communication strategy usually learned it through his experience of being integrated in English-speaking communities. K is the only one Nissan participant who was in English-speaking discourse for a long period of time (12 years). He acquired this socio-economic behaviour through his business practice.

Questionnaires to critical readers showed the same line of their interpretation. Twenty-eight respondents wrote that K's standing out in turn-taking frequency related to his long experience in overseas business. Foster and Ohta's study is evidence that American learners use co-construction more frequently than Japanese learners. Other Nissan participants might have had fewer chances to acquire co-construction of message by staying in a Japanese environment.

Some critical viewers interpreted K's frequent turns as a socio-economic behaviour. Three critical viewers pointed out a power issue which I did not consider in the early analysis. Three of them mentioned *daihyo to shite no tachiba* or *kanri sha to shite no chikar'*; both mean the power as a representative or manager of the Nissan team enabled him to take much more frequent turns than other Nissan participants. This was a reasonable analysis considering the boss–subordinate relationship that has been discussed in Japanese management studies.

Table 11.2 Transcription conventions

Meaning	Symbol	Example
Unintelligible text	(?)	Then what we have (?) ..now is the
Overlapping text	Word [word] word [word] word	French [language]? [French French]
Latching, i.e. two	=	Say = = it's non-sense whereas
Micro pause	(.)	I see Japanese TV (.) I (.)
Pause of indicated length	(0.5)	Might be difficult. (2.0)
Action	(nods)	Yes. (nods)
Outbreaths	(hhh)	It's (hhh) your idea.
English translation	*Japanese* (English)	Sodesu (Yes, it is.)
Japanese language	*italic*	*Ano*
Strongly raising tone	?	French?
Loudly	<< f >>	It's << not > utility

Thus, I claim here that K's use of co-construction and his power as a leader of Renault Sales team made him talk alone, which conveyed a different message to the Renault team than was intended by the Nissan team.

Conclusion

As I demonstrated, the contrast of participation styles between Renault and Nissan employees and amongst Nissan employees points to a problem of applying static views of a cultural characteristic to actual meeting behaviour. Such static view might say that all Japanese are group-oriented and all French are individualistic. However, observing linguistic data it is obvious that individuals do not behave in line with such static views. K, for example, insisted on his opinions, while other Nissan participants neither supported K nor expressed agreement with K's opinion. D and F alternatively took a turn and supported each other's points. K seemed individualistic and D and F looked very much group-oriented team members.

The research result also implies that the monolithic models of culture cannot account for complex business interaction which is influenced by several contextual factors as well as cultural and socio-economic factors.

It also needs to be noted that D, a French manager, did not talk as much as others. The variation among French participants might inform some important issue but valid analysis was not possible since I was not able to contact them for interviews.

This case study described part of the process of how the reciprocal relationship between English and certain management ideologies deconstructed and reconstructed a hybrid business discourse which consequently affected their final decision. The overall findings of the study indicate that specific management practices do not easily transfer to the emerging hybrid business discourse. It is hoped that the case demonstrates that socio-linguistic and business ideologies affect business interaction and that it leads to deeper insights about intercultural business communication in increasingly complex global business communities that will face more East–West contacts than ever.

12 An Italian perspective on international meetings, management and language

Gina Poncini and Elisa Turra

Introduction

In this chapter we explore management and language by using cases and examples drawn from our research on authentic interactions at business meetings in Italy as well as our interviews and ongoing contact with Italian managers from a range of industries. Indeed, while taking into account findings from our own research to shed light on how Italian managers use language in different settings, we also wanted to explore the perceptions of managers today. Is it possible to define or describe 'an Italian style of management'? Or rather, do Italian managers with international experience perceive an Italian style of management? If so, how do they articulate it and how can this be connected to research on authentic interactions? The chapter provides a brief background on the development of Italian capitalism and on the corporate sector in terms of its historical, economic and cultural context. By drawing on analyses of actual language use in business settings as well as interview data, it aims to provide insights into ongoing changes in 'management styles' and more specifically the use of language by managers.

Below are two examples which are snapshots of language use at actual business meetings in Italy. Though the settings differ, the extracts share a number of commonalities.

1.	Finnish Distributor:	the line for me is much more than – much better than before
2.	Italian Manager:	exactly, you know, it's there, all the collection
3.	Finnish Distributor:	very good, compliments

The Italian manager addresses the three Spanish participants:

4.	Italian Manager:	tutto a posto?
5.	Spanish Distributor:	dopo parliamo con (...) [...]
6.	Italian Distributor:	a posto

The Italian Manager addresses the Swiss participant:

7. Italian Manager: Pierre? toi? tu? you?
8. Swiss Distributor: I think it is (...) because (...)
9. Italian Manager: ok very good
   (Taken from Poncini 2002, 2003 and 2004. The original transcription
                conventions have been modified – see Appendix 12.3)

1. Marketing Manager: nel briefing il CEO ha chiesto il database con i trend
                           di marketing e i cluster sulla customer loyalty
2. Sales Manager: al meeting parteciperà il customer care?
3. Chief Operations
   Officer: sì e anche dei supplier perché il progetto è in out-
                           sourcing
4. Marketing Manager: il prossimo step è fare benchmarking sulle best
                           practices dei competitor per il BtoC
5. Chief Operations
   Officer: ok facciamo un download dalla homepage
                                          (Taken from work by Turra 2005)

In both examples the use of language is not only connected to the interactional context and communicative purpose. The use of language here also
reflects – and contributes to – ongoing changes in business and management
in Italy. Moreover, some linguistic choices can also be linked to historical
factors in Italy, as will be seen later. The first example took place at a
meeting organized by an Italian company for its international distributors,
from 12–14 countries, and conducted mainly in English – though not only
English is used. The second example is drawn from an internal meeting
conducted in Italian, with all participants native speakers of Italian – though
not only Italian is used. Discourse at each of the meetings reflects and
expresses relationships and practices particular to each group of participants.

Looking more closely at the examples in the opening, at the first meeting
cited above, the occasional use of languages other than English serves particular
purposes tied to the character of the meetings, which involve members of the
Italian company and distributors from up to 14 countries, with almost everyone
a non-native speaker of English using English as a *lingua franca*. Different
languages are used at certain points of the meeting to facilitate understanding, ensure correct product details, and highlight an interpersonal element
in the company's relationship with each distributor, all while underlining the
multicultural nature of the group. In the second example in the opening, the
heavy use of English business terminology while speaking Italian seems to
be more prevalent among young managers and professionals with degrees from
business schools and with international experience. But that is only part of the
context, which plays a key role in any communicative event. The age of the
managers and their position in the company, the age and size of the company,
its industry, business issues ... the list could go on. The effect of specific linguistic choices also deserves attention.

The next section provides a brief background on selected aspects of business in Italy and is followed by sections focusing more specifically on language and management.

Historical background and current influences: the family, management literature and international experience

According to a survey conducted in 2006 by a leading banking group (Capezzone 2006), 98 per cent of the companies in Italy are micro-companies and family firms with less than twenty employees. In the words of the president of a consortium of firms in the agro-food industry: 'Italy is considered a tiny giant as it is characterized by a fragmentation of numberless micro-companies which constitute at the same time the strength and the weakness of our economy' (interview by Turra 2006).

Economic historians and sociologists agree that the 'tradition of familialism', which is 'the use of kinship relations as the structuring principles of industrial organization' (Piore and Sabel 1984: 228), has always played a key role in the past, facilitating the accumulation of capital and the transition from a rural to an urban-industrial society. Collective family values and ties have enabled Italian manufacturers to compete successfully since the 1970s thanks to the creation of small firms relying on family labour, flexibility, diversification and extended networks. The persistence of small firms today, however, has led some scholars to view Italian capitalism as a non-advanced form of capitalism. In Weber's early work on medieval Italian capitalism, in fact, family firms are inevitably bound to decline, or to aggregate and evolve into bigger public companies.

Anthropologist Yanagisako (2002) believes that capitalism and corporate values in Italy are culturally traditional and different from other forms of Western capitalism, arguing that 'the familial character of Italian capitalism, ... enabled by the juridical and fiscal policies of the Government, is shaped by commitments to forms of collectivity, filial loyalty and patriarchal authority – all features associated with Asian capitalism' (Yanagisako 2002: 26).

Some scholars (Alemanni 2002: 52) have indicated two opposite views of the relationship between culture and management styles. The so-called *culture-free* approach believes that management styles mainly depend on economic and technological factors whereas culture is not considered a significant variable. The *culture-contingent* approach instead claims that management styles are strongly influenced by cultural identities and that corporate practices are *country-specific*. Comparative studies belonging to this approach show that it is possible to identify an Italian management style, characterized by continuity, flexibility and *cooptation*, which is based on a gradual replacement of the old leaders with new and younger leaders (Alemanni 2002: 53).

When reflecting on their experiences and the business environment today, the Italian managers interviewed for this chapter, however, hesitated about identifying a single 'Italian style of management'. Rather, they cited factors upon which a certain style may depend, and though they described different management styles, Italian managers may not necessarily use the 'Italian style' they describe. For example, when asked about whether he noted any differences between a management style in Italy and a management style in other countries in which he worked, the Chief Financial Officer (CFO) of an Italian branch of a pharmaceutical multinational corporation with headquarters in Germany stated:

> Differences in management styles do exist, for sure, in particular between the so-called 'international management style' and the 'local management style'. The local management style is related to the cultural background of each individual. The international management style is common to different nations.
>
> Managers belonging to the international management style have adopted the necessary conventions to develop dialogue, to manage differences and to focus on data and results. Italian management style instead is more emotional and focused on personal relationships whereas rules, processes and procedures are not strictly followed.
>
> (Interview by Turra 2007)

This difference between 'international' and Italian ('local') management styles also reflects the difference between what can be called 'the old generation' and 'the new generation' of corporate leaders in Italy. Organization and management literature from the US has had a strong influence on the curriculum of Italian business schools and on the management culture of younger managers. The contrast became more prominent at the end of the 1990s, with the advent of the new economy. Many organizational and management theories (Bender and Stromberg 2000; Pottruck and Pearce 2000; Valdani 2002) as well as studies on corporate discourse (Bargiela and Turra 2004) record how the new economy has considerably transformed work practices, including the hiring process. In Italy, for example, more attention is now given to the candidate's qualifications, and more opportunities are available to young people compared with the past. The market has become increasingly complex and unstable, and in such a hypercompetitive business environment organizations need to anticipate and rapidly adjust to the changes in their industries.

This new emphasis on constant change and innovation as opposed to continuity has accelerated the emergence of a young generation of Italian managers with international experience. Many of those who set up their own companies in the late 1990s were clearly trying to shape their company culture on the model of successful 'dot.coms' in the US. As the Italian founder and CEO of an Internet firm stated:

> When I founded Y.com I was inspired by the corporate culture and collaborative atmosphere of Microsoft. In this perspective the CEO

must foster group cohesiveness and create a knowledge-sharing and a collaborative working environment, so that all the people are well informed and motivated. I believe that in order to be able to carry out and implement authoritative decisions without meeting resistance, leaders need the support of the other managers and employees. This can be achieved by adopting specific participatory mechanisms such as meetings or short briefings aimed at empowering people and enabling them to work efficiently and harmoniously together.

(Interview by Turra 2002)

In order to improve and innovate constantly without meeting resistance from employees, many Italian managers with international experience realized they needed to create a positive atmosphere in the workplace, facilitating the exchange of information and viewpoints. The key words characterizing such an organizational change are 'collaboration', 'participation', 'devolution' and 'empowerment', which foster autonomy. These notions are also tied to the will to create a sense of community within the workplace, and in the case of multicultural corporate settings, a sense of 'groupness' (Poncini 2004).

This new organizational paradigm has gradually spread in Italy to companies operating in a wide array of sectors, and this, too, has been identified with the management style of a new generation of leaders with international experience. This comes through in an interview with a (now retired) worldwide export director of a leading Italian spirit company, who describes a style characterizing Italian managers and at the same time recognizes the changes under way:

In my experience there is a 'Latin' management style which includes Spain and Italy. These managers usually have a good education, coupled with a great capacity to communicate both with their reports and with the external business world. They have a high level of creativity and diplomacy, which can help in their business transactions. They prioritize – sometimes too much – human relations and emotions, which could lower, in some instances, their capacity to obtain the maximum result from a business negotiation.

Finally, even if this aspect is now changing in the younger generation, many managers are still reluctant to delegate part of their responsibilities, fearing to lose power. ... As to the Italian managers, their wish and/or need to keep everything under their strict control is now changing in the younger generations, certainly due to their experiences abroad and to the coming of a 'team-work' era, making a certain delegation almost compulsory.

(Interview by Turra 2006)

These comments share similarities with those made in other interviews: a 'local' or 'Latin' management style is recognizable as opposed to an 'international' or 'Anglo-Saxon' management style. Italian management style is described as *emotional* and sometimes excessively based on human relations. Several interviewees cited the reluctance of Italian managers to delegate part of their responsibilities because of their fear of losing power and their tendency to keep everything under their strict control. However, such peculiarities seem to be undergoing change in the younger generations, most likely due to their international experience and as part of the emergence of a new organizational paradigm based on team work, delegation and dialogue.

English specialized terminology in Italian business settings

The influence of English on the development of the language of finance in Italy was already evident in the 1930s (Devoto 1939) and continued with the language of marketing, management and technology. Unlike other languages such as French or Spanish, Italian has reacted very slowly to the process of creating Italian equivalents to English commercial and technical vocabulary. By the time a neologism was created in Italian, the English equivalent had already taken hold. Moreover, the curriculum of Italian business schools has always been 'Anglocentric', heavily drawing upon organization and management literature originating in the US and the UK, and this has contributed to increasing the use of specialized English terminology in Italian.

The linguistic repertoire used by Italian professionals operating in different corporate sectors is connected to their age, background and organizational culture. Here again, differences can be noticed between the 'old' and 'new' generation of professionals, and this is even more evident at the managerial level. Unlike the old generation, numerous members of the new generation of managers have attended a business school in Italy and many have studied or worked abroad. This generation makes a wider use of English words in general and technical terminology in Italian corporate settings (Turra in preparation). A 65-year-old owner of a well-known company operating in the agro-food sector comments: 'I've recently hired a new marketing manager. He's very young and he has studied abroad. However, when we have meetings, he keeps using technical words in English and I don't understand him. I'm afraid he's going to ruin my company!' (interview by Turra 2006).

It is interesting to note that the interviewee cited above not only comments on his own lack of understanding but also raises his concern that the new marketing manager may lack professional capabilities – or at least the ability to communicate his competence to the owner. This underlines the tension that can come into play even when managers sharing an Italian background adopt different styles.

Manifestations of these and other differences in the managerial styles of different generations reached a high point with the New Economy. This phenomenon is reflected in the use of linguistic resources and has led to a massive use of English loan words in Italian corporate contexts. Let's return to the example at the opening of this chapter, which was audio recorded in 2002 during a management meeting of an Italian Internet company.

Extract 1

1	Marketing Manager:	nel *briefing* il *CEO* ha chiesto il *database* con i *trend* di *marketing* e i *cluster* sulla *customer loyalty*
2	Sales Manager:	al *meeting* parteciperà il *customer care*?
3	Chief Operations Officer:	sì e anche dei *supplier* perché il progetto è in *outsourcing*
4	Marketing Manager:	il prossimo *step* è fare *benchmarking* sulle *best practices* dei *competitor* per il *BtoC*
5	Chief Operations Officer:	ok facciamo un *download* dalla *homepage*

(Taken from work by Turra 2005)

Much of this extract is intelligible without translation, even to an audience who is not familiar with the Italian language, as most of the content words used are in English. The participants in this meeting are all Italian native speakers based in northern Italy. Nevertheless the number of Italian words barely exceeds the number of English words (italicized in the extract). The Italian language is mainly used here to build the morpho-syntactic structure of the text, whereas key words and concepts are expressed in English.

Words like *marketing* or *benchmarking* have become part of the Italian vocabulary since their origin, as no Italian equivalent to these English words has ever been coined. However, many other specialized words are used in English even though there exists an Italian equivalent. This is the case of *customer loyalty*, *database*, *trend*, *cluster*, *meeting*, *download*, *step*, *best practices* and of some key positions such as *CEO* and *customer care*. No effective Italian equivalent to words such as *homepage* and *outsourcing* has ever taken hold, whereas other words such as *competitor* and *supplier* have Italian equivalents but are used as integrated loan words (Merlini 2005); that is, their singular forms in English are used as plurals in Italian without taking the form of the plural in English. The use of English specialized lexis in Italian interaction in corporate settings has now become a linguistic routine, especially for the younger generations of managers.

The process of creating a unitary nomenclature in Italian has always been very slow, not only in professional contexts, but also in the use of common words (Beccaria 1973). Specialized lexis in Italian in fact, is used in different ways in different institutions because its origins go back in time to the secret codes used by medieval professional corporations (Cogno 2004). The original secrecy associated with technical vocabulary has resulted in the development of different conventions used by different groups of people operating in the same sector. In the case of companies, employees that interact regularly with each other may also build up their shared linguistic repertoires. In the extract below, the CEO and an employee (SM) of the same Internet company are in a meeting characterized by the presence of external participants, including a French external consultant, EC, who does not work permanently in the company.

Extract 2

1	CEO:	quindi dato un cluster non solo lo seguiamo e iniziamo a
2		conoscere come si evolve ma soprattutto come possiamo
3		fare per aumentare la *fidelizzazione*
4	EC:	*fidelizzazione?*
5	CEO:	fideliz
6	SM:	frequenza all'ordine

Translation of Extract 2

1	CEO:	*so given a cluster not only do we follow it and (we) start to*
2		*realise how it evolves but above all how we can increase*
3		*loyalty*
4	EC:	*loyalty?*
5	CEO:	*loyal*
6	SM:	*frequency of purchases*

(Taken from Turra (in preparation)

The presence of an external consultant (EC) highlights the difference between an 'outsider's' use of specialized lexis and its use by 'internal' members of the company, who have developed a common repertoire over time. Indeed, the different use and meaning attributed to the word *fidelizzazione* (customer loyalty) in Extract 2 makes it possible to distinguish between 'internal' and 'external' participants. In lines 1, 2 and 3, the CEO describes a new marketing tool aimed at monitoring customers and increasing customer loyalty. However, the notion of customer loyalty is different for internal and external stakeholders, and this difference also implies differing opinions as to the most appropriate marketing strategy. Although the CEO implicitly assumes common ground when he uses the Italian word for *loyalty* for the first time, he is understood only by internal members of the company, whereas the external consultant (EC) asks a question and needs further clarification. The consultant has been working in Italy for over 20 years and is very fluent in Italian, but the use of specialized terminology shows that he does not share the same repertoire as the other participants.

A post-event interview (from Turra in preparation) conducted with the participants of the meeting that Extract 2 is drawn from shows that managers and professionals alike are aware that linguistic resources are gradually developed by people who work together on a daily basis: 'we have developed our own way of speaking our own terminology and jargon that sometimes nobody except us could understand'.

Lexical choices, in fact, can embody definite claims to specialized knowledge and institutional identities. Drew and Heritage (1992: 29) state that 'lexical choice is a significant way through which speakers evoke and orient to the institutional context of their talk'. Specialized terminology is used and interpreted in different ways by participants who operate in the same sector, but who have not developed a shared linguistic repertoire. The linguistic repertoire may vary depending on the type of company, its size and sector. However, within every single company different micro-discourse communities may coexist and generate different linguistic sets of linguistic resources.

Multicultural business meetings: a case study

This section is drawn from an in-depth study of meetings (Poncini 2002, 2003 and 2004) organized by an Italian company for its international distributors to present and discuss the next season's product collection, strategy and other issues. The company, which has been given the pseudonym Alta, was founded in 1984 with a single product, ski wax, and subsequently expanded its product lines to include technical eyewear and helmets for skiing and cycling, and sportswear for outdoor sports.

The meetings analysed normally lasted 2–3 days and were attended by approximately 25 distributors from 12–14 different countries located in Europe, Asia and North America, by some of the company's Italian staff and management (usually at least eight to ten 'company members'), and by a few other participants such as consultants or suppliers. Five twice-yearly meetings were observed from 1996 to 1999 and all but one were recorded. Two half-days segments from June 1997 and June 1998 were transcribed and analysed both quantitatively and qualitatively. (Appendices 12.1 and 12.2 provide sample seating arrangements and additional information about the meetings.) In a certain sense, the study can be seen as a case study of these particular meetings since the data used for this study were obtained from meetings organized from the same Italian company over a period of several years.

It is possible to view each meeting as a series of identifiable speech events, with *speech event* used as a general term to encompass the monologues and different kinds of discussions taking place at the meetings. The most frequent speech events consist of 'presentations/monologues', 'group discussions' involving the general group and 'small group discussions', during which distributors speak in small groups, interacting among themselves in their own language or speaking with someone from the company as they examine or try on circulating product samples. Distributors and two to four company members usually sit at the main table, with the company speaker or presenter(s) located in the middle towards the front (or 'top') of the U-shape, towards the front of the room. At times the speaker(s) walked around inside the U-shape, as do individuals modelling clothing.

Four sample extracts from the meetings are analysed and discussed, illustrating some of the key issues emerging from the study:

1. Extract 3 illustrates the main company speaker's use of 'we' to create a sense of group and solidarity, so that even new distributors can choose to include themselves in a vision of success. More generally, the analysis of pronoun use in the study shows that the group is characterized by fluid roles and flexible relationships, and there is shifting between individual and collective identity.
2. In Extract 4, the main company speaker uses implicit and explicit evaluative language and draws on shared values to persuade the distributors to follow a new procedure that aims to coordinate the worldwide image. Pronoun use in Extract 4 signals a shift from the distributors' status as 'independent' and autonomous business people to their being part of same group and able to share in the group's success.
3. Extract 5 provides an example of how everyday language rather than technical terminology is used at the meetings when the group decides on a product model to include in the collection for the upcoming season. It is an example of the speech event 'group discussion', sometimes characterized by overlapping speech – not the case during a 'monologue/presentation'. More generally, this is an example of shared repertoire and language use at the meetings.
4. The use of languages other than English was seen to facilitate communication at the meetings and at times serve a practical purpose, such as in the example shown in Extract 6.
5. The example shown at the opening of the chapter illustrates one of the speech events identified at the meetings – 'small group discussions'. During such events, the dyadic business relationship (e.g. company-Finnish distributorship, company-Spanish distributorship) emerges within the larger group. In addition, in addressing individual distributors or small groups, the main company speaker and other company members sometimes use languages other than English, underlining an interpersonal element of the interchange.

The role of personal pronouns: fluid roles and flexible relationships

The quantitative analysis revealed that Edo, the marketing manager and main company speaker at the meetings, uses 'we' with ambiguous referents (i.e. uses that may include or exclude the distributors) more frequently than other company speakers, thus building solidarity and a sense of groupness. His uses of 'we' were seen to allow distributors, even new ones, to include themselves in a positive vision of the company and its business. Other company speakers also used 'we' with ambiguous referents; however, they also showed a more frequent use of *we* with referents excluding the distributors. This usage seemed to be connected to their roles within the company and displayed a cooperative element rather than conflict, e.g. informing the distributors about a reciprocal company process.

Extract 3 illustrates the strategic role pronouns can play when participants at meetings represent different kinds of business relationships. A wide range of ambiguous referents are used for 'we', shifting from referents at the meeting to referents present at the Olympics earlier that year. The extract also shows how personal pronouns can contribute to building group solidarity and how, when used with positive evaluation, may contribute to the image not only of the company but also build the character of the group, as distributors may choose to include themselves with *we* referents connected to success. Edo is the marketing director, Iceberg Extra is a pseudonym for an eyewear model and Jean Louis is a pseudonym for Alta's service technician.

Extract 3

1	Edo:	[*Addressing entire group*] *we* can continue?
2		Iceberg Extra, Extra Iceberg [*eyewear model, also displayed on a promotional poster*]:
3		when we are at the Olympic Games we really improved very much [*laughs*]
4		and uh because we have a prototypes parts and we have to change it every day Jean Louis he have to work to work very hard
5		but the result we want to reach, we-we reached that
6		we had a very good exposure
7		we get a lot of uh medals with our racers
8		so was a very good result

Looking in-depth at a few occurrences of 'we' in the above extract illustrates a wide range of ambiguous referents. In line 1, referents for *we* must be present at the meeting; however, this occurrence could conceivably refer to different sets of participants: the entire group present (company members and distributors), or the company speaker and company members changing the display of products in the front of the room. In line 3, the first occurrence of 'we' shows a range of possible referents that may have been present at the Olympics: this could involve unspecified individuals physically present at the Olympics, but it could also involve the company and its products because as a sponsor of athletes, the company/brand name is visible on certain athletes' equipment and attire. For the second occurrence in line 3, the referents that improved (the eyewear model) are unspecified. In line 4 the activity becomes more specific, and someone who was present at the Olympics is indicated: Jean Louis, the only referent specified. He is the company's service technician who assists Alta-sponsored athletes at international competitions, so this first-name reference builds shared knowledge – not all distributors might know him – but also presents what is of value to the group because of the technical nature of the products they sell. Some distributors may be more interested in the 'general presence' at the Olympics of the company or individuals – including athletes – connected to the brand. Distributors may interpret many of these uses as inclusive, heightening a sense of groupness and shared values.

Lines 5–8 concern goal achievement and are characterized by the use of positive evaluation and uses of 'we' open to interpretation. Referents remain ambiguous for 'we' used in relation to an earlier defined objective, achieving this objective, and gaining exposure. In such cases, those present can choose to include themselves, with 'we' interpreted as all those involved in Alta products and activities, including distributors.

Using evaluative language to build consensus for a new procedure to coordinate the image worldwide

Extract 4 illustrates how Edo, the marketing manager, uses language to influence a change in distributors' behaviour by presupposing agreement with the procedure, which aims to coordinate the company's image worldwide. Rather than using direct commands requiring the distributors to change their behaviour (i.e. to use the new brand manual being presented by Francesca, from the company's advertising and promotion area), Edo uses both positive and negative evaluation (Thompson and Hunston 2000) that takes into account what is of value to the distributors. He also presupposes agreement through the use of *of course* and *as you know*, evoking this shared knowledge and making a bid for group solidarity. In addition, he uses words that begin to accumulate a positive or negative evaluative (in particular *same* takes on a positive connotation). Where he does specify actions, he assumes cooperation (line 5) from the distributors, who are positioned as independent businesspeople who can choose whether to cooperate (lines 13–14). In addition, the alternation in lines 4–7 of 'we' to refer to the company and *you* to refer to the distributors highlights a cooperative process and reciprocal roles. Indicators of relevance in English are in italics.

Extract 4

1	Edo:	*the point* it's-now it's to try to coordinate worldwide the image
2		*of course*, what makes sense in Italian not necessarily makes sense in Spanish, in-in Japanese. in English. in Finnish in-
3		the *very important* thing it's to understand the sense
4		and what we can do, the possibility we have, it's to send to you in a English language, the sense
5		and then *of course* everybody of you have to adapt it for your market
6		and what we can change it's only the black the black part the black text

7		after that we can send to you or we can send to you the come si dice l'impianto? eh?
		how do you say l'impianto? huh?
8	Francesca:	the films
9	Edo:	the films
10		or if it's collecting more than one countries, uh, and agree on the same on the same
11	?	language [*sounds like Giorgio*]
12	Edo:	language, we can make it for all of you
13		*this is up to your-up to you*
14		*it's your choice*

As a result of Edo's presupposing common knowledge and agreement, the steps in the reciprocal process take on an implicit positive connotation, potentially building greater consensus around them. Finally, Edo also builds solidarity by showing awareness of distributors' roles and independent activities.

Building a shared repertoire of language and practices at the meetings

The wider study of the meetings (drawn from Poncini 2003 and 2004: 168) includes an examination of specialized terminology that was also quantified by speech events ('monologues/presentations', 'group discussions' involving the wider group, and 'small group discussions'). The results indicate that the marketing manager and other company members tend to use more product-related technical vocabulary during 'monologues/presentations' compared with 'group discussions' (to be noted is that actual product models or posters displaying product features often accompany both kinds of speech events). Transcribed data show that the switch to 'everyday' language occurs above all in discussions where the group must make choices about product models for the international collection. Rather than using the product model name or lexis for technical features characterizing the options available, Edo, the marketing manager, uses nonverbal means to present the options, for example, holding up a product model and, as in line 1 of Extract 5, using everyday vocabulary such as names of colours to refer to choices. In any case, the lack of technical terminology is evident here and in the preceding discussions focused on choosing product models. Extract 5 illustrates features of such discussions. Edo has first moved around the table (see Appendix 12.1), and after addressing the Norwegians (transcription not shown), he explicitly addresses the entire group of distributors in line 1 and later in line 9.

Extract 5

| 1 | Edo: | [*addressing the entire group*] everybody agree? [*he holds up product model in question*]: |

2	?	[*many voices*] yes yeah
3	Edo:	they, the north countries, after discussion and agree together, they suggest to keep only one of those two
4	?	tutt'e due
		Both
5	?	white and yellow
6	?	keep the red one
7	Edo:	and keep (2) this one (.)
8	?	[*several voices*] yeah yeah keep the blue
9	Edo:	everybody agree?
10	?	yes
11	Edo:	now, second question [*laughs*]

In sum, when decisions have to be made concerning product models, there is reliance on everyday vocabulary combined with visual elements, including non-verbal communication such as holding up a product model and orienting the body towards part of table. This appears to facilitate the group's participation in such events.

Using languages other than English to facilitate communication and interactions

Company members following the meeting may also contribute to the unfolding of a monologue or discussion when they use Italian to address the company speaker. For instance, in Extract 6, Paola, a company employee who speaks German and French and follows certain international markets, is seated near German-speaking distributors (see Appendix 12.1). During the meetings she can usually determine whether nearby distributors have under-stood discussion items. Such understanding may go beyond the compre-hension of a foreign language per se (e.g. issues connected to the use of English as a *lingua franca*) and may involve wider business issues. In Extract 6 below, Paola uses Italian to address Edo, the marketing director, who consequently clarifies the two eyewear versions, Racing and Light, being discussed.

Extract 6

1	Edo:	how many go for Light?
2	?	me [*others also respond*]
3	Edo:	Light
4	Paola	[*loud enough to be heard by Edo, up front*]:
		spiega qual'è che non hanno capito la differenza qual'è il
		Light explain which one it is they haven't understood the
		difference which one is the Light one

(Taken from Poncini 2003)

Uses of Italian such as the one in the above example represent short 'asides' or 'insertions' in Italian that allow the discourse to proceed more smoothly and can thus contribute to achieving the goals of the meetings. These uses of Italian facilitate the work of the company speaker and other company members, who prepare and present numerous product models with varied features. The data also include instances of company members who use Italian in a lower tone of voice to remind a speaker to mention a product feature or to suggest a term in English if the speaker hesitates. Such uses of Italian ensure that pertinent and accurate information is included in presentations. Moreover, some uses of Italian enhance understanding and goal achievement by allowing contributions from company members able to assess distributors' understanding or reactions to presentations. Paola's use of Italian such as in Extract 6 above positions Edo as the addressed recipient and does not draw attention to the distributors' 'lack of understanding' or to Edo's 'lack of success in having them understand'; such uses can thus also fulfil a face-saving function.

Configurations of interaction also help ensure understanding and opportunities for distributors to communicate their concerns as the meeting progresses. For example, at times the marketing director approaches the meeting table or walks around the inside of the table, addressing each individual distributor or group of distributors representing a single market in a dyadic interaction. This is the case in the extract presented in the opening section of the chapter.

To close this section, in considering these analyses, it is possible to reflect on whether participants' use of language, e.g. the main speaker's use of ambiguous pronouns, is deliberately manipulative. However, ambiguity serves a function because when many individuals are involved, it is often difficult to specify all parties and not always necessary to know who they are. Consequently ambiguity does not necessarily bother us unless we need to know. Based on conversations with the main company speaker outside of the meetings, it does not appear he made a deliberate choice to use an ambiguous pronoun at the moment of choosing 'we' or 'you'. Rather, it seems that speakers in a leadership position have a vision of the company's future and its goals which goes deeper than a single linguistic choice as opposed to another in a particular instance. In the end, it is the cumulative effect of these choices – and not the individual occurrences – that plays a strategic role. In the meetings analysed, the cumulative effect of linguistic choices as well as the different configurations of interaction contribute to building a sense of groupness at the meetings – the meetings as a level of culture are characterized by fluid roles, flexible relationships and shared values.

Concluding comments

This chapter has explored language and management in Italy, drawing on studies which examine authentic business meetings. The analysis and discussion of extracts has shed light on the role of the immediate interactional context, the wider business relationship, ongoing changes in management styles and the use of English as a *lingua franca.*

In the case study of meetings organized by an Italian company for its international distributors and conducted mainly in English, different configurations of interaction, for example occasional small group discussions following monologues/presentations, were seen to help ensure understanding and achieve meeting goals. The main company speaker's use of evaluative language draws on shared values, and along with his use of personal pronouns helps build a sense of groupness while recognizing the distributors' individual activities. Moreover, the occasional use of languages other than English serves to facilitate understanding, present pertinent product details and underline the multicultural nature of the group.

In the meetings conducted in Italian, the heavy use of English business terminology seems to be more prevalent among young managers and professionals with degrees from business schools and with international experience. In this case, the use of English in meetings conducted in Italian reflects the difference between 'the old generation' and 'the new generation' of corporate leaders in Italy and is part of the progressive change from an Italian ('local') style to an 'international' management style.

While it is not possible to articulate definite answers to questions about 'an Italian style of management', what is of interest are ongoing changes and the way they are manifested in the communicative behaviour of Italian managers.

Appendix 12.1: seating arrangements and room set-up

Participation and seating arrangements may vary slightly from day to day. Some company members stay in the front of the room to assist with product displays.

Appendix 12.2: additional information about the meetings

In the early 1990s, Alta started to organize a meeting for its international distributors, to present and discuss the next season's product collection, strategy and other issues. The distributors are not Alta employees or agents; most own their own companies, and some work for larger distributors. Some distribute only Alta products, while others also distribute other companies' products for similar markets, so that meeting participants represent a variety of business relationships. In some cases, at the meetings the distributors decide as a group which product model versions are to be included in the international collection. Based on the products viewed and discussed, distributors decide which product models to include in the 'sample kit' their sales representatives will use, placing their orders for the season at the meeting or shortly thereafter.

Over the years, changes were made in line with the growth of the company, e.g. while many distributorships were involved in meetings where decisions were made about products, subsequently a smaller number representing the most important markets were involved.

Appendix 12.3: transcription conventions

Conventions for Poncini extracts, modified with respect to Poncini 2002, 2003, 2004:

Unintelligible speech (...)
Deleted text [...]
[*contextual information*]
Translations appear in italics below the original text.
Unidentified speaker = ? (in the column for speakers)

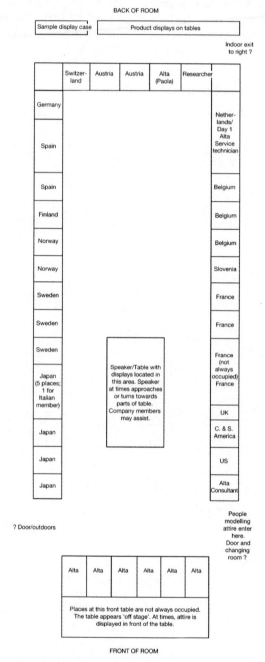

Figure 12.1 Seating arrangements and room set-up, June 1998.

13 Humour and management in England

Susanne Tietze

Introduction

A German manager and an English manager are in a conversation during a coffee break of a sales meeting. German manager says: 'I hear you are training for a marathon. I'm thinking of doing one myself. So, how many hours do you put in day?' English manager: 'I do at least three pints a day.'

This banter is taken from a sales meeting I observed and it symbolizes to me something quite typical for the (verbal) behaviour of English managers[1] – i.e. the way the use of humour is integrated into everyday behaviour and used as a way to bring about social relationships. The purpose of this final case study chapter is therefore to discuss some such usages in the context of English society, work organization and management. In this regard this case study chapter diverges from the form and content of the previous ones as it has a more personal tone and reflects to an extent my own experience of and fascination with the 'language of humour' which is so deeply ingrained in the identity of English people and therefore also into the 'doing of management'. In emphasizing the role of humour in England, it is not claimed that other national cultures do not possess or display humour (and this includes my own national culture, the German one), but merely that compared with other nations humour (and irony) are used more widely and play a different role in providing a lubricant for the complexities of social and organizational relationships.

I will first introduce the role of humour in social and organizational life and comment upon it as a form of language, which is part of making as well as subverting social realities. The chapter then provides some background to how and why humour is used in England and focuses specifically on the use of humour in management and organization.

Humour in social life

Humour is a form of communication, which creates feelings of amusements or the predisposition to laugh or giggle or smile, even if just inwardly sometimes. Watson (1994/2001, 2006) states that humour is woven into the fabric of all social life as it is a means to cope with the incongruities, ambiguities and the potential chaos that define human existence. Joking and the use of humour is therefore also common in many organizations and has been recognized as significant behaviour by organizational scholars (Collinson 1988; Grugulis 2002; Watson 2006), i.e. as behaviour which provides access to deeper or hidden meaning systems. Mulkay (1988) argues that the ubiquity of humour in the workplace exists because it is an alternative type of discourse which acts as a counterpoint to the serious discourse of business and commerce and that skilful joking facilitates the interplay between 'seriousness' and 'playfulness' in particular in problematic situations. The use of humour is then like a lubricating agent which smoothes difficult social and economic interactions and thus, ultimately, enables diverse groups of people to pursue joint objectives and goals.

Ackroyd and Thompson (1999) consider whether humour and jokes are part of an emerging agenda of new 'misbehaviour' and resistance, which replaces the traditional forms of 'misbehaviour' such as pilferage, sabotage or absenteeism and which possibly also act as a replacement for collective forms of resistance such as industrial action. Joking can after all be seen as a way to dissent and express disagreement with unacceptable points of views. Joking creates an 'unreal space' (Mulkay 1988) in which certain emotions can be voiced in such a way that is calculated to cause no offence. As joking and the use of humour is exempt from the normal rules of social conversations and exchanges, it is possible to articulate sensitive or critical points of views without having to face the consequences of ones verbal actions. Ironic or sarcastic comments on organizational initiatives or practices are commonplace in work contexts – the phrase 'you don't have to be stupid to work here, but it helps' and other similar stickers or comments found on computers or at workplaces are general comments which provide some relief from conforming to everyday routines which accompany organizational life. They hardly cause offence or evoke any changes. Their purpose it like that of a safety valve, which provides a bit of relief without challenging the status quo. According to most writers on work organizations, the main function of humour and humorous talk is to act as a social lubricant and to allow for the creation of some (limited) 'free space' in which individuals can voice their opinion, even if dissenting from the official point of view. Thus, humour is used as protecting the individual's identity from being appropriated by the overwhelming organizational fiat.

Humour can also be used to provide a sense of group cohesion as the frequency and quality of its use differentiates one group from another. Collinson (1988) showed that the quite intense use of humour and pranks on the shop floor was used by the workers to differentiate themselves from the more restrained and 'boring' office workers – thus the shop-floor workers defined themselves as being quite distinct from other organizational groups as well as from the company as a whole. Workers on the shop floor engaged constantly in humorous banter, teasing and 'piss-taking' which defined group and individual relationships – sometimes also resulting in deeply felt personal hurt and the open articulation of conflict.

In total, however, the main function of humour is to release tension by getting people to laugh (Gelfert 1998, 2002) and in this regard it has a great equalizing function as it momentarily cancels differences between people and groups of people by uniting them in a shared relief of tension and common experience of enjoyment.

Humour often takes a practical, observable form (e.g. playing of pranks, tomfoolery and clowning around), however much humour is expressed verbally. It is part of language and uses particular rhetorical forms to express and subvert messages and meanings. Quite often it draws on exaggeration, be it understatement or overstatement, and in doing so it 'plays' with the construction of reality. Irony is a case in point as it is a figure of speech, which reverses meaning, i.e. it means the opposite of what is being said.[2] Humour deals in ambiguity as it affords more than just one interpretation of reality – it can juxtapose contradictory or incompatible frames of reference and in doing so it can challenge existing organizational meanings. However, which reality it points to is difficult to establish as it creates an 'unreal, ambiguous' space in which individuals can express opinions and emotions which in 'serious discourse' would be difficult to state.

Humour in England

The identity of the English people is to a large extent based on their perception of having a superb (and superior) sense of humour – in particular certain 'brands' of humour, such as irony, black or gallows humour, wit and repartée feature strongly in the collective mind of the English people. There is, indeed, something distinctive about the use of humour – with the defining characteristic being the *value* that is put upon it and the *extent* to which its use is widespread in everyday talk and conversation. This does not mean that English people sit down and tell jokes all the time, rather humour is part and parcel of everyday exchange, of the kind of banter described in the opening exchange between a German and an English manager. In England there is no particular 'time and place' for humour; most English conversations will involve some degree of teasing, mockery, silliness or humorous self-depreciation. According to social anthropologist Kate Fox (2004: 61–62) humour is the 'default mode . . . : We do not have to switch it on deliberately, and we cannot switch it off. For the English, the rules of humour are the cultural equivalent of natural laws – we obey them automatically, rather in the way we obey the law of gravity.'

The rules of humour

- The importance of not being earnest rule: it is based on the distinction between 'serious' and 'solemn' and between 'sincerity' and 'earnestness'. Seriousness and sincerity are allowed, solemnity and earnestness are strictly forbidden. Serious matters can be spoken of seriously, but one must never take oneself too seriously (Fox 2004: 62).

- The 'Oh, come off it' rule (or the 'yeah, right' rule as a more modern version): the tiniest sign that someone might be overdoing the intensity of what they say and cross the line from sincerity to earnestness is spotted and evokes this scornful cry (Fox 2004: 63).
- The irony rule: the English 'patriotic pride' in their sense of irony as better developed and more subtle than that of any other nation or culture. The English may not always be joking or being ironic, but they are always alert to the *possibility* (Fox 2004: 65–66).
- The understatement rule: This rule implies that rather than risk exhibiting any hint of forbidden solemnity, unseemly emotion of excessive zeal, the English do the opposite and feign dry, deadpan indifference (Fox 2004: 66–67).
- The self-depreciation rule: this includes the prohibition of boasting and any form of self-importance and stresses the importance of self-depreciation and self-mockery. Of course, the English are not naturally more modest than other people and much of the self-depreciation is indeed not genuine, though it does signal that modesty is aspired to. The modesty that is displayed is generally false – or indeed ironic (Fox 2004: 67–70).

According to Hans-Dieter Gelfert (1998, 2002), a professor for English Studies and expert for comparative analysis, the reasons for the widespread use of humour in England (and the different use of humour in Germany) is to be found in the history of the country, which saw the emergence of a strong bourgeois nation much earlier than other European nations. In the late seventeenth century England developed the societal and cultural structures for an emancipated citizenship, i.e. a parliament and guaranteed civil liberties (Gelfert 1998: 179). Thus he sees an early emanicipatory phase of the English citizen, who uses (rebellious) laughter and wit as an equalizing process amongst different societal groups. The caricature of John Bull (eighteenth century) typifies a bottom-up attitude which is deeply suspicious of and defies all authority, which is pragmatic in character and relies on the principle of self-help. Humour, wit and laughter are the weapons to prick undue pomposity and undermine any insistence on pulling rank in order to ensure a degree of individual independence and social equality.

Playing with words

An old lady buys a stamp for a letter and asks: 'Must I stick this stamp on myself?'. The answer is forthcoming: 'No, stick it on the envelope.'

The English like to play with words and meanings. The use of puns, for example, enjoys widespread appreciation as it is a sign of (effortless) wit. Gelfert (1998: 91) states: 'as it is frowned upon to show off one's education, one cannot possibly quote from literature or science directly. However, hidden, subtle allusions can be used as they are considered to be witty and sophisticated, but avoid the direct demonstration of one's superior knowledge.'

According to the English comedian Stewart Lee (2006) much of English humour is in effect an outcome of its particular flexible sentences (which enables English comedians to use a technique called 'pull back and reveal', i.e. to conceal the subject of the sentence until the last possible moment) and its potential for confusion of meaning.

Humour and English management

Humour is used widely in the English workplace, too (Fox 2004). This does not mean that business people, managers or workers continuously swap jokes or play pranks on each other, but rather it functions like an undercurrent to social interactions in which teasing, banter, wit and irony are used frequently and with great relish. Empirical studies of English workplaces (e.g. Grugulis 2002; Tietze 1998; Watson 1994/2001) tend to confirm that humour and the use of irony is widespread and used a default mode, in particular in difficult and ambiguous situations. Grugulis' (2002: 387) work shows the use of humour in three private-sector organizations to be widespread, embedded in everyday contexts and conversations and shows it as a means to conveying 'ambitions, subversions, triumphs and failures' as well as being a copying mechanism in the face of the challenging task of gaining a particular vocational qualification. Tietze (1998) showed that the use of irony was widespread in the context of organizational change and used to convey unease with some changes as well as to cope with the ambiguities created by the upheaval. Watson's (1994/2001) ethnography of managers shows that the use of humour is widespread and it is a recurrent theme taking the form of stories, pranks that are played, insights that a made, rhetorical figures that are used. Humour appears to be the cultural backdrop in which all actions take place.

The commonalities between these three studies is that they detect humour as widespread and engrained in organizational behaviour. They confirm the assertions made earlier in this chapter that the use of humour is deeply embedded in the behaviour and identity of English organizations and people and that it provides a recognizable golden thread in the pattern of English social/organizational life. As a word of caution I must point out that none of the three cited studies has been conducted in a comparative spirit – i.e. the authors did not use 'Englishness' as a template to compare with 'Frenchness', let's say. So, much of my interpretation of the three studies is based on an imagined comparison, which I as the author bring to this chapter. In my mind's eye I constantly compared the situations described in the studies to similar, but imagined situations in a German context and I ask myself how they would have been played our there – my belief is that most situations would 'feel' quite different.

The social potential of humour as a utensil to relieve tension and to build bridges is of course also recognized and used by practising managers and consultants. Interestingly, several (comparative) studies (Barsoux and Lawrence 1990; Stewart *et al.* 1994) have shown that many managers see the use of humour as a legitimate managerial tool, but use it in a different fashion. In Stewart's *et al.* study (1994: 170) both German and British managers took recourse to humour, but the British managers cited its use as systematic and widespread, as an everyday tool to ease relationships, to 'cancel any hint of authoritarianism' (1994: 170) to soften brusque instructions or criticisms. Overall, the management style associated with these actions is one of 'persuasion', i.e. a style in which the mastery of language and the use of humour in the particular English sense are paramount to gain compliance and create a sense of convivial purpose.

From my own experience:

To soften a blow: 'Susanne, good news! You don't have to hold any meetings any more. Your request for a proper meeting table for your office has been turned down.' Facilities manager reports to my office with the news that I cannot have a meeting table.

To prick self-importance: 'You were the best of a bad bunch.' Answer by the chair of the appointment committee which appointed me to my first lecturing job to my request for feedback on my performance during the interview. We both knew that I had done well in the interview, but I still needed and wanted to hear it!

To point to different/less desirable habits: 'Oh look, Susanne, is here already. Where is her towel*?' A comment by a colleague strolling into a meeting room on my habit to be early for meetings and be ready to start the meeting on time.

*Germans are renowned, in English lore, to always want to reserve seats, in particular deck chairs, by putting a towel on them to claim ownership.

Conclusion

Gelfert (1998, 2002) argues that due to converging influences (e.g. of the European Union; globalization) the distinctiveness of English humour will lose some of its uniqueness. According to Fox (2004) this is not the case and contemporary behaviour in English society and workplaces continue to follow very much the same 'humour rules', which might change form, but which still abound. A case in point may be the success of the TV series *The Office*, a mock documentary, whose central character, the local branch manager, was obsessed with being funny, but unable to tread the fine line between hurt and humour. To me this series expressed much of the English ability to laugh at itself and also to have a good dig at the pomposity of much of the management discourse.

Be that as it may, the use of humour is widespread in English work organizations and its occurrence is a superb diagnostic device for researchers and managers, who have to find a 'way into' understanding the organizational fabric and its patterns as it creates its particular meanings clad in humorous and ironic messages. My advice for anyone who is going to work and live in England or who is going to work with a group of English people follows Fox's counsel (2004: 62):

> I cannot emphasize this strongly enough: if you are not able to grasp these vital differences [between seriousness/solemnity; sincerity/earnestness] you will never understand the English – and even if you speak the language fluently, you will never feel or appear entirely at home in conversations with the English. Your English may be impeccable, but your behavioural 'grammar' will be full of glaring errors.

Returning to the opening exchange between the German and the English businessmen we can now say that the English manager just behaved in a manner that is completely 'natural' to him: He answered a serious question in a humorous way and in doing so he tried to avoid being seen as an obsessed, over-eager 'swot'. He 'understated' the effort it takes to run such a long race rather than engage in a 'serious' conversation about training regimes and racing strategies. Later on in the evening the two men were indeed swapping stories of pulled muscles, racing days and preparatory eating regimes. So, 'serious exchange' did happen, but this was only possible after 'seriousness' had been mediated by humour in order to avoid any inkling of earnestness or self-importance.

To me, the pervasiveness and dominance of humour provides a flavour to conversations and social interactions which are distinctively English and which have always attracted me to this nation. These days, I can spot irony and understatement and have learned to stay clear of earnestness – no mean feat for a German.

Notes

1 I have chosen to write in this chapter about Englishness rather than Britishness: a) partly because while there might be a great deal of overlap between English, Welsh, Scottish and Northern Irish cultures, they are not identical; and b) partly because I am most familiar with English culture both in terms of being a resident as well as having researched work organizations, whereas I know Welsh, Scottish and Northern Irish cultures only from visits, readings and social meetings with Welsh, Scottish or Northern Irish people.

2 Irony is a fascinating and complex figure of speech and the brief comment in this chapter do not do it any justice. For a deeper understanding three sources spring to mind: Burke's (1941) essay 'The four master tropes', Winner and Gardner's (1993) essay 'Metaphor and irony: two levels of understanding' and Oswick *et al.*'s (2002) article 'Metaphor and analogical reasoning in organization theory'.

Part III

Conclusions

Introduction

The final chapters return to the main themes of the book and offer a new theoretical way forward, which could enable the field of management studies to use the insights from 'philology' as a trajectory to energise its endeavour to explore and understand management processes from a language perspective. In Chapter 14 (by Holden and Tansley) philology is used as the conceptual means to develop a comparative approach to management studies, which does not aim to replace the existing 'cultural school', but offers an alternative which grasps the frequently multi-linguistic situations managers find themselves in and have to cope with. Chapter 15 draws on translation studies as a synthesizing means to combine the various approaches which have been introduced in this book or have been used by scholars as a frame to researching language-based processes in (multinational) organizations. It is argued that in translating meaning is both lost and found, and that a framing of managerial activities as 'translation' (between languages as well as between meaning systems) is a constructive way forward to initiate a language-sensitive study of increasingly global processes of knowledge creation and exchange.

14 Management in other languages

How a philological approach opens up new cross-cultural vistas

Nigel Holden and Carole Tansley

Introduction

It was the leading literary critic George Steiner (1976: 88) who observed that 'languages generate different social modes, different social modes further divide languages'. In keeping with that our intention in this chapter is to reveal how management terms used in different languages, their etymologies and semantic zones, reflect different assumptions about notions of management, managers and managing, for such assumptions are not to be deduced from culture alone. We proceed by studying the evolution of the words 'manage', 'manager' and 'management' in English, which we will regard as our default language (an unusual designation for the undisputed language of international communication!). Next we shall examine the nominally equivalent words in French, German, Polish and Russian, paying attention to historical and contemporary influences on usages and associated semantic zoning.

We shall in effect be applying a philological approach to a discussion of the terminology of management in five European languages, contending that this methodology can reveal much about the way in which management in one cultural locale can to some extent be differentiated from management in another. Philology concerns itself with the scientific study of relationships between languages (genetic, grammatical, phonological) and pursues the investigation of historical forms of language to aid cultural understandings of societies at given times (Crystal 1997: 294–97). The approach will make manifest that management terminology is simply not a carbon-copy of itself across languages with isomorphic semantic zones and that lexical forms distinctive to one language bear socio-cultural and etymological imprints that are not entirely transferable to another language.

Just as nearly a century ago the Harvard philologist Wiener (1911: 242) observed that 'a close union must subsist between philology and economic history', so it is our conviction that *a close union must also exist between philology and the evolution of management both as a practice and a subject of social scientific study.* This must indeed be so, for management cannot be conducted without words: words often with long histories and *always* with moveable meanings in any language and variable meanings among them. This relationship between management and language is waiting to be examined through the systematic comparative study of management terminology in various languages.

There is no tradition in the field of management research and education for comparing managers using methodologies that rely on language as a principal cross-cultural hermeneutic device. However, a philological approach does not supplant the more established methodologies for cross-cultural comparison of managers of Hofstede (1980/2001, 1994a), Trompenaars (1993), Schwartz (1994), and the GLOBE project (House et al. 2004). But it can usefully enhance these and other schemes by supplying insights that only the exploration of language can unearth.

Hofstede is concerned with cultural differences based on contrasting values and has provided the most enduring framework for the cross-cultural investigation of managers. Trompenaars developed a scheme of six bi-polar cultural dimensions (which he calls 'dilemmas', whilst Schwartz, author of 'the most substantive challenge to Hofstede's model' (Koen 2005: 69) has developed a model involving three sets of bi-ploar cultural dimensions). The GLOBE project has evolved a Hofstede-influenced framework for the investigation of leadership differences in 62 countries. But none of these scholars makes language differences directly relevant to their schemes, although Hofstede (1980/2001: 27) notes: 'Language is the most clearly recognizable part of culture', adding that it is not 'a neutral vehicle', since 'our thinking is affected by the categories and words available in our language'.

These comments support the view that language, both as a descriptor of experience and a means of expression, is indeed be a major distinctive culture-specific influence on managers' *Weltanschauung*. In this chapter we take this as a given, contending that the philological method is *the* great unused methodology available to management scholars in general and possibly to critical theorists in particular (see Alvesson and Willmott 2003: 18–19) for exploring language's 'historically developed dimensions of interests – the attributes of concern or the lines along which things of the world will be distinguished' (Deetz 2003b: 31). All in all we are offering an interpretation of language that is somewhat at variance with 'the linguistic turn', which has been primarily social-science based in the field of management research; we have opted for a humanities-influenced approach.

In the following sections we chronicle the evolution of the words 'manage', 'manager' and 'management' in English. Then, with English as our base language, we will attempt to portray the equivalent terms in four European languages, namely French, Polish, Russian and German. We are, however, aware that our treatment of the word 'management' in a mere five European languages, including English, is purely illustrative of the potential of the philological approach. At the same time we are consciously avoiding the vexed matter of comparing *legal* definitions of the word 'manager', which reveal great variations in European languages (see Bournois and Livian 1997: 29–32). It will, however, become apparent that we are doing much more than a cross-linguistic survey of management words. Our treatment will in effect open up five notable vistas for reflection which we will comment on before the general conclusion. These vistas are: a) societal stances on management; b) etymological differences and linguistic change; c) capacity to create new terms; d) culture-specific semantic zoning; and e) the English language as intellectual comfort zone and blind spot.

The linguistics of core management words in English as an evolving diachronic and socio-cultural phenomenon

The words 'to manage' and the derived forms 'manager' and 'management' have existed in English for several hundred years. Other words such as 'managership' and 'managerial' are much later arrivals. In sixteenth-century European languages, including English, 'management' was exclusively concerned with the treatment of equine – emphatically not human – resources. Indeed, according to the *Oxford English Dictionary* (1970, Vol. VI: 104–5), the verb 'to manage' derives 'probably' from the medieval Italian word *maneggiare,* which in turn comes from the Latin expression *manu agere,* meaning to 'drive [animals] by hand' often for a public performance such as a parade (Neuberger 2002: 48; *Cassell's Latin–English English–Latin Dictionary* 1977).

The Italian word gave rise to the English word *manege,* which was first recorded in 1561. This word became 'manage' with the letter 'a' replacing the 'e' of the second syllable in 1586 (*Oxford English Dictionary* 2006). At that time the forebear of the modern word 'to manage' still referred to the handling and training of horses, though it would soon extend to hand-held weapons and musical instruments (Hofstede 1993: 82). Only by 1611 do we find the first attested occurrence of the word manage with reference to business, but this is not to say that manage was not used in this sense before this date. In *The Winter's Tale,* published in 1616, Shakespeare brings the words 'manage' and 'businesses' together in one sentence (IV.ii.15), possibly the first appearance of the collocation in the English language: 'Thou having made me businesses, which one without thee cannot sufficiently manage.'

The word 'management', first recorded in 1598, had acquired a meaning to do with 'businesse (viz.), handling, negotiation', whilst the word manager, meaning 'one skilled in managing affairs, money, etc', is first recorded in 1670 (*Oxford English Dictionary* 1970, Vol. VI: 106). Here we should note in passing that the formulation in this sense of the activity predates the designation of the doer by a good 70 years. To put that point in context: A character in Shakespeare's *Love labours Lost* (I. ii.176), published in 1588, referred to himself as the 'manager' of a rapier (Hofstede 1993: 82).

The first three letters *man-*are a continual reminder that the verb 'manage' and its later extensions (e.g. manager, management, managerial) derive from Latin word for 'hand', *manus.* As it happens, the historical record suggests a decidedly pre-modern form of the word 'manager', based on the *manus* root, namely the Latin term *manceps*, which referred to a head of a company commissioned by imperial Rome to supply bricks for roads and armour for the legions (Moore and Lewis 1999: 233–36).

This manager was a product of Roman family capitalism, and we may be certain that many aspects of their behaviour – meeting deadlines, appeasing the imperial client, cajoling their workforce, achieving quality standards, haggling with suppliers – would be readily identifiable to modern counterparts some 2,000 years hence. In passing we should note that well before imperial Rome – indeed as far back as 1500 BC – 'the Egyptians were using a number of management techniques, including: planning, organizing, and controlling; centralization and decentralization in organization; record keeping; the need for honest and fair play in management; and the use of staff advice' (Wilson and Thomson 2006: 6).

We can plot the development in 'the slow forge and working-house of linguistic creation' (Deutscher 2005: 77) of the *man*-root by means of what we call the 'manus time-line of core management terms in English' (see Figure14.1). It is important to emphasize that this time-line applies to English only. Equivalent time-lines for other languages will be quite different according to the evolution of management, as many would have to show the English words 'manage', 'manager' and 'management' in parallel with other words for these concepts in the language. The English word does not so much replace as displace those other words. In Figure 14.1 note first that the time-line covers some 2,000 years and that after the emergence of *manceps* in the first century BC it is some 1,700 years before the Latin *man*-root establishes itself in the English language with a meaning of management as broadly understood today.

The latest addition is the word *managism*, coined by Watson (2004: 75), referring to 'a discourse about directing work organizations that

Manus (Lat. 'hand') ➡ Manceps

Maneggiare (16th century Italian)
⬇

Manege Manage Management Manager Managing Manageress Managerial Managership Managerialism Managerialist

(1586) (1561) (1598) (1670) (1715) (1797) (1797) (1883) (1946) (1965)

Figure 14.1 The manus time-line of management in the English language. © Holden and Tansey.
   Source: Oxford English Dictionary, 1970, 1976 and 2006.

stresses the role of special techniques, practices, technologies, and terminologies'. The words in the time-line below are a selection. We have not included *managism* in our time-line, as we regard it as a non-standard term. We have also not incorporated derivatives such as manageable (hence manageability and manageableness), managee or managership among others, all of which are listed in the current version of the *Oxford English Dictionary* (2006).

Philologically speaking, we can trace a consolidation and an expansion of the Latin *man*-root as of the end of the sixteenth century, but, as Wilson and Thomson (2006: 6) note, management as an integrated concept was 'barely recognized' until 'the growth of large-scale industry after the 1870s'. The last generally accepted off-shoot of the *man*-root – managerialist – makes its first attested appearance in 1965 (*Oxford English Dictionary* 1976). The semantic loading on the words manage, manager and management is enormous, and especially cross-culturally, as we shall see.

The words 'managerialism' and 'managerialist' carry a strong hint of the jussory nature of management. According to the 1976 supplement of the Oxford English Dictionary, the first cited usage of the word 'managerialism' (in George Orwell) in 1946 referred to the Soviet Union, 'where "managerialism" has reached its fulfilment.' (*Oxford English Dictionary* 1976: 812–13). This is surely the only occasion when a coinage based on the *man*-root has been applied first to an ideological system hostile to capitalism, but not in fact to management per se. We should note in passing that the word manageress, first attested in the year 1797, has never referred to a female manager who is a carbon-copy of the male counterpart. Unlike the masculine form, the word manageress has never entered other languages. Finally it is impossible not to observe that a certain philological loop has been closed. Today's 'hands-on manager' is literally going back to his or her roots.

Through the philological lens: management in Europe

After this brief philological introduction, let us turn our attention in greater detail to the semantic diversity – and occasional semantic asymmetries – of the term management in various European languages. We start with the notions of management in English. What will emerge from the very treatment of a mere handful of words for management in English, German, French, Russian and Polish is that there is an unmistakable general unity of view as to the general nature of management.

Yet in all five languages we can find distinctions which are attributable to a motley collection of historical antecedents ranging from inter-country cultural influences which go back several centuries in some cases, conquest, contrasting intellectual traditions and values as well as language-specific capacities for word-building. The picture of management in Europe will be quite different from, and yet a valuable counterpoise to, traditional 'culture-driven' – indeed

Hofstede-guided (1980/2001) – explanations of management in cross-cultural contexts.

The philological lens allows us to see distinctions in a language which may not exist in our own. Every word we consider is a statement about management. Every word has its distinctive history, acquiring nuances distinctive to its passage within languages as well as between them. As will become evident in the following sections, the words for management in other languages give clue as to assumptions about management in practice and in the abstract, about hierarchy and structural relationships, as well as historical influences of management development in given business cultures. Knowledge of such things can be important both to researchers and practitioners for it can do something beneficial: to compel them to think more discerningly about the words they deploy in professional communication.

European variants on management's many meanings in English

The most conspicuous feature of the word management in English is that it covers four general meanings. The first area of meaning concerns management as a function concerned with the overall shaping of relationships, understandings and processes within a work organization to bring about the completion of the tasks undertaken in the organization's name in such a way that the organization continues in the future. Management is *what* is done at a point in time: management is execution (see Watson 2002: 67). Second, the word management refers to managers as opposed to workers: 'that group of employees which administers and controls an industry in contradistinction to the labour force in that industry or industry in general' (*Oxford English Dictionary* 1976: 812). Third, it refers to senior managers who constitute a collectivity monopolizing decision-making and strategic direction of a given enterprise. Fourth, it does not mean management as practice at all, but management studies. English is not bothered about this latter semantic distinction, but it is something that is carefully observed in German and the Scandinavian languages.

Whilst the English words 'manager' and 'management' have entered practically every European language, in French and German (and some other European languages) the words (i.e. *le manager/der Manager; le management/das Management*) are strongly associated with the management of professional sports people and celebrities. German has a female form, *die Managerin,* for which the translation 'manageress' would be inappropriate. One of the authors met *eine Managerin* at a conference in Vienna in November 2006. Working for the organization that arranged the conference, she would be in the UK 'an events manager', and definitely not 'an events manageress'. In contrast to these usages, as we shall presently see, the languages of Eastern Europe have bestowed upon 'manager' and 'management' as foreign words quite different associations: they are identified with the unfolding drama of the market economy.

Management in French

One of the most common words translatable by 'manage' in French is *diriger*, which is more widely used than its nominal counterpart in English 'to direct'. We are probably on safe semantic ground to suggest that the idea behind *diriger* is that of being in command. Etymologically connected with *diriger* are the words *la direction* and *le directeur* and its feminine counterpart *la directrice*. In French the words *le directeur* (f. *la directrice*) extends beyond the general remit of the corresponding word in English, as it is not so strongly associated with membership of the board of a company. Thus the French for marketing manager is *directeur du marketing*. But one could also be *responsable du marketing*, where *responsable* is a noun (i.e. meaning 'the person responsible for ... ').

Cognate with *directeur* is the word *dirigeant,* who inhabits the highest echelons of corporate management. *Le dirigeant* sits on the board and has as such a distinct leadership role, being part of the top-level team that defines vision and strategy. A *directeur* may have a leadership function based on skills and attributes, but hierarchy is everything. Thus the head of HR – *directeur des ressources humaines* – would be a *dirigeant* as long as he is a board member. If this suggests a certain operational overlap between *le directeur* and *le dirigeant,* there is one area where there is no doubt as to the distinction between them: a *dirigeant* has the non-reciprocal power to fire a *directeur.* Note too that *un dirigeant* is expected to combine eloquence with sartorial and physical presence (Fr. *allure*) (Solé 2006: 30).

When it comes to management as prosecution of policy the French use a word with no etymological connections to *diriger.* The word in question is *la gestion,* which derives from the Latin verb *gerere,* a polysemous word, which can be translated as 'to manage' in the sense of business affairs (*Cassell's Latin–English English–Latin Dictionary* 1977). *La gestion* is an abstract term for management; it invokes processes and procedures rather than 'getting things done through people'. It is to be seen in the expression *la gestion quotidienne de l'entreprise,* which is the exact translation of the English 'the day-to-day running of the company'.

A widely used word for managerial staff is *cadres* (plural), which we find in expressions like *cadres supérieurs*, meaning top management, and *cadres moyens,* meaning middle managers. As a rule *cadres* come under directeurs in the French organization. In a standard French–English dictionary the first meaning of *cadre* in the singular will be 'picture frame'. By extension the word acquired a meaning in military science, referring to 'the permanent establishment forming the framework or skeleton of a regiment, which is filled up by enlistment when required' (*Oxford English Dictionary* 1970, Vol. II: 6). This word passed into Imperial Russia before the 1917 Revolution. It became a concept cherished by Lenin and Stalin (Fink and Lehmann 2007: 139–43). The *kadry* (plural) were selected by the Communist Party for their operational competence and ideological loyalty to form the top management of institutions and enterprises (Kotelovoi 1984: 250).

We might add here that the Anglicisms *le management* and *le manager* and even *le leader* do occur in French to refer to the running of companies. However, as Solé (2006: 29) pungently notes, no one seriously questions these English words, which merely form 'a volapük, an artificial and shallow *(pauvre)* language' which by dint of its snobbism, business trendiness *(affairiste)* and expressive paucity reduces our capacity to think.

Russian and Polish: management languages under construction

In Polish and Russian, the standard verbs for management (*kierować* and *upravlyat'*, respectively) that were used in the socialist era contained a semantic kernel suggesting directing, controlling, guiding. In those times the flavour of the word was 'administration'. The Russian word *upravleniye*, meaning management/administration, despite its wide usage in the Soviet era, is still a standard translation for the English word management. For example, a recent Russian book on human-resource management, which carries wide discussion of HRM practice in the EU and USA, uses *upravleniye* and not the loan-word *menedzhment* in the title (Maslov 2004).

However, the essential distinction between management in the Western sense and *upravleniye* as management is made explicit in one of Russia's most widely used textbook on management (Gerchikova 2005). This book states: 'management (i.e. *menedzhment*) is *upravleniye* in market conditions' (Gerchikova 2005: 2). As we shall see, a contemporary Polish dictionary of management terms (in fact 2,300 of them) makes the point even clearer about 'management' in transitional economies.

Polish has several words for manager, the most multi-purpose one being *kierownik* (derived from the German word *kehren*, meaning to turn in a particular direction). Not surprisingly the word *menedżer* has taken up residence in Polish. But what is the difference between a *kierownik* and a *menedżer*? It is frankly hard not to come to the point of view that that the terms *menedżer* in Polish and *menedzher* in Russian represent an ideal form of manager who is, as it were, at peace with the market-economy system and has a 'new self-image' to boot (Kostera *et al.* 1995). A Polish dictionary (Penc 1997: 245) explains that the key point about a *menedżer* is that he is not only efficient (*skuteczny*), but also *'efektywny'* (effective), whereby one of the dullest words in the English-language lexicon management passes into the language of a former communist regime with a something resembling a concrete connotation. It is very important to appreciate here that the English words 'management' and 'manager' have not replaced native words, but they have displaced them by widening the semantic possibilities for the discussion of the nature of management in its socialist and post-socialist guises.

Polish has two main words for management and they form a useful distinction. The word *kierowanie* is the nominal equivalent of the Russian *upravleniye*, but has the meaning of management in a fairly overt strategic sense, involving long-term planning. It does not necessarily imply the power to wield organizational resources except people who come under the direct control of the respective *kierownik*. For reference specifically to the management of functions Polish has another word. This word *zarządzanie* is the word that is used in expressions like: management of human resources, management of change, marketing management. One way of explaining the distinction between *kierowanie* and *zarządzanie* is to note that the Polish translation of the expression 'style of management', which implies a relationship with people, involves the former and not the latter word.

Furthermore, Polish distinguishes between management as the activity of top management (i.e. *kierowanie*) and top managers as a group (i.e. *kierownictwo*). According to Penc (1997: 188) *kierownictwo* which means management in the sense of a collective of managers: that is, according to Penc (1997: 188) it is the word that is used in expressions like 'top management', 'middle management' and 'lower management'. We should also mention that Polish avails itself the word *dyrektor*, which refers to a senior manager, but not necessarily the member of a governing board of an organization. This word, still in wide currency, was used in the socialist period with its corresponding collective noun *dyrektorowanie*. But the latter word has a decidedly socialist ring about it; its days are numbered. One almost praises these distinctions in Polish until encountering in the same Polish text the words *menedżment*, *kierowanie* and *zarządzanie*, all of which can only be translated by our semantically overworked word 'management'.

As noted above, the word *cadres* passed into the languages of the countries of East and Central Europe which were Sovietized after 1945. 'Cadres decide everything', had declared the wily Stalin in 1935 (Utechin 1961: 85). No – they did what *he* decided. The word did not disappear with the collapse of the communism as of the late 1980s. Indeed it is still much in evidence. For example, a compendious Polish–English dictionary (Szercha 1994) lists the word, though in the singular (*kadra*). Another Polish dictionary of management and business terms devotes half a page to *kadry* (pl) suggests that the kadry 'possess independence, take decisions and manage [*kierować*] teams' (Penc 1997: 182)

Out of this great tussle with terminology emerges a little appreciated fact: that some 15 years and more after the demise of the communist regimes in the Soviet Union and East and Central Europe the local languages of management, spreading across some 12 zones and embracing more than 300 million people, are far from able to cope with market-economy concepts and terminology. Entire cultures, economies *and* languages are in a vivid sense under reconstruction. The comments below about Russian applies to these languages, which of course also embrace the languages of all the former Soviet republics: 'the evolving language of the market economy will not be Russian; it will be 'russgliskii'' (Rathmayr 2004: 155), that as yet uneasy amalgam of Russian and English, which, as Pshenichnikova (2003) has noted, will form 'a sub-language that has the potential to develop as a self-sufficient functional variation within the system of literary Russian ... it will fulfil the social, economic and linguistic demands of a new generation of managers in market economy Russia.' (cited in Holden and Fink 2007). It may take another generation before the languages of management in all the former socialist countries are lexically and conceptually equipped for the market-economy system.

German: a concrete language of management

Now let us turn our attention to German. The redoubtable word-building capacity of German ensures that it can make distinctions which are truly concrete. This is in contrast to French which favours distinctions that are *fine*. German is in a class of its own in the robustness of its management language. For example, we can note that the English term 'management', 'manager' and 'manage' in general organizational senses is translatable by nearly 50 words. German has different words for managing large estates i.e. as owned by aristocrats (*bewirtschatften*), or conflict (*handhaben*). The English word manager is an offered translation for words like impresario as well as 'special' classes of managers such as 'theatre manager' (der *Intendant*), 'estate manager' (*der Gutsverwalter*) and even 'decision maker' (*Entscheidungsträger*) (Duden 1996; Hentze 1995; Langenscheidts Handwörterbuch Englisch 2001; see also Chapter 7 in this volume). The German diversity reveals how chronic is the semantic overloading of these three terms in English.

It is of more than of passing significance that the Prussian intellectual traditions – notably 'the application of the scientific method ... and development of rational-legal modes of order' – of the mid-nineteenth century were a direct influence on the development of business education in the United States of America (Mintzberg 2004: 21). But, as Craig (1991: 318) has pointed out, the associated language of German nineteenth-century scholarship was loftily pedantic, riven with what he termed 'professorial profundity'. When Hampden-Turner and Trompenaars (1994: 20) noted that the language of management in the USA is characterized by the 'sheer extent of codification and preformulation', it may well be that that trait is a vestige, and a marked one at that, of nineteenth-century German professorial thinking.

In German, although there are several words for managing in organizational contexts, it is not easy to suggest that there is one that stands out as being, as it were, especially generic. However, two words with primary meaning 'to lead' are of importance: *führen* and *leiten*. When these verbs are used to build various German words for manager and management, the verb *führen* tends to be more significantly associated with the exercise of greater power and authority. The derived nouns for management tell the story. The word *Leitung* often refers to management in non-commercial organizations in contrast to *Führung*, which embraces not only management in the commercial sphere but in other endeavours ranging from politics to sport. The noun *Führung* refers to the process of management as a strategically guiding activity. But this is not the word for management as a collective of dynamic leaders. For this German uses the word *Führungskräfte*, a combination of 'leading' and 'power', the *kräfte* element implying the notion of resource (cf. *Arbeitskräfte* 'work' + s for euphony + 'power' = workforce).

Connoisseurs of the term leadership may be interested to note that the German word *führen* 'to lead' is a factitive verb, derived from the old German word *faran*, meaning 'to travel' (the English word 'fare' as in 'fare you well' is cognate with *faran*). Factitive verbs are those which indicate the causation of a process (Priebsch and Collinson 1962: 250–51; Neuberger 2002: 7–11). Thus the deep semantics of *führen* suggest the idea of causing others to travel as companions or followers, which suggests that in German a leader should be an inspirational personage.

We might interject here that there is a Russian word for manager with associations of leading. The word *rukovoditel'*, which is a compound based on the Russian word for hand *ruka* and the word for leader or guide *voditel'*. Its nominal semantic ground happens to be very close to the Latin *manceps*: but if Russian managers 'lead' by the hand, Romans 'take' by the hand. The word *rukovodite'l* can apply to leaders in the economy or in politics and was established in these meanings in the Soviet period.

Discussion

In the foregoing sections we have applied a philological approach to portray language as an ever-evolving societal resource which managers draw upon, augment, embroider and, as Watson (2004: 73) has noted, even use as a device for obscuring any 'outward and audible sign of inner state of angst and potential managerial incapacity'. Seen in this light, language can not only throw fresh light on the nature of human and organisational communication in the modern business world, but explain even well-known phenomena in a new light. We will touch on five key factors which shape experience at societal, organizational and personal level, manifest themselves in distinctive ways according to the actual language of management in question: a) societal stances on management; b) etymological differences and linguistic change; c) capacity to create new terms; d) culture-specific semantic zoning; and e) the English language as intellectual comfort zone and blind spot. We shall refer to some European languages and to Japanese, which is arguably the most important 'non-Western' language of management.

Societal stances on management

That management is perceived differently in different cultures as a social good as well as an economic function is well established (Hampden-Turner and Trompenaars 1994; Hofstede 1980; Koen 2005). Recent writings about Russia suggest that Russians are preferring to create a native lexis of management as a reflection of the centuries-long Russian wariness of dependence on the West for all forms of progress, even including management terminology (Holden and Fink 2007; Jacobs, 2001; Pshenichnikova 2003; Rathmayr 2002). In Germany, a manager does not have to be regarded for his social skills; he or she must able to impress both superiors and subordinates with his outstanding functional knowledge. That person must therefore speak German with formal, function-related authority (Ganter and Walgenbach 2002; Nees 2000). This appears to be a strongly German trait plainly manifest in the language behaviour.

This contrasts with management in France, where a manager is expected to speak French not only with grammatical precision but also with disputatious adroitness (see Barzini 1984: 121). In Japan a manager would be expected to speak Japanese with grammatical precision (and write it neatly) in such a way as to *avoid being* disputatious, as this could cause much loss of face. In their own cultural ambiences the French manager and the Japanese manager must be *equivalently* skilled in their use of language for desired effect. It would seem that contrastive studies of the use of management language as an instrument of professional assertiveness could identify some remarkable culturally ordained differences in communication style.

Etymological differences and linguistic change

The English word for management derives from the Latin for hand, but with equestrian associations. German uses two separate verbs for leading (*führen* and *leiten*) as a basis for many words for management. A French word 'cadre' is derived from military science and was absorbed into Russian as management concept for communist society. The English verb 'manage' has spawned other words. But there is no equivalent process with verbs 'to manage' in other languages.

The English word 'manage' has spread across certain types of control function which according to some people are strictly speaking not management (e.g. cross-cultural management for 'coping with cultural differences'; image management for promotion and manipulation of images; talent management for bringing to prominence people with valuable skills and knowledge). The word management first described an activity. It then referred to a collective of managers. It later extended its meaning to denote management as an object of academic study. In British labour history, management was the 'boss class'. It otherwise acquired a host of subsidiary meanings ranging from the care of patients and medical conditions to the cultivation of land and the process of manuring. English seems to be unique in allowing its 'central' word for management to embrace such an enormous semantic range. In American society in contrast to British society it might be said that being a manager is prerequisite to becoming a leader.

But the most striking feature of this linguistic change is that the academic management community and professional associations of management in the USA and UK, as the two most influential English-speaking countries, have taken so little care about the evolving terminology of management. As suggested by Watson (2004), management does not take care of its specialist language as do other professionals such as lawyers, engineers or medical practitioners. There is no guardian body of management terminology, no authoritative body in the English-speaking world that inveighs against the resulting 'managerial pseudojargon' (Watson 2004: 67–82) and the tendency to 'repetition of emphatic phrases [that] can cause an inflationary process that devalues their currency' (Deutscher 2005: 62). Emblematic of the general indifference is that a leading dictionary of management does not even have an entry for management (Cooper and Argyris 1998) or that there is massive indifference to the fate of English-language management terminology in other languages.

Capacity to create new terms

Related to linguistic change is the generation of management and business neologisms, of which American English is the catalyst par excellence. No other language of management, including that of British management, can compete with America's inventive resourcefulness and global reach of its terminology. As noted earlier, the new mintings are often created for effect; no-one cares whether they are straightforward to translate in other languages. Words like 'excellence', 'change', 'bottom line', 'cash and carry', 'shopping experience' and 'white knight tax' often defeat translators especially in countries like China and the former socialist countries of Europe, which have not yet digested the language of the market economy. In textbooks on international management it is common for authors to advocate 'tolerance to ambiguity'; yet a major cause of interlingual ambiguity is created by terminological unprofessionalism, which may be seen as the most striking philological feature of English as a language of management.

New coinages which are verbs are especially troublesome to translate into other languages. For complicated morphological reasons foreign languages can absorb nouns more easily into their grammatical systems than verbs. For example, Rathmayr (2002) found that in a list of 166 business 'loan' words from English in Russian, only four were verbs. In a rare instance of a foreign language being more succinct than English the Russians have coined a verb 'to internet', meaning to surf the Internet. It should not be forgotten that English has no problem converting nouns into verbs. But in Polish it is impossible to convert the native word for market (*rynek*) into the verb 'to market', let alone a noun based on that noun meaning 'marketing'. The verb 'to network' in Polish is, literally, 'to connect to a network' (France *et al.* 2006: 218).

Culture-specific semantic zoning and the problem of equivalence

From the treatment of various words for management in various languages it is evident that these words occupy differing semantic zones and are associated with culture-specific connotations. For example, we suggested earlier that there is in Germany and France a tacit view about how managers should display their competence in their native language. We argued too that the English words manager and management are displacing rather than replacing corresponding native words in Russian and Polish. For its part, the Japanese language maintains (through the complexities of their writing system) a marked visual distinction between imported management terminology and native word-stock.

For example, the Japanese have borrowed the English term 'knowledge management', but there is also a corresponding Japanese expression. The English expression (i.e. *norejji manajimento*) refers to knowledge management as performed by foreigners; the Japanese expression is exclusive to the Japanese, whose way have the advantage of performing that activity with a device denied to all foreigners, namely the 'unique' Japanese brain (Holden 2001a: 158). In short, terms for management behaviour in the widest send of the word are not semantically equivalent across languages and the differences are encoded in language-distinctive ways. The semantic zones are not isomorphic, as each language is a unique repository of managerial notions and experience, occupying distinctive semantic territory and communicating distinctive realities.

The words for manager and management in various languages are not then semantic clones of each other. They are relative to each other. More precisely, they enjoy *equivalence*, which co-varies cross-culturally according to several factors highlighted above. Equivalence is a known concept in various fields such as law, psychology and ethics and a notable branch of linguistics, namely translation studies. The translator's ultimate task is to achieve equivalence in a target language of a text in the source language (Sager 1994). For her part, Baker (2005) has identified five different categories of equivalence at word level and above word level: grammatical equivalence, textual equivalence (thematic and information structures),

212 Management in other languages

textual equivalence (cohesion), pragmatical equivalence. At word level she identifies 11 different forms of equivalence (Baker 2005: 21–26), which cover such phenomena as the non-lexicalization of source language concepts in the target language, the prevalence of different distinctions in meaning between the source and target languages, the semantic complexity of the source-language word.

To the management specialist, even the one concerned with the impact of culture on management, such an array of forms of equivalence may appear to be confusing, hair-splitting, or even trivial. But the most important point to grasp about equivalences is that they are not to be presupposed, but rather are to be discovered in the exploration of management cultures. In other words, the discovery of equivalences stems from insight or intuition. Foreign-language knowledge is the best tool we have for the discovery of equivalence among management cultures. The purpose of this chapter has been to support that conviction.

The English language as an intellectual comfort zone and blind spot

Very few English-speaking management scholars have any interest in language either as an historical accretion or as mode of expression of managers in languages. Such a state of affairs, directly linked to the general monoglottism of the USA and UK management scholarship, leads to the intellectual impoverishment of management studies, whereby the English language, far from acting as a great universal distributor of management knowledge, operates at best as a filter and at worst a distorting mirror of that knowledge. As Caulkin (2005: 5) has noted: 'English is a one-way membrane that all too often filters out the rest of the world.'

As we have already inferred, English is not the language of instant management enlightenment for once-benighted socialist countries. It is a source of persistent confusions; confusions as mistranslations in Western textbooks and misunderstandings in cross-cultural business interactions that are replicating themselves thousands of times a day from Central Europe to Vladivostok (Holden and Fink 2007; Kuznetsov and Yakavenka 2005). These impediments to knowledge transfer and business development are for the most part unanticipated and undetected, costing corporations cumulatively massive sums of money in misdirected resources through knowledge depletion, talent waste and strategic readjustment (Hurt and Hurt 2005). Firms who think such things are attributable to 'cultural differences' are completely missing the big picture. Language barriers do more than prevent mutual understanding; they create false trails, protract dialogue, block the establishment of common cognitive ground between *Weltanschauungen*.

We suggest that the linguistically induced ethnocentrism in the English-speaking world is not only the biggest constraint on the intellectual

development of international management studies. It is an as yet unacknowledged form of 'mechanistic pooling' (Knights and Wilmott 1997),
whereby the world of management as enacted via the English language is
blinded silo-like to corresponding enactments *in any other language.*

Conclusion

In this chapter we have demonstrated how management language is not
only a contemporary manifestation, but it is also historically and culturally
conditioned in multiple socio-cultural locales. Geert Hofstede, doyen of the
study of culture and management, noted that the term management is used
across the world but its meaning differed from one country to another and
that 'it takes considerable historical and cultural insight into local conditions to understand its processes, philosophies, and problems ... Management is not a phenomenon that can be isolated from other processes taking
place in a society.' (Hofstede 1993: 89)

Consistent with that point of view, we have adopted a philological
approach, whereby the linguistic, the cultural and the historical facets of
management can be analytically conjoined. We suggested this can be
achieved by comparing and contrasting etymologies and semantic zoning
across five European languages. The pursuit of philology and management
is not for those who prefer orderly frameworks and who are not inclined to
look beyond the parapets of the English language. It is for those who
endorse Solé's (2006: 30) conviction that 'The less we question our language,
the more we become prisoners of the world view which it conveys.'

Managers, it may be said, are in a very real sense creations of their own
use of language; their discursive world reflects and is reflected in the specific
language of their native culture. For management scholars to explore the
language of management as presented in this contribution would be a
challenge of a very high intellectual order. Philologically speaking, managers, whatever country they are operating in, do truly extraordinary things
with language in their professional endeavours, whilst their particular languages (English, French, Russian, Japanese and so forth) are culturally distinctive kinds of mental repositories and descriptors of organizational
behaviour as well as management know-how and performance. Much to its
intellectual detriment the world of management education and research has
shown little interest in such things.

15 Conclusion

International management and translation

In this final chapter I review the case studies and applications (and other examples) presented in the book. The drawing together of the empirical evidence will be framed through a particular theoretical lens, which as it is proposed, carries the potential of a unifying framework for a systematic comment on empirical richness. Its ideas are taken from 'translation theory' (or studies) as 'the formulation of concepts designed to illuminate and to improve the practice of translation' (Venuti 2004: 13). However, rather than presenting the technical vocabulary of translation studies in depth and introducing myriad new terminology in the concluding chapter, I shall first draw on the main positions and expositions of translation studies and to synthesize the ideas of the book.

The chapter will briefly comment on approaches taken to the subject matter of translation and then proceed to introduce one particular theoretical contribution which posits translation studies as central to understanding language strategies in international business (Janssens *et al.* 2004). The metaphorical perspectives on language strategies (mechanical, cultural and political) suggested by these authors together with the four dimensions of language use (see Chapter 2) are used to draw the applications of Part II together in such a way as to highlight the relative and constructionist character of the events and outcomes captured in Chapters 7–13. In concluding, it is suggested that translation theory/studies is an adept and appropriate point of reference to understand processes of knowledge transfer as it is aimed at creating 'common cognitive ground'; which is exactly what translation, a form of interlingual communion, is (Holden and von Kortzfleisch 2004: 129).

Translation: the transfer of meaning

If language were simply a nomenclature for a set of universal concepts, it would be easy to translate from one language to another. One would simply replace the French name for a concept with the English name. If language were like this the task of learning a new language would be much easier than it is. ... languages are not nomenclatures, ... the concepts of one language ... may differ radically from those of another. ... Each language articulates or organizes the world differently. Languages do not simply name existing categories, they articulate their own.

(Culler 1976: 21–22)

Translation theory is built on particular assumptions about language use (Venuti 2004); the two main one being 'instrumental' and 'hermeneutic' (cf. Kelly 1979). The instrumental one sees a clear and unambiguous relationship between language and empirical reality and translation equals the transfer of objective information. Cleary, the above quote by Culler and the position of this book are more aligned with the second category, the hermeneutic one. According to this approach, language is seen as interpretation, constitutive of thought and meaning and meanings are bound to changing cultural and social contexts. Translation theory here includes interpretive processes and explains meaning differences in terms of social functions and effects. Likewise, the reasoning and examples of this book have shown that acts of translations and meaning transfer occur in particular contexts, which shape and impact upon the communicative process – i. e. the communicated content is subject to interpretation. This is not just so for translating between two different languages, but also for communicating within one language. It is proposed that translating activity is akin to communication as every act of linguistic exchange requires acts of interpretation and 'meaning-making' (Tietze *et al.* 2003). George Steiner (1976: 49; emphasis in original), the great scholar and commentator on translation, suggests that: '*inside and between languages, human communication equals translation. A study of translation is a study of language.*'

The relevance of translation studies for international management is therefore twofold as: a) the organizational reality of international and multinational organizations is produced through communicative processes in which multiple languages interact. In this regard international managers need to be able to translate or mediate between different languages; b) international managers also need to mediate or translate inside the same language (in many cases this is English) as any form of communication is subject to interpretation and the use of a 'common corporate language' is by no means a guarantee that meaning and knowledge are shared unequivocally and evenly. On the contrary, the use of a common corporate language may create the illusion of the generation of common meaning and purpose; yet as many empirical studies have shown, this would be a false conclusion to draw.

Thus, the differentiating element between 'managers' and 'international managers' is that the former translate within the same language; the latter translate between the same language as well as between different languages. Increasingly in multinational organizations such 'translation activity' is not restricted to the top echelon of managers or those on expatriate assignments – rather through information technology, new organizational forms and network structures many more managers and other personnel interact frequently in multiple languages as well as using English as a business lingua franca. Network structures in particular require the interaction of personnel and managers beyond their traditional functional or departmental role – in other words, even if working in a shared mother tongue, cross-functional and departmental interactions require strenuous translation activity between organizational groups.

Perspectives on language strategies

The three scholars Janssens, Lambert and Steyaert (2004) traced translation studies through its development and suggested that taking recourse to its approaches can inform the understanding of language strategies as they see the 'organizational reality of international companies as being produced through the communicative process in which multiple languages interact' (2004: 415). They develop a metaphorical approach to framing the language strategies of international companies, which each metaphor (mechanical, cultural, political) capturing specific elements of language and culture – thus offering alternatives for conceptualising international communication.

Their approach is summarized here and amalgamated with the four dimensions of language use (descriptive/categorizing; phatic; performative; hegemonial) as there are considerable similarities between both attempts to provide a systematic means to capture complex and shifting language processes.

The *mechanical perspective* aims at formulating abstract rules for translation of the original text to ensure equivalence between it and the translated text. It is based on a fixed and static view of communication and exchange of meaning, which is controlled by the person/s who commissioned the translation and the translator. Language is taken to be a technical system through which to transfer information; meaning is reproduced, rather than produced. Language strategies based on this perspective are likely to select a common corporate language as it is considered to be a neutral code. Should translators be needed, they are seen as 'talented' technicians and expected to produce uniform texts across the company (Janssens *et al.* 2004: 419–420).

The *cultural perspective* views acts of translation as a mediation between different cultures as they are viewed to form part of a larger socio-cultural context. Translation is intercultural activity and aims to relate two different meanings systems. In doing so, translation can be viewed as a cultural process and 'mistakes' that deviate from the original texts are indeed necessary to create new understanding in the different culture. Translation functions as a zone between the original text and the translated one, where meaning is produced, not merely reproduced. Language strategies based on this thinking will allow for multiple languages to exist and use them according to the requirements of different situations and demands. Translation requirements are often performed by native speakers as they are considered to be most conversant with the specificities of their culture and able to adjust texts as necessary, so that potential users can understand them. Translators are mediators between different cultural meaning systems (Janssens *et al.* 2004: 422–424).

The *political perspective* is similar to the cultural perspective as it acknowledges the existence of different linguistic-cultural meaning systems, but also sees them embedded in political decision-making processes as in every translation processes at least two traditions meet, which implies at least a modicum of conflict and attempt to dominate one another. Thus, decisions whether to use a common corporate language and which one to select are inevitable constitutive and reflective of the exercise of power of one cultural-linguistic group over another. Within this tradition translation is neither a mechanical switching of codes, nor an equal transfer of cultural knowledge, but every translation and communication process is informed by degrees of negotiation, manipulation, influence or resistance. Language strategies based on this perspective see language and cultures as reflecting differences in status and power. Thus, decisions about which language/s will be used in the corporation are choices about which groups or individuals will be involved in the international communication process and which ones are likely to be more marginalized or ignored. Language fluency in the dominant language/s becomes a source of expert power. Translators are then part of the negotiation process who can guard the interest of particular groups as parley between the different values systems and discourses that they encounter (Janssens *et al.* 2004: 424–428).

In Chapter 2 several dimensions of language use have been established: descriptive/categorizing; phatic; performative; and hegemonial. These can be partly aligned with the metaphorical frames suggested by Janssens *et al*. The descriptive dimension is related to the mechanical frame as social and organizational worlds are divided into categories, subjects and groups which provide labels and 'words' for the ordering of the world and for translation activities from one language into another. Their cultural frame can be likened to the phatic dimension with its communicative intent to share a common purpose and identity amongst diverse groups. The hegemonial dimension can be associated with the political frame as the emergence of order is seen in the light of political and power-imbued processes.

The four dimensions also include a performative axis, which stresses that each act of using language is an act of reproducing the world or even of producing a different world. It stresses the generative, creative function of language, without which any form of change remains difficult to explain. This dimension is an overarching one and contains the other three dimensions in it.

International managers have been defined (see Chapter 4) as having excellent language proficiency – including rhetorical skill such as use of persuasion, humour, negotiation and motivation. In addition, they were seen to be equipped with the understanding of their organizations' business objectives and purpose to create and provide a trajectory for the multi-cultural and linguistic activities they have to steer.

The words chosen for this language-sensitive definition of international managers (persuasion, humour, etc.) indicate that there are mechanical as well as cultural and political elements to their work as they have to communicate and generate sufficient shared understanding to generate action in line with – or indeed sometimes challenging – the objectives and purposes of the organization. It is therefore not far fetched to extend the above metaphorical frames to international managers and view them as engaged in acts of translations, in which meaning is produced, reproduced and negotiated – or imposed. Their particular role in communicating and translating meaning is to preserve the business focus while they are sustaining and creating the global networks in which communicational exchanges and meaning transfer increasingly occur – thus, rendering the translation process more large-scale and complex. Ultimately, the responsibility of international managers is to ensure that knowledge between different groups, be they functional, departmental, professional, cultural and linguistic is exchanged in order to sustain the competitiveness and value of the products and services provided by their organization. This process has become known as 'knowledge transfer' which Holden and von Kortzfleisch (2004) liken to acts of translation. Translation is seen as 'the oldest universal practice of conscientiously converting knowledge from one domain (i.e. a language group) to another' (Holden and von Kortzfleisch 2004: 129) – yet, these authors, too, argue that knowledge transfer, like translation, is a culturally and politically sensitive activity, which occurs in frequently ambiguous circumstances. Yet, the purpose of international knowledge transfer remains to 'find cross-cultural equivalence' (Holden and von Kortzfleisch 2004: 133), i. e. a state in which a shared view, purpose and priority can emerge and is shared between different cultural and linguistic groups. International managers can therefore be likened to translators, who have to ensure that flows of knowledge connect in such ways to allow for consensual and purposeful activity to emerge. As translators they have access to at least two languages, of which English is likely to be one, but they also need access to different occupational, departmental or functional meaning systems as they translate both *between and within* languages.

Revisiting applications

Chapters 7–13 were applications of the ideas introduced in Part 1. They were diverse in scope, content and style, deliberately reflecting the richness of approaches to understanding the activities of international managers and cultural and linguistic collaborations. They shall be briefly revisited here in order to integrate them into the final intellectual suggestions of this book.

Chapter 7 investigated the German language in its historical and cultural context and showed that German managers are inclined to use their language as an authority-marking vehicle used to achieve *Klarheit* (clarity) through displays of expounded knowledge. The purpose of communication is then less to built community (phatic dimension) as to use language to share (technical) information (descriptive/categorizing function) and to impress an audience, which points to a political-hegemonial use of language exercised through the skilled display of knowledge.

Chapter 8 tracks the linguistic and knowledge developments in Russia since the collapse of the Soviet Union in 1991 through a linguistic and translation lens and points to key difficulties to finding 'equivalent' terminology as meaning is shown to be situated in specific economic and historical contexts. The outcome of knowledge transfer (unilateral one from 'West to East'; indicating a hegemonial flow of knowledge) is an uneasy amalgam of Russian and English (*russgliskii*). The chapter is an excellent case to show that the mere technical translation of words (descriptive/categorizing dimension) does not suffice to transfer knowledge as a) integrating the English language structure and terminologies into the Russian language proofed difficult and b) the meaning systems (discourses) of business and commerce did not exist to support the transfer or meaning.

Chapter 9 looked at the nexus of ties between language/s and careers in multinational corporations. It showed that requirements for language skills will remain high in the corporate world – despite the advance of English as the lingua franca of business and management and its frequent adoption as the common corporate language. Summarizing the existing research on this topic, it is shown that decisions to use particular languages carry strong emotional messages (phatic dimension) and can create unity as well as disunity, is imbued in hegemonial processes (allowing 'voice' to some language speakers, but not to others) and can either propel forward or hinder individual careers as well as support or undermine organizational performance. In one study discussed in the chapter (Piekkari *et al.* 2005) the introduction of Swedish as the common corporate language following a merger had serious consequences for some Finnish staff as they could not longer participate in occupational and organizational affairs as they lacked the idiom and skills to actively participate in relevant professional debates (descriptive dimensions).

Chapter 10 tracked the emergence of a new structural reality in a Dutch chemical multinational, AKZO. Overall, the case study demonstrates the performative dimension of language as a new and unknown concept, the business unit, was introduced by the CEO. This word and the structural concept behind it derived from a different cultural-commercial context (American) and the events as they unfold in the case study (captured in different language events and meetings) show that the organization had to work hard at adopting this new structure and at making sense of what the word 'business unit' meant to AKZO. The transition from the divisional structure to a business unit structure was reflected and constituted by language-based processes, monologues and dialogues and the skilled rhetorical interventions and actions of the CEO. The totality of re-describing the company's structure (descriptive/categorizing dimension), political manoeuvrings and negotiations (hegemonial dimension) together with efforts to create a unifying structure and sense of purpose (phatic dimension) resulted in a creating of a new reality for AKZO (performative dimension) in so far as tasks and roles were redesigned and reallocated in an ultimately radical re-ordering of the organization.

Chapter 11 analysed the linguistic exchanges in a French–Japanese business meeting, which was held in English as the joint lingua franca. In this regard the chapter provides a good example of the use of English between two groups of non-native speakers of English. Yet it also shows that cultural and group-oriented behaviour (phatic dimension) continues to inform the communicative exchanges between the participants and that experience in using the English language in overseas business provides an advantage to speakers (hegemonial dimension) as they can articulate their views with greater ease.

Chapter 12 draws on a variety of empirical materials to shed light on the use of languages and changes in management styles in an Italian context. The notion of 'groupness' as it derives from some of the empirical material is an interesting concept and relates to the phatic dimension of language. Here, it is shown how multilingual groups have to create a shared sense of purpose and identity ('groupness') which is achieved through rhetorical means such as the use of pronouns, style and tone of speech and speech events, the use of English as well as other languages, informal translation activities. Interestingly, the occasional use of languages other than English serves to facilitate understanding and share pertinent product details – details which might have been overseen if English had been adhered to all the time (descriptive dimension); their use also stresses the existence of the multicultural character of the group and is an important symbolic indicator of tolerance and respect.

Chapter 13 is a study of the use of humour and humorous language in an English context. It is thus a chapter exploring the phatic dimension of language use (as using the language of humour has strong group defining and building capabilities) and how it is utilized in business contexts and managers. In social and organizational life humour is used in manifold ways as a playful device to comment on and play with the shapes and forms of social reality (performative function), to forge group cohesion (phatic function), to support or subvert hierarchies (hegemonial function).

From the point of view of international management, these applications point to several important 'language lessons': a) there is the importance of English as the business lingua franca, which is increasingly the channel through which international communications flow; b) yet, the use of English has not undermined the existence or influence of other languages; c) culture and historical context provide the bedrock within which knowledge is transferred and translated – relying on the unifying power of one language only, frequently English, means glossing over continued differences in meaning; d) having access to rhetorical skills and being able to use language/s in a sophisticated manner, which includes the appropriate and context-sensitive use of all four dimensions of language will be characteristic of the future work of international managers as they are the knowledge brokers in networks of global information flow.

Conclusion

This book started by stressing the importance of language ('language matters') for understanding the increasingly global and networked realities of business and management. It was argued that through such networks knowledge is flowing – yet, that knowledge is always coded in semantic systems of syntax and generated in cultural, political and historical contexts. If knowledge is to flow between differently constituted parts of the network, great skill is required to ensure that it is shared in such ways to facilitate mutual understanding. Translation is a vital part of making knowledge flow and ensuring that shared meaning is achieved. International managers are such knowledge workers and language experts who translate *between* languages as well as *within the same* language to ensure that the transfer of ideas and information is successful. Defining them as such is not to detract from the technical expertise they have or the hierarchical roles they inhabit; rather it is to point to the neglected area of international management and business, i.e. to language processes, which provide the ground and trajectory for knowledge activity to occur.

The reality of many organizations and communities is likely to become increasingly multilingual and multicultural. English is a superb source to generate mutual intelligibility between diverse groups. There is no reason to either condemn it as part of a hidden ideological agenda to subvert other languages and cultures; nor is there any reason to celebrate powers it does not possess, i.e. the power to create harmonious understanding and to end all misunderstanding. Yet, combined with the lexis of business and management discourses it wields influence to shape business agendas, transform interactions and mould careers and lives. The craft of the international managers is a language-based one in which effectiveness of performance is dependent on the skilled use of a common communicative tool, while remaining sensitive to linguistic diversity and difference and to translate such sometimes opposing forces into united understanding and action.

The study of these processes has made some progress as scholars have begun to investigate the language and cultural realities of multinational organizations. Yet, much more advance could be made by scholars from different traditions working together to enhance theoretical insights and to contribute grounded knowledge of emergent and existing language strategies.

References

Abalkin, L. (1989) 'Vorwärts wie eine Schildkröte', *Der Spiegel* (15).

Abramishvili, G. (1991) Interview in *Ekonomika i Zhizn*, 45: 8.

Ackroyd, S. and Thompson, P. (1999) *Organizational Misbehaviour*, London: Sage.

Adam, B. (1995) *Timewatch. The Social Analysis of Time*, Cambridge: Polity Press.

Adler, N. (1991) *International Dimensions of Organizational Behaviour*, Boston, MASS.: PWS-Kent Pub. Co.

Agar, M. (1994) *Language Shock. Understanding the Culture of Conversation*, New York: William Morrow and Company.

AKZO (1964–1986) berichten.

——(1982) 'A new spirit', Arnhem.

——(1982 and 1984) *Annual Reports*, Arnhem.

——(1986) Nightingale Report to Loudon, *Weaknesses and Synergies*, 28 March.

——(1987) Archival documents, draft corporate history.

——(1987–94) News and Views, Arnhem

—— (1987) First management letter BU organization no. 1, Dec.

——(1991) Business Units–The basis of the AKZO organization, Arnhem.

Alemanni, B. (2002) 'The Cems and the training of European managers', in L. Schena and L.Soliman (eds) *Prospettive linguistiche della Nuova Europe*, 51–54, Milan: Egea.

Alvesson, M. and Kärremann, D. (2000) 'Taking the linguistic turn in organizational research. Challenges, responses, consequences', *The Journal of Applied Behavorial Science*, 36 (2): 136–158.

Alvesson, M. and Willmott, H. (1992) *Critical Management Studies*, London: Sage.

Alvesson, M. and Willmott, H. (1996) *Making Sense of Management: A Critical Introduction, London: Sage.*

——(2002) 'Identity regulation as organizational control: producing the appropriate individual', *Journal of Management Studies,* 39 (5): 619–644.

——(2003) *Studying Management Critically*, London: Sage.

Anderman, G. and Rogers, M. (eds) (2005) *In and Out of English: For Better, For Worse?*, Clevedon: Multilingual Matters Ltd.

Anderson, C. (2003) 'Phillipson's children. Review article', *Language and Inter-cultural Communication*, 3 (1): 81–95.

Applebaum, A. (2003) *Gulag: A History of the Soviet Camps*, London: Allen Lane.

Ardagh, J. (1987) *Germany and the Germans: An Anatomy of Society Today*, London: Hamish Hamilton.

Arens, E. (1994) *The Logic of Pragmatic Thinking*, New Jersey: Humanities Press.

Armbrüster, T. (2005) *Management and Organization in Germany*, Aldershot: Ashgate Publishing.

Association of Business Schools (2001) *Pillars of the Economy: The Contribution of UK Business Schools to the UK Economy*, London: Association of Business Schools.

Austin, J.L. (1962) *How to Do Things with Words*, Cambridge, MA: Harvard University Press.

Baker, M. (2005) *In other Words: A Course Book on Translation*, London: Routledge.

Bargiela-Chiappini, F. (2001) 'Management, culture and discourse in international business', in M. Stroinska (ed.) *Relative Points of View. Linguistic Representations of Culture*, 144–160, Oxford: Berghahn Books.

——(2005) 'Book review: Gina Poncini discursive strategies in multicultural Business Meetings', *English for Specific Purposes*, 24: 447–452.

——(2006) '(Whose) English(es) for Asian business discourse(s)?', Editorial, *Journal of Asian Pacific Communication*, 16 (1): 1–23.

Bargiela-Chiappini, F., Bülow-Moller, Nickerson, C., Poncini, G. and Zhu Yunxia (2003) 'Five perspectives on intercultural business communication', *Business Communication Quarterly*, 66 (3): 73–96.

Bargiela-Chiappini, F. and Nickerson, C. (2003) 'Intercultural business communication: a rich field of studies', *Journal of Intercultural Studies*, 24 (1): 15.

Bargiela, F. and Turra, E. (2004) 'Organizational change from old to new economy: exploring consensus and conflict in business meetings', paper presented at the conference 'Discourse, Ideology and Ethics in Specialized Communication', Milan, October.

——(in press) 'Organisational change in corporate meetings', in S. Sarangi and G. Garzone (eds), *Discourse and Ideology in Specialised Communication*, Bern: Peter Lang.

Barner-Rasmussen, W. and Björkman, I. (2005) 'Surmounting interunit barriers', *International Studies of Management and Organization*, 35 (1): 28–46.

Barry, D., Carroll, B. and H. Hansen (2006) 'From text or context? Endotextual, exotextual, and multi–textual approaches to narrative and discursive organizational studies', *Organization Studies*, 27 (8):1091–1110.

Barsoux, J.L. and Lawrence, P. (1990) *The Challenge of British Management*, Basingstoke: Macmillan.

Baruch, Y. (2006) 'Career development in organizations and beyond: Balancing traditional and contemporary viewpoints', *Human Resource Management Review*, 16: 125–138.

Barzini, L. (1984) *The Europeans*, London: Penguin Books.

Bass, B. (1999) 'From transactional to transformational leadership. Learning to share the vision, *Empowerment in Organizations*, 5: 14–15.

Bate, P. (1994) *Strategies for Cultural Change*, Oxford: Butterworth.

Beccaria, G. (1973) *Linguaggi settoriali in Italia*, Milano: Bompiani.

Beeton, I. (1861) *The Book of Household Management* (Facsimile 1968), London: Jonathan Cape.

Bender, R. and Stromberg, K. (2000) *Culture. Com. Building Corporate Culture in the Connected Workplace*, Ontario: John Wiley and Sons.

Berger, P. and Luckmann, T. (1966) *The Social Construction of Reality*, New York: Doubleday and Co.

Bloch, B. (1995) 'Career enhancement through foreign language skills', *International Journal of Career Management*, 7 (6): 15–26.

Bloch, B. and Starks, D. (1999) 'The many faces of English: intra-language variation and its implications for international business', *Corporate Communications*, 4 (2): 80–88.

Block, D. (2002) 'McCommunication': a problem in the frame for SLA', in D. Block and D. Cameron (eds) *Globalization and Language Teaching*, 117–33, London: Routledge.

Block, D. and Cameron, C. (eds) (2002) *Globalization and Language Teaching*, London: Routledge.

Boddewyn, J.J. (1997) 'The conceptual domain of international business: territory, boundaries, and levels', in B. Toyne and D. Nigh (eds) *International Business: an Emerging Vision*, 50–61, Columbia: University of South Carolina Press.

Boden, D. (1994) *The Business of Talk: Organisations in Action*, Cambridge: Polity Press.

Boje, D.M. (1991) 'The story telling organization: a study of story performance in an office-supply firm', *Administrative Science Quarterly*, 36: 106–126.

Bol'shaya Sovietsaya Entsiklopedia (Great Soviet Encyclopaedia) (1970–78), Vol. 15. Moscow.

Bourdieu, P. (1990) *The Logic of Practice*, Cambridge: Polity Press.

Bournois, F. and Livian, Y.-F. (1997) 'Managers, 'cadres', 'leitende Angestellte': Some landmarks about managerial group titles and definitions', in Y-F. Livian and J. G. Burgoyne (eds) *Middle Managers in Europe*, 25–33, London: Routledge.

Bowers, R. (1986) 'English in the world: aims and achievements in English Language Teaching', *TESOL Quarterly*, 20: 393–410.

Brannen, M.Y. (2004) 'When Mickey loses face: recontextualization, semantic fit and the semiotics of foreigness', *Academy of Management Review*, 29 (4): 593–616.

Brighton, A. (2002) 'Management speak: a master discourse?', *Critical Quarterly*, 44 (3): 1–3.

Brodbeck, F., Frese, M. and Javidan, M. (2002) 'Leadership made in Germany: Low on compassion, high on performance', *Academy of Management Executive*, 16 (1):16–29.

Bruntse, J. (2003) 'It's Scandinavian: Dansk-svensk kommunikation i SAS' (Danish-Swedish communication in SAS), unpublished Master's thesis, Institute for Nordic Philology: University of Copenhagen.

Burchfield, R. (ed.) (1976) *A Supplement to the Oxford English Dictionary*, Oxford: Clarendon Press.

Burke, K. (1941) 'Four master tropes', *Kenyan Review*, 3: 421–438.

Burnham, J. (1941) *The Managerial Revolution*, Bloomington, IN: Indiana University Press.

Burr, V. (2003) *Social Constructionism*, London and New York: Routledge.

Bygate, M. (1987) *Speaking*, Oxford: Oxford University Press.

Cabinet Office (2001) *Foreign Economic Data*, Tokyo: Japan Cabinet Office.

Cameron, D. (2000) *Good to Talk? Living and Working in a Communication Culture*, London: Sage.

——'Globalization and the teaching of "communication skills"', in D. Block and D. Cameron (eds) *Globalization and Language Teaching*, 67–82, London: Routledge.

Canagarajah, A.S. (1999) *Resisting Linguistic Imperialism in English Teaching*, Oxford: Oxford University Press.

Capezzone, Daniele (2006) 'L'impossibile crescita', *Economy* 4 (51): 23.

Cassell's Latin–English English–Latin Dictionary (ed. D.P. Simpson) (1977) London: Cassell & Company Limited.

Caulkin, S. (2005) 'English, language of lost chances', *Observer,* 24 July, 10, (Business).

Champy, J. (1995) *Reengineering Management,* London: HarperCollins.

Chandler, A.D. (1994) 'The functions of the headquarters unit in multibusiness firms', in R.P. Rumelt, D.E. Schendel and D.J. Teece (eds) *Fundamental Issues in Strategy Research,* 323–360, Cambridge,MA: Harvard University Press.

Charles, M. and Marschan-Piekkari, R. (2002) 'Language training for enhanced horizontal communication: A challenge for MNCs', *Business Communication Quarterly,* 65 (2): 9–29.

Chew, K.S. (2005) 'An investigation of the English language skills used by new entrants in banks in Hong Kong', *English for Specific Purposes,* 24: 423–435.

Chia, R. (1996) *Organizational Analysis as Deconstructive Practice,* De Gruyter: London and Berlin.

Chiapello, E. and Fairclough, N. (2003) 'Understanding the new management ideology: a transdisciplinary contribution from critical discourse analysis and new sociology of capitalism', *Discourse and Society,* 13 (2): 185–208.

Clyne, M. (1984) *Language and Society in the German-speaking Countries,* Cambridge: Cambridge University Press.

——(1995) *The German Language in a Changing Europe,* Cambridge: Cambridge University Press.

Cogno, E. (2004) *Come risolvere i problemi. Tecniche per trasformare gli ostacoli in opportunità con il pensiero an*titetico, Milano: Franco Angeli.

Collinson, D.L. (1988) 'Engineering humour: masculinity, joking and conflict in shop floor relations', *Organization Studies,* 9 (2): 181–199.

Conger, J.A. and Kanungo, R.N. (1998) *Charismatic Leadership in Organization.* London: Sage.

Cooper, C.L. and Argyris, C. (eds) (1998) *The Concise Blackwell Encyclopaedia of Management,* Oxford: Blackwell.

Craig, G. (1991) '*The Germans',* New York: Meridian.

Crystal, D. (1997) *The Cambridge Encyclopaedia of Language,* Cambridge: Cambridge University Press.

——(2000) 'On trying to be Crystal-clear: A response to Phillipson', *Applied Linguistics,* 21 (3): 415–423.

——(2003) *English as a Global Language,* 2nd edn, Cambridge: Cambridge University Press.

Culler, J. (1976) *Saussure,* Glasgow: Fontana/Collins.

Currie, G. and Knights, D. (2003) 'Reflecting a critical pedagogy in MBA education', *Management Learning,* 34 (1): 27–49.

Czerniawska, F. (1998) *Corporate Speak. The Use of Language in Business,* London: Macmillan.

Dalby, A. (2002) *Languages in Danger,* Harmondsworth: Penguin.

Dalton, M. (1959) *Men who Manage. Fusions of Feeling and Theory in Administration,* New York: John Wiley & Sons.

Davis, M. (2004) Unicode Technical Note #13: GDP by Language (http://unicode. org/notes/tn13/) Accessed 28 February 2007.

de Cock, C. (1998) 'Organizational change and discourse: hegemony, resistance and reconstitution', *M@n@gement,* 1 (1): 1–22.

Deetz S. (2003a) 'Reclaiming the legacy of the linguistic turn', *Organization,* 10 (3): 421–429.

——(2003b) 'Disciplinary power, conflict suppression and human resources management', in Alvesson and Willmott (eds) *Studying Management Critically*, 23–45, London: Sage.

DeFillippi, R.J. and Arthur, M.B. (1994) 'The boundaryless career: a competency-based perspective', *Journal of Organizational Behavior*, 15 (4): 307–324.

Dehler, G. E., Welsh, M.A. and Lewis, M.W. (2001) 'Critical pedagogy in the "new paradigm"', *Management Learning*, 32 (4): 493–511.

Derrida, J. (1978) *Writing and Difference*, Chicago: University of Chicago Press.

Deutscher, G. (2005) *The Unfolding of Language: The Evolution of Mankind's Greatest Invention*, London: Arrow Books

Devoto, G. (1939) 'Lingue Speciali–Dalle cronache della finanza', *Lingua Nostra*, June, Florence: Sansoni.

Dijk, P. van, J. Kamp and R. Rensen (1985) *De stijl van de leider*, Amsterdam: Bert Bakker.

Donnelon, A. (1996) *Team Talk*, Boston: Harvard Business School Press.

Dowling, P.J. and Welch, D.E. (2004) *International Human Resource Management: Managing People in a Multinational Environment*, 4th edn, London: Thomson Learning.

Drew, P. and Heritage, J. (1992) *Talk at Work. Interaction in Institutional Settings*, Cambridge: Cambridge University Press.

Drucker, P. (1954/1993) *The Practice of Management*, London: Heinemann.

Duden Deutsches Universal Wörterbuch A–Z (1996) Mannheim: Dudenverlag.

du Gay, P. (1996) 'Making up managers: Enterprise and the ethos of bureaucracy', in S.R. Clegg and G. Palmer (eds), *The Politics of Management Knowledge*, 19–35, London: Sage.

Duden (1996) *Deutches Universal Wörterbuch A–Z*, Mannheim: Dudenverlag.

Duranti, A. (2005) *Linguistic Anthropology*, Cambridge: Cambridge University Press.

Dzhincharadze, A.K. (ed.) (1991) *Marketing: tolkovyi terminologicheskii slovar-spravochnik*, Moscov: Infokont.

Eccles, R.G. and N. Nohria (1992) *Beyond the Hype*, Harvard: Harvard Business School Press.

Economist (1999) 'DaimlerChrysler: crunch time', 25 September, 91–92.

Elgin, S.H. (2000) *The Language Imperative*, Cambridge, MA: Perseus Books.

Fairclough, N. (1989) *Language and Power*, London and New York: Longman.

——(2002) 'Language in New Capitalism', *Discourse & Society*, 13 (2): 163–166.

——(2006) 'Discourse analysis in organization studies: the case for critical realism', *Organization Studies*, 26 (6): 915–940.

Fairclough, N. and Thomas, P. (2004) 'The discourse of globalization and the globalization of discourse', in D. Grant, C. Hardy, C. Oswick and L. Putnam (eds), *The Sage Handbook of Organizational Dis*course, 379–396, London: Sage.

Fairhurst, G.T. and Sarr, R.A. (1996) *The Art of Framing. Managing the Language of Leadership*, San Francisco, CA: Jossey-Bass.

Faria, A. and Guedes, A. (2005) 'What is international management? A critical analysis', paper presented at Critical Management Studies Conference, Judge Institute, University of Cambridge, UK, July.

Fayol, H. (1949) *General and Industrial Management*, London: Unwin.

Feely, A.J. (2003) 'Communication across language boundaries', in M. Tabey (ed.) *International Management: Theories and Practices*, 206–235, London: Pearson Education.

Feely, A.J. and Harzing, A.W. (2003) 'Language management in multinational companies', *Cross Cultural Management*,10 (2): 37–52.

Filin, F.P. (ed.) *Entsiklopedia russkogo yazyka*, Moscow: Russkii Yazyk.

Financial Times (1993) 'A cross-cultural minefield', 2 August.

Fink, G. and Holden, N. J. (2002) 'Collective culture shock: contrastive reactions to radical systemic change', Research Institute for European Affairs, Vienna University of Economics and Business Administration. Working paper, 45.

——(2005) 'Introduction: The global transfer of management knowledge', *Academy of Management Executive*, 19 (2): 5–8 May.

Fink, G. and Lehmann, M. (2007) 'People's twist: The cultural standard of loyalty and performance in former socialist economies', in D. Pauleen (ed.), *Cross-cultural Perspectives on Knowledge Management*, 135–154, Westport, CT: Libraries Unlimited.

Ford, J.D. and Ford, L.W. (2003) 'Conversations and the authoring of change', in D. Holman, D and R. Thorpe (eds), *Management and Language*, 141–156, London: Sage.

Forester, N. (2000) 'The myth of the international manager', *International Journal of Human Resource Management*, 11 (1): 126–142.

Foster, P. and Ohta, A.S. (2005) 'Negotiation for meaning and peer assistance in second language classroom', *Applied Linguistics*, 26 (3): 402–430.

Fox, K. (2004) *Watching the English. The Hidden Rules of English Behaviour*, London: Hodder and Stoughton.

Fox, R. and Fox, J. (2004) *Organizational Discourse*, Westport: Praeger Publishers.

France, S. C., Mann, P. and Kolossa. B. (eds) (2006) *Pons Biznesowy sownik tematyczny*, Poznan: Wydawnictwo LektorKlett.

Fredriksson, R. (2005) 'Effects of language diversity in an MNC', unpublished Master's thesis, International Business, Helsinki School of Economics.

Fredriksson, R., Barner-Rasmussen, W. and Piekkari, R. (2006) 'The multinational corporation as a multilingual organization: the notion of a common corporate language', *Corporate Communications: An International Journal*, 11 (4): 406–423.

Freundlich, D. (1994) 'Foucault's theory of discourse and human agency', in C. Jones and R. Porter (eds) *Reassessing Foucault*, 152–180, London: Routledge.

Funder, A. (2003) *Stasiland: Stories from behind the Berlin Wall*, London: Granta Books.

Gabriel, Y. (2000) *Storytelling in Organizations. Facts, Fictions and Fantasies*, Oxford: Oxford University Press.

Ganter, H.-D. and Walgenbach, P. (2002) 'Middle managers: Differences between Britain and Germany', in M. Geppert, D. Matten and K. Williams (eds) *Challenges for European Management in a Global Context: Experiences from Britain and Germany*, 165–88, London: Palgrave Macmillan.

Garton Ash, T. (1997) *The File: A Personal History*, London: Flamingo.

Gee, J. P. (1996) 'Discourses and literacies', in J.P. Gee (ed.) *Social Linguistics and Literacies: Ideology in Discourses*, 122–160, London: Falmer Press.

Gee, J.P., Hull, G. and Lankshear, C. (1996) *The New Work Order. Behind the Language of the New Capitalism*, Boulder, CO: Westview Press.

Gelfert H.D. (1998) *Max und Monty. Kleine Geschichte des deutschen und* englischen *Humors*, München: Beck.

——(2002) *Typisch english. Wie die Briten wurden, was sie sind*, München: Beck.

Geppert, M., Matten. D. and Williams, K. (2002) *Challenges for European Management in a Global Context: Experiences from Britain and Germany*, London: Palgrave Macmillan.

Gerchikova, I.N. (2005) *Management (in Russian)*, Moscov: Unity.

Gesteland, R. (2006) *Cross-cultural Business Behaviour: Negotiating, Selling, Sourcing and Managing across Cultures*, Copenhagen: Copenhagen Business School Press.

Gherardi, S. and D. Nicolini (2000) 'To transfer is to transform: the circulation of safety knowledge', *Organization*, 7 (2): 329–348.

Gibson, C.B. and Zellmer-Bruhn, M. (2001) 'Metaphors and meaning: An intercultural analysis of the concept of teamwork', *Administrative Science Quarterly*, 46: 274–303.

Gioia, D.A, Donnellon, A. and Sims, P.J. (1989) 'Communication and cognition in appraisal: a tale of two paradigms', *Organization Studies*, 10: 503–530.

Goeudevert, D. (2003) *Wie Gott in Deutschland: Eine Liebeserklärung*, München: Econ Verlag.

Golubkov, Y. (1999) *O nekotorykh aspektakh kontseptsii marketinga I ego terminilogii/On some conceptual aspects of marketing and marketing terminology. Marketing v Rossii I za robezhom, 6. Available from http://www.cfin.ru/press/marketing/1999–6/index.shtml.*

Goodwin, C. (1981) *Conversational Organization: Interaction between Speaker and Hearer*, New York: Academic Press.

Graddol, D. (2004) *English Next*, London: British Council.

Gramsci, A. (1971) *Selections from the Prison Notebooks*, London: Lawrence and Wishart.

Grant, D., Keenoy, T. and Oswick, C. (eds) (1998) *Discourse and Organization*, London: Sage.

Grant, D. and Oswick, C. (eds) (1996) *Metaphor and Organizations*, London: Sage.

Gray, J. (2002) 'The global coursebook in English language teaching', in D. Block and D. Cameron (eds) *Globalization and Language Teaching*, 151–167, London: Routledge.

Green, S.E. (2004) 'A rhetorical theory of diffusion', *Academy of Management Review*, 29 (4): 653–669.

Gregersen, H.B., Harrison, D.A. and Black, J.S. and Ferzandi, L.A. (2004) 'You can take it with you: individual differences and expatriate effectiveness' in N. Boyacigiller and T. Kiyak (eds) *Proceedings of the 46th Annual Meeting of the Academy of International Business*, East Lansing, MI: Academy of International Business, 185.

Grey, C. (1999) 'We are all managers now; we always were: on the development and demise of management', *Journal of Management Studies*, 36 (5): 561–585.

——(2005) *A Very Short, Fairly Interesting and Reasonably Cheap Book about Studying Organizations*, London: Sage.

Grey, C. and Mitev, N. (1995) 'Management education: a polemic', *Management Learning*, 26 (1): 73–90.

Grugulis, I. (2002) 'Nothing serious? Candidates' use of humour in management training', *Human Relations*, 55 (4): 387–406.

Guirdham, M. (1999) *Communicating across Cultures*, Basingstoke: Macmillan.

Gudykunst, W.B. (1998) *Bridging Differences: Effective Interrupt Communication*. London: Sage.

——and Lee, C.M. (2002) 'Intercultural communication theories', in: W.B. Gudykunst and B. Mody (eds) *International and Intercultural Communication*, 2nd edn, 25–51, Thousand Oaks: Sage.

Guidelines for Translation of Social Science Texts (2006) *American Council of Learned Societies*, New York. Available from: www.acls.org/sstp.htm.

Haffner, S. (1998) *The Rise and Fall of Prussia*, London: Phoenix.

Hall, E.T. (1973) *The Silent Language*, New York: Anchor Books.

Hall, J.K. and Eggington, W. (eds) (2000) *The Sociopolitics of English Language Teaching*, Clevedon: Multilingual Matters ltd.

Halliday, M.A.K. (2003)'Written language, standard language, global language', *World Englishes*, 22 (4): 405–418.

Halsall, R. (2007) 'The discourse of cosmopolitanism in the global corporation', unpublished working paper, Aberdeen Business School.

Hampden-Turner, C. and Trompenaars, F. (1994) *The Seven Cultures of Capitalism: Value Systems for Creating Wealth in the United States, Britain, Japan, Germany, France, Sweden, and the Netherlands*, London: Judy Piatkus.

Hancock, P. and Tyler, M. (2004) '"MOT your life": critical management studies and the management of everyday life', *Human Relations*, 57 (5): 619–645.

Hardy, C. (2004) 'Scaling up and bearing down in discourse analysis: questions regarding textual agencies and heir contexts', *Organization*, 11 (3): 415–425.

Hardy, C., Palmer, I. and Phillips, N. (2000) 'Discourse as strategic resource', *Human Relations*, 53 (9): 1227–1248.

Harris, S. and Bargiela-Chiappini, F. (2003) 'Business as a site of language contact', *Annual Review of Applied Linguistics*, 23: 155–169.

Hasan, R. (2003) 'Globalization, literacy and ideology', *World Englishes*, 22 (4): 433–448.

Hatch, M.J. (1997) *Organization Theory: Modern, Symbolic and Postmodern Perspectives*, Oxford: Oxford University Press.

Held, D., Goldblatt, D. and Perraton, J. (1999) *Global Transformation*, Cambridge: Polity Press.

Henderson, J. (2005) 'Language diversity in international management teams', *International Studies of Management and Organizations*, 35 (1): 43–54.

Hentze, J. (1995) *Personalwirtschaftslehre 2*, Berne: Verlag Paul Haupt.

Higher Education Statistics Agency. Online documents at URL www/hesa.ac.uk/holisdocs/pubinfo/students/subject0102.htm. (accessed 19 January 2004).

Hinton, D.A. (2002) 'Triangulating the circle: the three laws of management speak', *Critical Quarterly*, 44 (3): 55–62.

Hirst, P. and Thompson, G. (1996) *Globalization in Question*, Cambridge: Polity Press.

Hofstede, G. (1993) 'Cultural constraints in management theories', *Academy of Management Executive*, 7 (1): 88–89.

——(1994a) *Culture and Organizations: Intercultural Cooperation and its Importance for Survival–Software of the Mind*, London: HarperCollins.

——(1994b) 'The Business of international business is culture', *International Business Review*, 3 (1): 1–14.

——(1980/2001) *Culture's Consequences: Comparing Values, Behaviors, Institutions and Organizations across Nations*, Thousand Oakes: Sage.

Holden, N.J. (1991) 'Shades of meaning in Soviet business and management', *European Business Review*, 91 (3): 9–14.

——(2001a) 'Why globalizing with a conservative corporate culture inhibits localization of management: the telling case of Matsushita Electric', *International Journal of Cross Cultural Management*, 1 (1): 53–72.

——(2001b) 'Knowledge management: Raising the spectre of the cross-cultural dimension', *Knowledge and Process Management*, 8 (3): 155–163.

——(2002) *Cross-Cultural Management. A Knowledge Management Perspective.* Harlow: Prentice Hall.

——(2003) 'Making Russian managers: a review of management education in the USSR, and its prospects in post-Soviet society', *Journal of Education Management,* 7 (4): 10–16.

——(2005) *Kross-kulturnyi menedzhment: kontseptsiya kognitivnogo menedzhmenta,* Moscow, Izdatelstvo Yuniti-Dana.

Holden, N.J. and Fink, G. (2007) 'Russia's path to the market economy: its language in slow pursuit', in U.Doleschal, E. Hoffmann and T. Reuther (eds) *Sprache und Diskurs in Wirtschaft und Gesellschaft: interkulturelle Perspektiven,* Frankfurt a. M. Bern, Wien: Peter Lang Verlag.

Holden, N.J. and von Kortzfleisch, H.F.O. (2004) 'Why cross-cultural knowledge transfer is a form of translation in more ways than you think', *Knowledge and Process Management,* 11 (2): 127–136.

Holden, N. J., Cooper, C. L. and Carr, J. (1998) ***Dealing with the New Russia: Management Cultures in Collision,*** Chichester: John Wiley and Sons.

Holman, D. and Thorpe, R. (eds) (2003) *Management and Language,* London: Sage.

Holland, R. (2002) 'Globospeak? Questioning text on the role of English as a global language', *Language and Intercultural Communication,* 2 (1): 5–24.

Holliday, A. (1997) 'The politics of participation in international English language education', *System,* 25: 409–423.

Holman, D. and Thorpe, R. (eds) (2003) *Management and Language,* London: Sage.

House, J. (2003) 'English as a lingua franca: A threat to multilingualism?', *Journal of Sociolinguistics,* 7 (4): 556–578.

House, R. J., Hanges, P. J., Javidan, M., Dorfman, P. and Gupta, V. (eds) (2004) *Leadership, Culture and Organizations: The GLOBE Study of 62 Societies,* Thousand Oaks, CA: Sage Publications, Inc.

Hurt, M. and Hurt, S. (2005) 'Transfer of management practices by French food retailers to operations in Poland', *Academy of Management Executive,* 19 (2): 36–49.

International Financial Review (2006) 'City looks abroad for graduate trainees', September 30: 6.

Jackson, N. and Carter, P. (2000) *Rethinking Organisational Behaviour,* Harlow: Prentice Hall.

Jacobs, E. (2001) 'The influence of Western concepts on Russian marketing theory', *British Journal of Management,* 12: 149–157.

James, H. (2000) *A German Identity: 1770 to the Present Day,* London: Weidenfeld and Nicolson.

Jandt, F.E. (1998) *Intercultural Communication. An Introduction,* London: Sage.

Janssens, M., Lambert, J. and Steyaert, C. (2004) 'Developing language strategies for international companies: the contribution of translation studies', *Journal of World Business,* 39 (4): 414–430.

JETRO (1999) *Communicating Japanese in Business,* Tokyo: Japan External Trade Organization.

Johansson, S. and Graedler, A.L. (2005) 'Anglicisms in Norwegian: when and where?' in G. Anderman and M. Rogers (eds) *In and Out of English: For better of for Worse?,* 185–200, Clevedon: Multilingual Matters Ltd.

Jones, K. (1995) 'Masked negotiation in a Japanese work setting', in A. Firth. (ed.) *The Discourse of Negotiation: Studies of Language in the Workplace,* 141–158, Oxford: Pergamon.

Joseph, J.E. (2004) *Language and Identity. National, Ethnic, Religious*, Houndsmill, Basingstoke: Palgrave Macmillan.

Kachru, B.B. (1985) 'Standards, codification and sociolinguistic realism: the English language in the outer circle', in R. Quirk and H.G. Widdowson (eds) *English in the World: Teaching and Learning the Language and Literatures*, 11–30, Cambridge: Cambridge University Press.

—— (1986) 'The power and politics of English', *World Englishes*, 5 (2/3): 121– 140.

——(ed.) (1992) *The Other Tongue: English Across Cultures*, 2nd edn, Urbana, IL: University of Illinois Press.

——(1994) 'Englishization and contact linguistics', *World Englishes*, 13 (2): 135–154.

Kanter, R.M. (1990) *When Giants Learn to Dance*, London: Unwin Hyman.

——(1995) *World Class: Thriving Locally in the Global Economy*, London: Simon and Schuster.

Karsten L., van Veen, K. and van Wulfften Palthe, A. (2008) 'What happened to the popularity of the polder model? Emergence and disappearance of a political fashion', *International Sociology*, 23 (1): 37– 67.

Keeley, T.D. (2001) *International Human Resource Management in Japanese Firms: Their greatest Challenge*, Hampshire: Palgrave.

Kelly, L.G. (1979) *The True Interpreter: A History of Translation Theory and Practice in the West*, Oxford: Blackwell.

Kempe, F. (1999) *Father/Land: A Search for the New Germany*, London: Profile Books.

Kipping, M. (1999) 'American management consulting companies in Western Europe, 1920 to 1990: products, reputation and relationships', *Business History Review*, 73: 190–220.

Klaverstijn, B. (1986) *Samentwijnen: via fusie naar integratie*, Arnhem: ENKA B.V.

Kleinberg, J. (1999) 'Negotiated understanding: The organizational implication of a cross-national business negotiation', in S.L. Beechler, and A. Bird (eds) *Japanese Multinationals abroad: Individual and Organizational Learning*, 62–91, New York: Oxford University Press.

Knights, D. and Willmott, H. (1997) 'The hype and hope of interdisciplinary management studies', *British Journal of Management*, 8: 9–22.

Koen, C.I. (2005) *Comparative and International Management*, London: McGraw-Hill Education.

Kogut, B. and U. Zander (1996) 'What firms do? Coordination, identity and learning', *Organization Science*, 7 (5): 502–518.

Kordsmeier, W., Arn, J. And Rogers, B. (2000) 'Foreign language ne U.S. businesses', *Journal of Education for Business*, January/February: 169–171.

Kostera, M., Proppé, M. and Szatkowski, M. (1995) 'Staging the new romantic hero in the old cynical theatre: on managers, roles and change in Poland', *Journal of Organizational Behavior*, 16 (6): 631–646.

Kotelovoi, N.Z. (1984). *Novye slova I zhacheniya: slovar'-spravochnik po materialam pressy I literatury 70-x godakh* (Reference dictionary of new words and meanings from the press and literary sources in the 1970s). Moscow: Pusskii Yazyk.

Kranz, J. and Gilmore, T.N. (1990) 'The splitting of leadership and management as a social defence', *Human Relations*, 43 (2): 183–204.

Krogh, G. von and J.Roos (1994), 'An essay on corporate epistemology', *Strategic Management Journal*, 15: 53–71.

Krogh, G. von, K. Ichijo and I. Nonaka (2000) *Enabling Knowledge Creation*, Oxford: Oxford University Press.

Kubota, R. (2002) 'The impact of globalization on language teaching in Japan', in D. Block and D. Cameron. (eds) *Globalization and Language Teaching*, 67–82, London: Routledge.

Kuznetsov, A. and Kuznetsova, O. (2003) 'Institutions, business and the state in Russia', *Europe-Asia Studies*, 55 (6): 907–922.

——(2005) 'Business culture in modern Russia: Deterrents and influences', *Problems and Perspectives in Management*, 2 (2): 25–31.

——(2006) 'Closing the gap between big business and society in Russia: the role of corporate social responsibility', Conference proceedings: 'Building International Communities through Collaboration' BAM 2006, Belfast, September 12–14.

Kuznetsov, A. and Yakavenka, H. (2005) 'Barriers to the absorption of management knowledge in Belarus', *Journal of Managerial Psychology*: Special Issue on the application and absorption of management knowledge, 20 (7): 566 –577.

——(2006) 'The role of educator in the international transfer of management knowledge', in Conference proceedings: 'Building International Communities Through Collaboration' BAM 2006, Belfast, September 12–14.

Langenscheidts Handwörterbuch Englisch (2001) Berlin: Langenscheidt

Lakoff, G. and Johnson, M. (1980) *Metaphors We Live By*, London and Chicago: University of Chicago Press.

Lee, S. (2006) 'Lost in translation', *Guardian*, 23 May: 8–11.

Lincoln, J.R., Kerbo, H.R. and Wittenhagen, E. (1995) 'Japanese companies in Germany: a case study in cross-cultural management', *Industrial Relations*, 34 (3): 417–440.

Linnell, P. (1998) *Approaching Dialogue*, Amsterdam: Benjamins.

Louhiala-Salminen, L, Charles, M. and Kankaanranta, A. (2005) 'English as a lingua franca in Nordic corporate merges: two case companies', *English for Specific Purposes*, 24: 401–421.

Luo, Y. and Shenkar, O. (2006) 'The multinational corporation as a multilingual community: language and organization in a global context', *Journal of International Business Studies*, 37 (3): 321–339.

Maanen, J. van (1995) 'Style as theory', *Organization Science*, 6: 133–143.

Malinowski, B. (1923) 'The problem of meaning in primitive language' in C.K. Ogden and I.A. Richards (eds) *The Meaning of Meaning*, 451–510, London: Kegan Paul, Trench, Trubner and Cok.

Mant, A. (1977) *The Rise and Fall of the British Manager*, London: Macmillan.

Marglin, S.A. (1974) 'What do bosses do?', *Review of Radical Political Economics*, 692: 60–112.

Marriott, H. (1995) 'The management of discourse in international seller-buyer negotiations', in K. Ehlich and J. Wagner (eds) *The Discourse of Business Negotiation*, 103–126, Berlin: Mouton de Gruyter.

——(1997) 'Australian–Japanese business interaction: Some features of language and cultural contact', in F. Bargiela-Chiappini and S. Harris (eds) *The Language of Business: An International Perspective*, 49–71. Edinburgh: Edinburgh University Press.

Marschan-Piekkari, R. and Welch, C. (eds) (2004) *Handbook of Qualitative Research Methods in International Business*, Cheltenham, UK: Edward Elgar.

Marschan-Piekkari, R., Welch, D.E. and Welch, L.S. (1999a) 'Adopting a common corporate language: IHRM implications', *International Journal of Human Resource Management*, 10 (3): 377–90.

——(1999b) 'In the shadow: the impact of language on the structure, power and communication in the multinational', *International Business Review*, 8 (4): 421–440.

Martin, E. (2006) *Marketing Identities through Language. English and Global Imagery in French Advertising*, Basingstoke: Palgrave Macmillan.

Martinez, Z.L. and Toyne, B. (2000) 'What is international management, and what is its domain?', *Journal of International Management*, 6 (1): 11–28.

Maslov, V. I. (2004) *Strategicheskoye upravleniye personalom v usloviakh effektivnoi organizatsionnoi kultury* [Strategic human resource management and effective corporate culture] Moscow: Finnpress.

McCraw, Th. K. (1997) *Creating Modern Capitalism*, Harvard: Harvard: University Press.

McAuley, J., Duberley, J. and Johnson, P. (2007) *Organization Theory. Challenges and Perspectives*, Harlow: Pearson Education ltd.

McKinlay, A. and Starkey, K. (eds) (1998) *Foucault, Management and Organization Theory: From Panopticon to Technologies of the Self*, London: Sage.

Mendenhall M. E. and Oddou G. (1986) 'The cognitive, psychological and social contexts of Japanese management', *Asia Pacific Journal of Management*, 4 (1): 24–37.

Merlini, L. (2005) 'Globalizzazione e prestito linguistico', in G. Bellini, L. Merlini and S. Vecchiato (eds) *Pablo Neruda in Bocconi. Uno sguardo alle lingue professionali*, 99–103, Milan: Egea.

Mey, J.L. (1993) *Pragmatics. An Introduction*, Oxford: Blackwell.

Micklethwait, J. and Woodridge, A. (2000) *'A Future Perfect: The Challenge and Hidden Promise of Globalisation*, London: William Heinemann.

Mintzberg, H. (2004) *Managers not MBAs: A Hard Look at the Soft Practice of Managing and Management Development*, London: Financial Times/Prentice Hall.

Mintzberg, H., B. Ahlstrand and J. Lampel (1998) *Strategy Safari, a Guided Tour through the Wilds of Strategic Management*, London: Prentice Hall.

Mirkin, Y. and V. Mirkin (eds) (2006) *English–Russian Banking, Investment and Financial Markets Dictionary*, Moscow: Alpina Business Books.

Moore, K. and Lewis, D. (1999) *Birth of the Multinational: 2000 Years of Ancient Business History from Ashur to Augustus*, Copenhagen: Copenhagen Business School Press.

Morris, R. (1996) *Marketing: situatsii i primery*, Moscow: Banki i birzhi/Yuniti.

Mueller, F. and Carter, C. (2005) 'The scripting of total quality management within organizational biography', *Organization Studies*, 26 (2): 221–247.

Mulholland, J. (1997) 'The Asian connection: Business requests and acknowledgement', in F. Bargiela-Chiappini and S. Harris (eds) *The Language of Business: An International Perspective*, 94–116, Edinburgh: Edinburgh University Press.

Mulkay, M. (1988) *On Humour*, Cambridge: Polity Press.

Mulligan, E. (1999) *Lifecoaching: Change your Life in Seven Days*, London: Piatkus Books.

Musson, G. and Tietze, S. (2004) 'Places and spaces. The role of metonymy in organizational talk', *Journal of Management Studies*, 40 (8):1 301–1324.

Musson, G., Cohen, L. and Tietze, S. (2007) 'Pedagogy and the "linguistic turn": developing understanding through semiotics', *Management Learning*, 38 (1): 45–60.

Nakane, C. (1986) 'Criteria of group formation.' in T.S. Lebra and W. P. Lebra (.eds) *Japanese Culture and Behaviour: Selected Readings,* 171–87, Honolulu, HI. University of Hawaii Press.

Nakasako, S. (1998) 'Japan. (Forum: International Perspectives on Business Communication Research)', *Business Communication Quarterly*, 61 (3): 101–106.

Nees, G. (2000) *Germany: Unravelling an Enigma*, Yarmouth, Maine: Intercultural Press.

Neuberger, O. (2002). *Führen und führen lassen*, Stuttgart: Lucius & Lucius.

Neustupny, J. V. (1985) 'Problems in Australian–Japanese contact situations', in J. B. Pride, (ed.) *Cross-cultural Encounters: Communication and Miscommunication,* 44–84, Melbourne: River Seine.

Ngugi wa Thiong'o (1981) *Decolonising the Mind: The Politics of Language in African Literature,* Portsmouth: NH: Heinemann.

NHK (2000) '*Eigo ga kaisha ni yatte kita: Business man tachi no shiren*' Tokyo: Nippon Hosou Kyokai (NHK).

——(2007) *Eigo ga kaisha ni yatte kita*' *Business man tachi no shiren* http://www.nhk.or.jp/special/libraly/00/l0010/l1028.html. Accessed on 22 February.

Nickerson, C. (2005) 'English as a lingua franca in international business contexts'. Editorial, *English for Specific Purposes,* 24 (4): 367–380.

Nonaka, I. and Takeuchi, H. (1995) *The Knowledge-creating Company,* New York: Oxford University Press.

Ohmae, K. (1990) *The Borderless World. Power and Strategy in the Interlinked Economy,* New York: Free Press.

——(1991) *The End of the Nation State: The Rise of Regional Economics,* London: HaperCollins.

——(1994) *The Borderless World. Power and Strategy in the Global Marketplace,* London: HarperCollins.

——(2000) *The Invisible Continent: Four Strategic Imperatives of the New Economy,* London: Nicholas Brearly.

Ostler, N. (2005) *Empires of the Word. A Language History of the World,* London: HarperCollins Publishers.

Oswick, C., Keenoy, T. and Grant, D. (2002) 'Metaphor and analogical reasoning in organization theory: beyond orthodoxy', *Academy of Management Review,* 27 (2): 294–303.

Oxford English Dictionary (1970) Vol. VI, Oxford: Clarendon Press.

Oxford English Dictionary (1976) Vol VI, Oxford: Clarendon Press.

Oxford English Dictionary (2006) OED online, http://dictionary.oed.com/cgi/wordlist/00300812?query_type = word&quetwor … 22/03/2006.

Park, H., Hwang, S.D. and Harrison, J.K. (1996) 'Sources and consequences of communication problems in foreign subsidiaries: the case of United States firms in South Korea', *International Business Review,* 5 (1): 79–98.

Parker, M. (2002) *Against Management,* Cambridge: Polity.

Pavlenko and Blackledge (eds) (2004) *Negotiation of Identities in Multilingual Contexts,* Clevedon: Multilingual Matters.

Penc J. (1997). *Leksykon biznesu: sownik angliesko-polski ponad 2300 terminów.* Warsaw: Agencja Wydanwnicza 'Placet'

Pennycook, A. (1994) *The Cultural Politics of English as an International Language,* London: Longman.

——(2000) 'The social politics and cultural politics of language classrooms', in: J.K. Hall and W.G. Eggington (eds) *The Sociopolitics of English Language Teaching,* 89–103, Clevedon: Multilingual Matters.

Peters, T. and Waterman, R. (1982) *In Search of Excellence. Lessons from American's Best run Companies,* New Yorker: Harper & Row.

Petrov, B.N., Kaspin, I.V. and Segal, M.M. (1991) *Kratkii anglo-russkii slovar terminov dlya delovykh lyudei: marketing,* Leningrad: Vyborgskaya Storona.

Pettigrew, A.M. (1985) *The Awakening Giant: Continuity and Change in ICI,* Oxford: Blackwell.

Pettigrew, A.M. and Whipp, R. (1995) *Managing Change for Competitive Success*, Oxford: Blackwell Publishing.

Phillipson, R. (1992) *Linguistic Imperialism*, Oxford: Oxford University Press.

——(1999) 'Voice in global English: Unheard chords in crystal loud and clear'. Review of D. Crystal (1997) 'English as a Global Language', *Applied Linguistics,* 20 (2): 265–276.

——(2003) *English-Only Europe? Challenging Language Policy*, London and New York: Routledge.

Piekkari, R. (2006) 'Language effects in multinational corporations: a review from an international human resource perspective', in G. Stahl and I. Bjrkman (eds) *Handbook of Research in International Human Resources Management*, 536–550, Cheltenham, UK and Northampton, MA: Edward Elgar.

Piekkari, R. and Zander, L. (2005) 'Language and communication in international management', *International Studies of Management and Organizations,* 35 (1): 3–9.

Piekkari, R., Vaara, E., Tienari, J. and Säntti, R. (2005) 'Integration or disintegration? Human resource implications of a common corporate language decision in a cross-border merger', *The International Journal of Human Resource Management*, 16 (3): 330–344.

Piore, M. and Sabel, C. (1984) 'Italian small business: Lessons for U.S. industrial policy', in J. Zysman, and L. Yson (eds) *American Industry in International Competition*, 391–421, Ithaca: Cornell University Press.

Pollard (1965) *The Genesis of Modern Management*, London: Penguin.

Poncini, G. (2002) 'Investigating discourse at business meetings with multicultural participation', *The International Review of Applied Linguistics*, 30: 345–373.

——(2003) 'Multicultural business meetings and the role of language other than English', *Journal of Intercultural Studies*, 24 (1): 17–32.

——(2004) *Discursive Strategies in Multicultural Business Meetings*, Bern: Peter Lang.

Pondy, L. (1978) 'Leadership is a language game', in M.W. McCall and M.M. Lombardo (eds) *Leadership: Where Else can we Go?* 78–90, Durham, NC: Duke University Press.

Pottruck, D. and Pearce, T. (2000) *Clicks and Mortars: Passion-driven Growth in an Internet-driven World*, San Francisco: Jossey-Bass.

Prahalad C.K. and R.A. Bettis (1986) 'The dominant logic: a new linkage between diversity and performance', *Strategic Management Journal*, 7: 485–501.

Priebsch, R. and Collinson, W.E. (1962) *The German Language*, London: Faber & Faber.

Pshenichnikova, I. (2003) 'The challenges of socialization in business education: The case of the School of Management. St. Petersburg University', *Anthropology of East Europe Review,*21 (2), Available from: http://condor.depaul.edu/~rrotenbe/aeer/v21n2/Pshenichnikova.pdf.

Puig, N. (2004) 'Between accommodation and tension AKU/HKI/AKZO in Spain 1925–91', BINT Research Program, Utrecht: November.

Putnam, L.L., Phillips, N. and Chapman, P. (1996) 'Metaphors of communication and organization', in S.R. Clegg, C. Hardy and W.R. Nord (eds) *Handbook of Organizational Studies*, 375–408, Thousand Oaks, CA: Sage.

Pyles, T. and Alego, J. (1993) *The Origins and Development of the English Language*, 4th edn, Texas: Harcourt Brace.

Rathmayr, R. (2004) 'Kontsept DENGI peterburgskogo naseleiniya v nachale 1990-x godov. Zhanr intervyu: Osobennosti russkoi ustnoi rechi v Finlandii i Sankt-Peterburge', in M. Leinonen (ed.), Slavica Tamperensia VI, 137–150, Tampere: Tampere University Press.

——(2002) 'Anglizismen im Russischen: Gamburgy, Bifteky und die Voucherisier-ung Russlands', in R. Muhr and Kettemen (eds) *Eurospeak: Der Einfluss der Englischen auf europäische Sprachen zur Jahrhundertswende*, Wien: Peter Lang Verlag.

Rea, H. and Chapman, M. (1995) 'Languages and learning in international busi-ness', Conference paper, Association of International Business Conference, Brad-ford, UK, April.

Reed, M. and Anthony, P. (1992) 'Professionalizing management and managing professionalization: British managers in the 1980s', *Journal of Management Stu-dies*, 29 (3): 591–613.

Reeves, N. and Wright, C. (1996) *Linguistic Auditing*, Clevedon: Multilingual Matters.

Reynolds, M. (1999) 'Grasping the nettle: possibilities and pitfalls of a critical management pedagogy', *British Journal of Management*, 10 (2): 171–184.

Richards, A.D. (1991) *A Strategic Focus: A Comparative Analysis of the European Chemical Industry*, Credit Suisse First Boston (CSFB).

Risner, K. (2006) *Language and Culture. Global Flows and Local Complexity*, Cleve-don: Multilingual Matters.

Ritzer, G. (1996) *The McDonalidization of Society*, 2nd edn, London: Sage.

Roberts, C., Dabies, E. and Jupp, T. (1992) *Language and Discrimination: A Study of Communication in Multi-ethnic Workplaces*, London and New York: Longman.

Robbins Report (1963) *Higher Education: Report of Committee of Higher Education*. London: HMSO.

Rother, T. (2003) *Die Krupps durch fünf Generationen Stahl*, Bergisch Gladbach: Bastei Lübbe Taschenbücher.

Sager, J.C. (1994) *Language Engineering and Translation: Consequences of Automa-tion*, Amsterdam: John Benjamins Publishing.

Salskov-Iversen, D. Hansen, H.K. and Bislev, S. (2000) 'Governmentability, globali-zation and local practice: transformations of a hegemonic discourse', *Alternatives*, 25: 183–222.

Samovar, L.A. and Porter R.E. (eds) (2000) *Intercultural Communication. A Reader*, Belont, CA: Wadsworth Publishing Company.

SanAntonio, P.M. (1987) 'Social mobility and language use in an American company in Japan', *Journal of Language and Social Psychology*, 6 (3–4): 191–200.

Sapir, E. (1949) *Selected Writings*, ed. D.G. Mandelbaum Berkeley, Los Angeles: University of California Press.

Sato, C. (1982) 'Ethnic style in classroom discourse', in M. Hines and W. Ruther-ford, (eds) *On TESOL' 81*, 11–24,Washington DC.: TESOL.

Sayer, A. (2000) *Realism and Social Science*, London: Sage.

Schmidt, G. and Williams, K. (2002) 'German management facing globalization: The 'German model' on trial', in M. Geppert, D. Matten and K. Williams (eds) *Challenges for European Management in a Global Context: Experiences from Brit-ain and Germany*, 281–293, London: Palgrave Macmillan.

Schneider, S. and Barsoux, J.L. (2001) *Managing across Cultures*, Harlow: Prentice Hall.

Schön, D. (1993) *The Reflective Practitioner. How Professionals think in Action*, London: Maurice Temple Smith.

Schroll-Machl, S. (2003) *Die Deutschen–wir Deutsche: Fremdwahrnehmung und Selbstsicht im Berufsleben*, Goettingen: Vandenhoek & Ruprecht.

Schwartz, S.H. (1994) 'Beyond individualism and collectivism: new cultural dimensions of values', in U. Kim, H.C. Triandis, C. Kagitcibasi, S. C. Choi and G.

Yoon (eds) *Individualism and Collectivism: Theory, Method, and Applications*, 85–99, Thousand Oaks: Sage.

Scollon, R. and Wong Scollon, S. (2001) *Intercultural Communication. A Discourse Approach*, 2nd edn, Oxford: Blackwell.

——(2003) *Discourses in Place. Language in the Material World*, London: Routledge.

Selmer, J. (2004) 'Do you speak Chinese? Language proficiency and adjustment of business expatriates in China' in N. Boycilliger and T. Kiyak (eds) Proceedings of the 46th Annual Meeting of the Academy of International Business, East Lansing, MI: Academy of International Business, 104.

Sereny, G. (2001) *The German Trauma: Experiences and Reflections 1938–2001*, London: Penguin Books.

Seth, V. (2005) *Two Lives*, London: Abacus.

Shakespeare, W. ({1588/2005}) (ed. T.J.B. Spencer) *Love's Labour's Lost*, London: Penguin Books.

——(1616) (ed. T. J. B. Spencer) *A Winter's Tale*, London: Penguin Books.

Shotter (1993) *Conversational Realities. Constructing Life through Language*, London: Sage.

Shotter, J. and Cunliffe, A. (2003) 'Managers as practical authors: everyday conversations in action,' in D. Holman and R. Thorpe (eds) *Management and Language*, 15–38, London: Sage.

Simon, H.A. (1960) *Administrative Behaviour*, New York: Macmillan.

——(1996) *Hidden Champions: Lessons from 500 of the World's Best Unknown Companies*, Boston, MA: Harvard Business School Press.

Sinclair, A. (2000) 'Teaching managers about masculinities', *Management Learning*, 31 (1): 83–101.

Sklair, L. (2001) *The Transnational Capitalist Class*, Oxford: Blackwell.

Smith, H. (1991) *The New Russians*, London: Vintage.

Solé, A. (2006) 'Parlez-vous management? Mots, pensée et liberté', *Business Digest*, 164, June: 29–30.

Sonnenmeier, R., (1993) 'Co-construction of messages during facilitated communication', *Facilitated Communication Digest*, 1 (2): 7–9.

Sørensen, E.S. (2005) 'Our Corporate Language is English: An Exploratory Survey of 70 DK-sited Corporations' Use of English', unpublished Masters thesis, Faculty of Language and Business Communication, Aarhus School Business.

Sparrow, P. (1999) 'International Recruitment, selection and assessment' in P. Joynt and R. Martin (eds), *The Global HR Manager: Creating the Seamless Organization*, 87–114, London Chartered Institute of Personnel and Development (CIPD).

Spencer-Oatey, H. (2000) *Culturally Speaking: Managing Rapport through Talk across Cultures*, London: Continuum.

Squires, G. (2001) 'Management as a professional discipline', *Journal of Management Studies*, 38 (4): 473–487.

Stahl, G.K., Miller, E.L. and Tung, R.L. (2002), 'Toward the boundaryless career: a closer look at the expatriate career concept and the perceived implications of an international assignment', *Journal of World Business*, 35 (4): 417–436.

Steiner, G. (1976) *After Babel: Aspects of Language and Translation*, Oxford: Oxford University Press.

Stevenson, P. (1997) *The German-speaking World: A Practical Introduction to Sociolinguistic Issues*, London: Routledge.

——(2002) *Language and German disunity: A Sociolinguistic History of East and West in Germany, 1945–200,* Oxford: Oxford University Press.

Stewart, R., Barsoux, J. L., Kieser, A., Ganter, H.D. and Walgenbach, P. (1994) *Managing in Britain and German,* Basingstoke: Macmillan.

Stürmer, M. (2002) *The German Empire 1871–1919,* London: Phoenix.

Sumihara, N. (1993) 'A case study of cross-cultural interaction in a Japanese multinational corporation operating in the United States: decision-making processes and practices', in R.R. Sims, and R.F. Dennehy (eds) *Diversity and Differences in Organization: An Agenda for Answers and Question,*135–148, Westport, CT: Quarum Books.

Suutari, V. and Brewster, C. (2000) 'Making their own way: International experience through self-initiated foreign assignment, *Journal of World Business,* 35 (4): 417–436.

Szercha, M. (ed) (1994) *The Great Polish-English Dictionary,* Warsaw: Wiedza Powszechna.

Tanaka, H. (2006) 'Emerging English-speaking business discourse in Japan', in F. Bargiela-Chiappini (ed.) Special issue of *Journal of Asian Pacific Communication,* 16 (1): 115–25.

——(in press). 'Corporate language policy change: the trajectory of management discourse' in: Dolón, R., Labarta, M. and Todolí, J. (eds) *What is Critical Discourse Analysis?* Quaderns de Filogogia: Monografic Volume 11, Valencia: Universitat de València.

Tarone, E., (1980) 'Communication strategies, foreigner talk, and repair in interlanguage', *Language Learning,* 30 (2): 417–431.

Taylor, F.W. (1947) *The Principles of Scientific Management,* New York, London: Harper & Brothers.

Taylor, J.R. and Van Every, E.J. (2000) *The Emergent Organisation: Communication as Site and Surface,* Hillsdale, NJ: Lawrence Erlbaum.

Terjesen, S. (2005) 'Senior women managers' transition to entrepreneurship: leveraging embedded career capital', *Career Development International,* 10: 246–259.

Thompson, G. and Hunston, S. (2000) 'Evaluation: An introduction', in S. Hunston and G. Thompson (eds) *Evaluation in Text: Authorial Stance and the Construction of Discourse,* 1–27, Oxford: Oxford University Press.

Thrift, N. (2002) 'Think and act like revolutionaries: episodes from the global triumph of management discourse', *Critical Quarterly,* 44 (3): 19–26.

Tietze, S. (1998) 'The role of language in the process of creating meaning in a professional organization', unpublished PhD thesis, Sheffield Hallam University, UK.

——(2004) 'Spreading the Management Gospel–in English', *Language and Intercultural Communication,* 4 (3):175–189.

Tietze, S. and Musson, G. (2005) 'Recasting the home–work relationship: A case of mutual adjustment?', *Organization Studies,* 26 (9): 1331–1353.

Tietze, S., Cohen, L. and Musson, G. (2003) *Understanding Organizations through Language,* London: Sage.

Tollefson, J.W. (2000) 'Policy and ideology in the spread of English', in J.K. Hall and W.G. Eggington (eds) *The Sociopolitics of English Language Teaching,* 7–21, Clevedon: Multilingual Matters.

Tooze. A. (2006) *The Wages of Destruction: The Making and Breaking of the Nazi Economy,* London: Allen Lane.

Top-Manager (2006) Special issue: Sobstvenniki and menedzhery (Owners and managers), 4 (15).

Townley, B. (1994) *Reframing Human Resource Management. Power, Ethics and the Subject at Work,* London: Sage.

Trompenaars, F. (1993) *Riding the Waves of Culture: Understanding Cultural Diversity in Business,* London: Economist Books.

Turra, E. (2005). 'Riunioni aziendali: realtà e simulazioni a confronto. Analisi delle risorse pragmatiche e interazionali tra drammatizzazione e culture di riferimento', in G. Bellini, L. Merlini and S. Vecchiato (eds) *Pablo Neruda in Bocconi. Uno sguardo alle lingue professionali,* 210–223, Milan: Egea

——(in preparation) *Exploring consensus and conflict: an interactional analysis of Italian business meetings,* PhD dissertation, Lancaster: Lancaster University, UK.

Twain, M (2003) 'The awful German language', in *A Tramp Abroad* (first published in 1880), 315–329, New York: The Modern Library.

Utechin, S. V. (1961) *Everyman's Concise Encyclopaedia of Russia,* London: J. M. Dent.

Valdani, E. (2002) *L'impresa pro-attiva,* Milan: McGraw-Hill.

Vandermeeren, S. (1999) 'English as lingua franca in written corporate communication: findings from a European survey', in F. Bargiela-Chiappini and C. Nickerson (eds) *Writing Business: Genres, Media and Discourses,* 273–291, Harlow: Pearson.

Venuti, L. (ed.) (2004) *The Translation Studies Reader,* 2nd edn, Abingdon, Oxon: Routledge.

Watson, T.J. (1994/2001) *In Search of Management,* London: Routledge.

——(1995) 'Rhetoric, discourse and argument in organizational sense-making', *Organization Studies,* 6 (3): 805–821.

——(1996) 'How do managers think? Identity, morality and pragmatism in managerial theory and practice', *Management Learning,* 27 (3): 323–341.

——(2002) 'Speaking professionally–occupational anxiety and discursive ingenuity among Human Resource specialists', in S. Whitehead and M. Dent M. (eds) *Managing Professional Identities,* 123–145, London: Routledge.

——(2004) 'Managers, managism, and the tower of babble: making sense of managerial pseudo-jargon', *International Journal of the Sociology of Language,*166: 67–82.

——(2006) *Organising and Managing Work,* Harlow: Pearson Education.

Watson, T.J. and Harris, P. (1999) *The Emergent Manager,* London: Sage.

Weber, M. (1978) *Economic and Society: An Outline of Interpretive Sociology.* Vol. 1, ed. Guenther Roth and Claus Wittich, trans.Ephraim Fischoff et al., Berkeley and Los Angeles: University of California Press.

Weick, K. (1995) *Sensemaking in Organizations,* Thousand Oaks, CA: Sage.

Welch, D., Welch, L. and Piekkari, R. (2005) 'Speaking in tongues. The importance of language in international management processes', *International Studies of Management and Organization,* 35 (1): 10–27.

Welch, C.L., Welch, D.E. and Tahvanainen, M. (forthcoming) 'Managing the HR dimensions of international project operations', *International Journal of Human Resource Management.*

Wesley, R. (1996) 'Isabella Beeton: Management as 'everything in its place'', *Business Strategy Review,* 7 (1): 37–46.

Westwood, R. and Linstead, S. (2001) *The Language of Organization,* London: Sage.

Whitehead, S. and Dent, M. (eds) (2002) *Managing Professional Identities,* London: Routledge.

Whittington, R. and M. Mayer (2000) *The European Corporation,* Oxford: Oxford University Press.

Wiederhold, T. (2003) *Gerhard Fieseler–eine Karriere: Ein Wirtschaftsführer im Dienste des Nationalsozialismus*, Kassel: Verlag Winfried Jenior.

Wiener, L. (1911) 'Economic history and philology', *Quarterly Journal of Economics*, 25 (2): 239–278.

Willmott, H. (1984) 'Images and ideals of managerial work: a critical examination of conceptual and empirical accounts', *Journal of Management Studies*, 21 (3): 349–368.

——(1987) 'Studying managerial work: a critique and a proposal', *Journal of Management Studies*, 24 (3): 249–270.

——(1994) 'Management education: provocations to a debate', *Management Learning*, 25 (1):105–136.

——. (1997) 'Management and organization studies as science?', *Organization*, 4 (3): 309–344.

Wilson, J. F. and Thomson, A. (2006). *The Making of Modern Management: British Management in Historical Perspective*, Oxford: Oxford University Press.

Winner, E. and Gardner, H. (1993) 'Metaphor and irony: Two levels of understanding' in A. Ortony (ed.) *Metaphor and Thought*, 2nd edn, 425–447, Cambridge: Cambridge University Press.

Wissema, H. (1992) *Unit Management, Entrepreneurship and Coordination in the Decentralised Firm*, London: Pitman Publishing.

Wöhe, G. (1986) *Einführung in die Allgemeine Betriebswirtschaftslehre*, München: Verlag Vahlen.

Wolfe Morrison, E. and Milliken, F.J. (2003) 'Speaking up, remaining silent: the dynamics of voice and silence in organization', *Journal of Management Studies*, 40 (6): 1353–1358.

Wolpert, L.J.S. (2002) 'Mangement van organisatie vernieuwing, een analyse van de constructie processen van business–unitvorming binnen AKZO', unpublished PhD thesis, University of Groningen, Holland.

Wright, C., Kumagai, F. and Bonney, N. (2001) 'Language and power in Japanese transplants in Scotland', *Sociological Review*, 49 (2): 236–253.

Yamada, H. (1992) *America and Japanese Business Discourse,* Norwood, NJ: Ablex.

——(1997) 'Organisation in American and Japanese meetings: Task versus relationship', in: F. Bargiela-Chiappini, and S. Harris (eds) *The Language of Business: An International Perspective*, 117–35, Edinburgh: Edinburgh University Press.

Yanagisako, S.J. (2002) *Producing Culture and Capital Italian Family Firms,* Princeton, NJ: Princeton University Press.

Yoshihara, H. (2001) 'Global operations managed by Japanese and in Japanese', in J H. Taggart, M. Berry and M. McDermott (eds) *Multinationals in a New Era*, 153–165, Chippenham: Palgrave.

Yoshihara, H., Okabe, Y., and Sawaki, S. (2000) *Eigo de keisei suru jidai (International Management in English),* Tokyo: Yuhikaku.

Yoshino M.Y. and Fagan, L. (2003) 'The Renault–Nissan Alliance', Harvard Business Online, http://harvardbusinessonline.hbsp.harvard.edu/b01/en/common/item_detail.jhtml;jsessionid = ORN4U3CIWHKZUAKRGWCB5VQBKE0YOISW?id = 303023&_requestid = 88913 (Accessed on 12 February 2007)

Index

English humour 11, 101, 189, 191–93, 194–95

English language: as cause of offence 80; as common corporate language 130–31, 133–34, 135, 160, 215; difficulty of 33n; as global language 8–9, 75–76, 78, 82, 83n, 84, 93, 95, 155–56; and globalization 4–5, 76, 79, 84, 85; hegemony of 48, 78–79, 81–82, 87, 93–94; as intellectual comfort zone 212–13; as lingua franca 8, 27, 59, 63–67, 69, 71–74, 76–77, 82, 83n, 84–89, 154–55, 172, 176–78, 184, 185–86, 220; and linguistic imperialism 8, 77–79, 85–86; loan words 76–77, 116, 120, 122, 123, 176–79, 205, 211; and management discourses 80–82, 84–85, 92–96; in universities 73–74, 212–13; *see also* Business English Lingua Franca; Global English; Standard English

English-speaking countries 64–65, 73, 126, 210

ENKA group 142, 143, 144–47

equivalence 211–12, 216, 218

etymology: of management words 200–202, 209–10

evaluative language 182–83

expatriates 57, 128, 131–33, 154–55, 161–62

factory system 35, 52n

Fagan, Perry L. 160

Fairclough, Norman 5, 49, 50, 94, 139

Fairhurst, Gail T. 21

Faria, Alex 4

Fayol, Henri 35

Feely, Alan J. 27, 55–56, 57–58, 77

Fernández-Armesto, Felipe 73

Filin, F. P. 115

Financial Times 126

Fink, Gerhard x, 112, 114–27, 205, 207, 209, 212

Finnish language 27–28, 55, 61–64, 132, 134–35

Ford, Henry 118

Ford, Jeffrey D. 21

Ford, Laurie W. 21

Forster, Nick 97

Foster, Pauline 159–60, 168

Foucault, Michel 44, 86

Fox, John 48

Fox, Kate 191–92, 193, 195

Fox, Renata 48

France 62, 72, 80, 209

France, Stephen 211

Fredriksson, Riikka 53, 60, 61, 131, 135

free markets 3, 14–15, 16–17, 79, 114–15, 121, 206–7

French language 39–40, 59–60, 71, 80, 203–5, 209

Freundlich, Dieter 44

Funder, Anna 103, 112

Gabriel, Yiannis 21

Ganges river 26–27

Ganter, Hans-Dieter 107, 209

Garton Ash, Timothy 103

Gee, James Paul 5, 27, 49, 66, 86–87, 156

Gelfert, Hans-Dieter 190, 192, 194

General Electric 130, 131

Gerchikova, I. N. 124, 205

German Democratic Republic 106, 112

German language: characteristics of 102, 103–4, 107–8, 113n; and management 9, 99, 102–3, 107–12, 194, 203, 207–8, 209, 218–19; and multinationals 61

German national characteristics 104, 105–6, 107–8, 189, 194, 195

Germany 9, 73, 127n; Japanese subsidiaries in 133, 135; management in 104–13, 209

Gesteland, Richard 108

Gherardi, Silvia 149

Ghosn, Carlos 160

Gibson, Cristina B. 60

Gilmore, Thomas N. 36

Gioia, Dennis A. 21

Glanzstoff (textile company) 142

glass-ceiling effect 10, 100, 130, 134–35, 137

global discourses 5, 34, 48–50, 66, 84–85, 86, 89

Global English (GE) 78–79, 83n

global identities 5, 49, 97

global languages 8–9, 70n, 71–72, 75–76, 78, 82, 83n, 84, 93, 95

globalization: and Asian economies 154, 155; and humour 194; and language 4–6, 76, 79, 85, 98, 154; and management 48–49; and social constructionism 20; theses of 3–4, 69, 96–97

GLOBE (Global Leadership and Organisational Behaviour Effectiveness) study 106–7, 199

eBooks

eBooks – at www.eBookstore.tandf.co.uk

A library at your fingertips!

eBooks are electronic versions of printed books. You can store them on your PC/laptop or browse them online.

They have advantages for anyone needing rapid access to a wide variety of published, copyright information.

eBooks can help your research by enabling you to bookmark chapters, annotate text and use instant searches to find specific words or phrases. Several eBook files would fit on even a small laptop or PDA.

NEW: Save money by eSubscribing: cheap, online access to any eBook for as long as you need it.

Annual subscription packages

We now offer special low-cost bulk subscriptions to packages of eBooks in certain subject areas. These are available to libraries or to individuals.

For more information please contact
webmaster.ebooks@tandf.co.uk

We're continually developing the eBook concept, so keep up to date by visiting the website.

www.eBookstore.tandf.co.uk

DH

658.
049
TIE

5001255832